CHASING THE
EMERALD
BUDDHA

AN ALTERNATIVE JOURNEY THROUGH
THAILAND, LAOS & ANGKOR

Sailingstone TRAVEL

Written by Ken Lawrence.
All photographs by the author.

Sailingstone Press LLC
680 S Cache Street, Suite 100
Jackson, WY 83001

sailingstonetravel.com

Copyright © 2019
Sailingstone Press LLC

All rights reserved.

No part of this publication
may be re-produced,
distributed, or transmitted
in any form or by
any means, including
photocopying, recording,
or other electronic or
mechanical methods,
without the prior written
permission of the publisher.

First edition.

ISBN-13: 978-0-9984278-1-2
ISBN-10: 0-9984278-1-0

LCCN: 2019915399

Disclaimer: The author
and publisher have made
every effort to ensure the
accuracy of the information
within this book at the
time of publication. The
author and publisher do not
assume and hereby disclaim
any liability to any party
for any loss, damage, or
disruption caused by errors
or omissions, whether such
errors or omissions result
from accident, negligence,
or any other cause.

Publisher's Cataloging-in-Publication Data:

Names: Lawrence, Ken, 1986- author.
Title: Chasing the Emerald Buddha : an alternative journey
   through Thailand, Laos & Angkor / Ken Lawrence.
Description: Jackson, WY : Sailingstone Press, 2019. | Includes
   bibliographical references and index.
Identifiers: LCCN 2019915399 | ISBN 978-0-9984278-1-2
   (paperback)
Subjects: LCSH: Emerald Buddha (Statue) | Laos--Description
   and travel. | Thailand--Description and travel. | Cambodia-
   -Description and travel. | Southeast Asia--Description and
   travel. | Southeast Asia--History. | Art, Asian. | BISAC:
   TRAVEL / Asia / Southeast. | TRAVEL / Museums, Tours,
   Points of Interest. | TRAVEL / Special Interest / Adventure. |
   HISTORY / Asia / Southeast Asia.
Classification: LCC DS522.6 .L39 2019 (print) |
   DDC 915.904/54--dc23.

Contents

Introduction
- Foreword 4
- Using this Guide 8
- Background Info 12

Lanna 27
- Chiang Rai 31
- Lampang 47
- Chiang Mai 63

Laos 81
- Luang Prabang 85
- Vientiane 107

Bangkok 123
- Thonburi 125
- Rattanakosin 141

From India to Angkor 161
- Emerald Buddha: Origins 163
- Nakhon Si Thammarat 179
- Angkor 199
- Isaan 223

Central Thailand 229
- Ayutthaya 233
- Lopburi 245
- Kamphaeng Phet 255

- Afterword 270
- Practical Travel Info 276

The Chronicle of the Emerald Buddha Retelling

1434 - 1784:
32, 48, 64, 86, 108, 126, 142

150 BC - 14ᵀᴴ Century:
164-65, 172, 180, 218, 246, 268

Historical Maps

1430s: 24-25

From India to Sri Lanka: 169

1060s: 176-177

The Emerald Buddha's Complete Journeys: 274-275

Foreword

Battles have been fought over it. Multiple temples have been named after it. Chronicles detailing its journeys have been found on ancient palm leaf manuscripts in numerous languages. Today, it's revered as the protector of an entire nation and a symbol of a powerful dynasty. Despite being a carving of only 66 centimeters tall, there's no denying that the Emerald Buddha and its journeys have significantly shaped the course of Southeast Asian history.

Presently, the statue sees countless visitors on a daily basis. The green image is the centerpiece of Wat Phra Kaew, Bangkok's most prominent temple and tourist attraction. If you've visited Bangkok before, there's a high chance you've seen the Emerald Buddha. But few foreign visitors are aware of the incredible journey it took to get there.

Admittedly, during my first visit to Wat Phra Kaew over a decade ago, the statue didn't leave a huge impression on me. Everything in and around the temple complex has been built on such a grand scale while also teeming with intricate detail. Despite the temple's name literally translating to 'Temple of the Emerald Buddha,' it didn't quite sink in that it was all constructed with the little green statue as its focal point.

During a later trip to Thailand, I visited the Lanna region for the first time. And at Chiang Rai's main temple, I was surprised to learn that it too once hosted the same jade statue now kept in Bangkok. It seemed like an interesting bit of trivia, but beyond that, I didn't give it too much thought. After all, Buddha statues are everywhere in Thailand!

But later in Chiang Mai, after a visit to the massive stupa of Wat Chedi Luang, I learned that the Emerald Buddha had been there too! Now I was intrigued. Not only did I wonder why this statue traveled around so much, but I was curious as to whether our journeys would overlap yet again. And indeed they would.

Looking deeper into the story recorded in the 'Chronicle of the Emerald Buddha,' I was amazed at how many other destinations the statue had visited - many among them top tourism hotspots.

My travels would later take me to the tropical beaches of South Thailand, the awe-inspiring ruins of Cambodia's Angkor and the laid-back World Heritage town of Luang Prabang. Back in Thailand, I went on to explore the ancient Siamese capital of Ayutthaya and lesser-known ruins like Kamphaeng Phet. Sure enough, the Emerald Buddha had visited all of these places before me.

Though first written down over five hundred years ago, the Chronicle of the Emerald Buddha, I realized, made for a pretty useful travel guide. I then went on to explore other locations from the Emerald Buddha's backstory which led me to discover a myriad of hidden gems.

But the Chronicle is more than just an account of a single relic's travels. It opens up a whole new world to the reader, taking them back in time to the heyday of the region's most legendary kingdoms. Accordingly, many of Southeast Asia's most influential historical figures also make appearances.

And believe it or not, just about every major temple mentioned in the Chronicle is still standing! That means that the story, though centuries old, can still be directly experienced by the modern traveler. If you're hoping to learn more about Indochina's rich culture, history and architecture during your adventures, then the Emerald Buddha's story serves as the perfect gateway to the region.

What is the Emerald Buddha?

66cm

48.3cm

- **Official Name:** Phra Kaew Morakot (พระแก้วมรกต), or Phra Phuttha Maha Mani Rattana Patimakon (พระพุทธมหามณีรัตนปฏิมากร)

- **Material:** Jade, or possibly green jasper.

- **Posture:** *Dhyana mudra*, or meditation posture. Its legs are in the *virasana*, or Half Lotus position. The right is folded over the left, with both soles pointing upward.

- **Origins:** Over 2,000 years ago in Pataliputra, India. Not all scholars agree, however.

The 66 cm-high Emerald Buddha isn't actually made of emerald, but from a single block of jade. 'Emerald' is often used in the Thai language to refer to the color green, and so the name stuck.

The statue's origins are mysterious. According to legend, it was created in Pataliputra, India, over 2,000 years ago. And as described in the ancient chronicles, the statue has changed hands as many as fifteen times!

Currently, the Emerald Buddha is regarded as the palladium of Thailand - the protector of the entire nation. Thailand (then Siam) has had it since the 18th century. In fact, when Chao Phraya Chakri, or King Rama I, chose Bangkok to be the site of his new capital, Wat Phra Kaew was his very first construction project. Ever since, the jade image has been synonymous with the Chakri dynasty, which still rules to this day.

While Thailand is now a constitutional monarchy, the Emerald Buddha's residence continues to host a number of important ceremonies. The coronations of new kings and even the Supreme Patriarchs of Thai Buddhism take place in front of the Emerald Buddha. During World War II, the statue's significance spilled over into the political realm, with the jade image acting as a witness to important war pacts. And even in recent years, major political alliances and treaties have been made official in the statue's presence.

Clearly, the Emerald Buddha is much more than an old relic. It remains an integral part of Thai society. And throughout its history, many have considered it more than just a mere statue, but something almost 'alive.'

The Chronicle of The Emerald Buddha

Accounts of the Emerald Buddha's journeys appear in at least five different ancient manuscripts found in various regions. Collectively, they're referred to as the 'Chronicle of the Emerald Buddha.'

The different versions are mostly alike but with some notable differences. And they all likely stem from a much older, long-lost version of the tale. But in actuality, nobody knows for sure.

The most famous version of the Chronicle is the 'Chiang Mai Manuscript.' It was written in the ancient Pali language, accompanied by a translation in the local *yuon* dialect. Yet its author, not to mention its exact age, remains a mystery. According to estimates, it dates back to sometime in the 15th or 16th centuries.

The Emerald Buddha story also appears in another Chiang Mai manuscript, albeit in much shorter form, that we know more about. Compiled by a monk named Ratanapañña in 1516, the Jinakalamali text comprises of various tales and historical accounts of Thailand's northern Lanna region. The Emerald Buddha's story is just one small chapter of many, but the series of events largely correlates with other versions. And beyond that, there are even a few more Emerald Buddha manuscripts from Chiang Mai.

But why so many manuscripts from this one region? The Emerald Buddha did, in fact, stay in Lanna for over a century. But beyond that, when it came to transcribing historical events, the ancient kingdom of Lanna was among the best at it. In fact, much of what we know about ancient Thai history in general comes from manuscripts discovered at Chiang Mai temples.

Aside from northern Thailand, there's also a version from Luang Prabang, Laos, in addition to a Siamese version. While the Siamese version is largely based off the Chiang Mai text, the story varies in a number of instances which we'll cover in time. Furthermore, the Emerald Buddha story is referenced in manuscripts found in Cambodia as well as the Shan States of Myanmar.

As the region's most significant Buddha statue, it's only fitting that so many texts would be dedicated to the Emerald Buddha. But it's certainly not the only relic with its own manuscript. Buddha statues like the Phra Bang and Phra Sihing, among others, also have chronicles of their own.

And all of these chronicles, in addition to most religious and historical texts, were originally written down on dried palm leaf. A common practice throughout South and Southeast Asia, the process dates back to at least the 5th century BC. And it remained prevalent in both the Hindu and Buddhist worlds up until the 19th century, when printing presses

A relief carving at the Bayon temple in Angkor shows a Brahmin priest reading a palm leaf manuscript

A palm leaf manuscript bundle and storage box ⌄

became increasingly common.

Palm leaf manuscripts like the Chronicle of the Emerald Buddha were first cut into rectangular sheets and then cured. Afterwards, a hole was cut through the bundle so that it could be bound together with string. The various 'pages' would then unfold, almost like a book.

Finally, the words were written down in ink and the bundle was placed together in a special box. Oftentimes, a single document could take months to complete. And depending on climate and other factors, these manuscripts could survive anywhere from decades to centuries.

In 1933, a French diplomat named Camille Notton was the first person to translate the various palm leaf manuscripts about the Emerald Buddha into English. Notton was a Thai language expert who spent a number of years in both Chiang Mai and Bangkok in the early 20th century. His passion for Thai history, culture and art grew so deep that he even took the time to learn Pali!

Notton's book also acts as a compilation of the different versions of the Chronicle, and he conveniently notes the important variations between them. To this day, his book remains the only full-length translation of all these ancient texts.

In 1968, the full Jinakalamali text was translated into English by N.A. Jayawickrama, under the elaborate title of *The Sheaf of Garlands of the Epochs of the Conqueror*. As mentioned, the chapter about the Emerald Buddha is a much shorter and more condensed version of the tale, but it's interesting to compare and contrast it with the story described in Notton's book.

Using both Notton's and Jayawickrama's translations as a base, I've rewritten the entire Chronicle of the Emerald Buddha for the modern reader. Overall, I've kept both the story and style of writing consistent with the original translations. Some differences include replacing archaic location names with modern ones, and also error corrections in regards to names and dates. I've also omitted long passages of a purely religious nature that don't have a direct bearing on the plot. And each retelling of the Chronicle is followed by additional commentary to further explain the story from within a historical and cultural context.

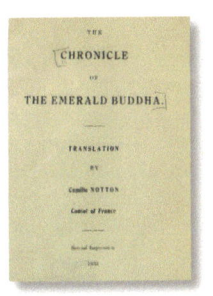

Notton's translation is sadly long out of print

Bear in mind that the Chronicle retelling is not located all in one place. At the beginning (or sometimes end) of each section, you'll find the part of the story which correlates to that geographical location.

For reasons that should become clear in time, we'll be starting with the second half of the story first. Later, *after* we catch up to the present, we'll cover the statue's origin story and its first 1,000 years. While you'll find sections on India, Sri Lanka and Myanmar, there are no accompanying travel guides for those countries.

History and mythology buffs may choose to start from the Emerald Buddha's creation story on p163. But regardless of where you begin reading, be sure to read through the entire tale at least once before embarking on your journey - even if you won't be able to travel to every location.

As we know where the Emerald Buddha is now, this journey is not a treasure hunt or something akin to the quest for the Holy Grail (though there will be plenty of mysteries to ponder). Instead, think of the Chronicle as a key to understanding the complex, interwoven history and culture of three fascinating countries.

Using this Guide

This book is a new type of travel guide which leads people on the path once taken by the region's most significant relic. With that said, it's still a lot like your typical travel guide in many other respects. You'll find practical transport information, maps and a curated list of the best things to see and do in each location.

One way in which this book differs from others is how the geographical locations are arranged and organized. For example, our story will take us in and out of Thailand on multiple occasions. But that doesn't mean that you have to, or even should, visit the locations in that order.

As we'll cover on p276, travelers following this guide should plan out their trip as they would any other - by taking logistics and timing into consideration.

Before your journey, however, it's highly recommended that you read through the Emerald Buddha's entire story at least once. Then, during your travels, simply open up to the relevant section just as you would with any other guidebook.

At the beginning of each section, you'll find a retelling of the Chronicle of the Emerald Buddha which pertains to that geographical location, followed by some additional commentary. You'll then find location-specific travel info such as transport and accommodation tips, together with a city map.

The heart of each section is the curated list of the top attractions that visitors shouldn't miss. In addition to the former homes of the Emerald Buddha, you'll also find info on plenty of other significant sites to visit around town.

Turn the page to learn more about regional weather along with packing tips. And from p276, you'll find lots of useful info for planning your itinerary.

Chronicle Retellings

This book contains a retelling of the entire Chronicle of the Emerald Buddha. Readers will find the relevant portion of the story at the beginning (but occasionally end) of each section.

Convenient navigation guides are there for those who want to read through the story in one go.

Each portion of the story is accompanied by **additional commentary** to help explain it from a historical and cultural perspective.

Using this Guide

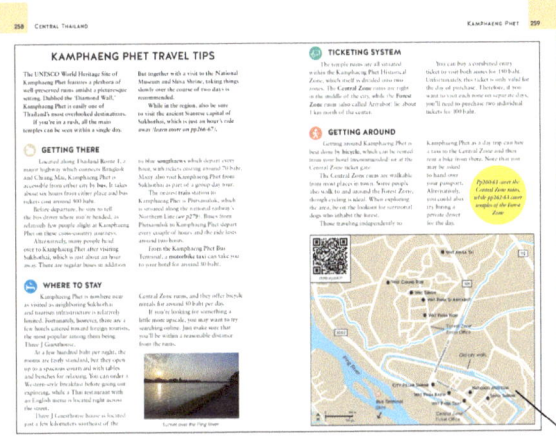

Travel Tips
Each section contains numerous practical travel tips along with a city map. Learn how to get to each destination, which neighborhoods to stay in and the best ways to get around town. Occasionally, you'll also find info on local cuisine or what to shop for.

cteb.xyz/KP

Each location has its own **scannable QR code** (and shortened URL) which links to a special web page containing **additional content and updates**. You'll find a digital version of the area map and links to relevant travel articles from our web site. Furthermore, these pages will also regularly be updated should any significant changes or developments occur.

Area maps feature the main highlights covered in each section. They might also include some additional landmarks that are worth visiting if you have extra time.

Detailed Descriptions

Learn all about each landmark's history, along with what details to look out for. We'll also delve into the meanings behind the local art and architecture.

- 📍 1 19 Trairat Rd.
- 7:00 – 18:00
- 📅 Daily
- ฿ 50

The address, opening hours, schedule and entry fee (for foreigners, at least) is listed for each major attraction.

Color photographs can be found on nearly every page. Every location mentioned in this book is accompanied by at least one, if not several!

PLANNING YOUR TRIP

This book features locations spread out among three different countries, and visiting every single destination would take around three weeks at the very least. But don't feel that you need to visit each place to appreciate the story or themes presented throughout.

Some travelers might only stick to Thailand, while others may just have time for the highlights in each country. Meanwhile, some lucky souls might even get to travel throughout the region for months on end. But whatever your travel itinerary may look like, there are a number of things you should take into consideration when planning your trip.

April's Songkran festival is both a religious holiday and a fun way to cool off during the region's hottest month (see p79)

WEATHER & TIMING

Thailand, Laos and Cambodia all have similar subtropical climates. Some months are hotter than others, however, and the hottest months may be too much for some to handle. If you're coming from a colder country, it may take some time to get adjusted. Depending on the region, the temperature can vary slightly, but it's almost always hot to some degree.

Generally speaking, **the best time to visit Thailand, Laos or Cambodia is between November and February.** These months are mostly dry and relatively cool - or rather, less stifling hot than the other months!

April is the hottest month in the region. Places like Bangkok and Siem Reap (Angkor) can get as hot as 35° C (95° F), not to mention the humidity. But April is also when the annual Songkran festival takes place in all three countries, which makes for a memorable cultural experience and a great way to cool off.

If you're visiting from March-May, beware of **'burning season,'** especially in Thailand's Lanna region. Before the rainy season begins, local farmers burn their crop fields over a period of months, while forest fires (both intentional and accidental) are also common. As a result, the air quality can get very bad, so much so that distant mountains may entirely disappear behind the haze. While the severity can vary from year to year, the northern mountainous regions are generally best avoided in March.

In much of Indochina, May to late November is the **rainy season**. While not as ideal as the dryer, cooler months, don't completely rule out a trip during this time. It often just rains for a few hours a day (albeit very heavily), or sometimes only at night. If you're out during a downpour, you can often just wait out the rain for a little while at a coffee shop or restaurant. The forests are also especially lush and green around this time.

One exception is the Gulf of Thailand (home of Ko Samui), where the wettest months are from September to January. Keep this in mind when planning your travels in South Thailand *(see p196)*.

If your schedule is flexible, the rainy season won't be a problem. But those with just a few days in each location should play it safe and stick to the dry (and non-smoky) time of year.

USING THIS GUIDE

WHAT TO BRING

One of the nice things about visiting such a warm region is that you can pack relatively light. Here's a list of items you shouldn't travel without:

- Passport with at least six months validity *(see p281)*
- Universal electric adapter
- Hat, sunglasses and sunscreen
- A rain jacket or poncho
- Footwear you can easily slip off (for temples)
- Closed-toed shoes for hiking or exploring ruins
- Swimwear
- Long sleeves for bus rides

BUDGET

The story and travel destinations covered in this book can be enjoyed by anyone with a passion for culture, history and adventure. It doesn't matter if you'll be staying at 5-star hotels or in cheap hostel dorm rooms.

With that said, Thailand, Laos and Cambodia are all ideal for budget-friendly travelers, while those with a taste for luxury will find some amazing deals.

In many cities, a basic noodle or rice dish can go for just $1 or $2 USD, while a decent coffee costs about the same. Fancier restaurants might cost four or five times that, which is still very reasonable by Western standards. Expect to pay around $20 for two at a nice restaurant.

A bottle of beer, meanwhile, generally costs a few dollars, but the cost goes way up at fancier bars. Note that food and drink prices will also increase substantially on islands.

While in Thailand, you shouldn't miss out on getting plenty of Thai massages,

FOOD

Indochina is a food lovers' paradise. In all three countries, you'll encounter a huge variety of rice and noodle dishes, many of which you'd never be able to find back home. While food isn't a major focus of this book, it's always worthwhile to visit local restaurants and try out regional cuisine. Not only is it delicious, but it's a great way to get a feel for local life.

Vegetarian restaurants are common in well-touristed areas, but not so much in smaller towns. Luckily, fresh produce is abundant at all local markets.

‹ 'Kai Yaan' is Isaan-style grilled chicken with spicy papaya salad. It's just one of many local favorites you'll encounter during your travels.

which only cost around $5 or $6 an hour. But while tipping isn't common practice in the region, massage parlors are an exception.

In all three countries, you can generally find a basic room with a private bathroom for around $10 a night. Nicer hotels go for around $20-30, while major hotel chains in the bigger cities still cost less than what you'd find back home.

Hotels can easily be booked through web sites like Booking.com. Vacation rental apartments are also prevalent, though local laws are constantly changing. At the beginning of each section in this book, you'll find recommendations on the most convenient parts of the city to stay in, regardless of budget.

> If it's your first time in the region, planning out your trip can be tricky. From **p276**, you can find suggestions on how to piece your itinerary together, along with general transportation info for each country.

The Religions of Southeast Asia

Though written from a Buddhist perspective, the story of the Emerald Buddha is a story for everyone. And the tale places as much emphasis on world history and geography as it does religion. With that said, a basic understanding of Indochina's religions is essential to understanding the story and its nuances.

And as Eastern religion and philosophy still play a huge role in contemporary society, knowing its core tenets will greatly enrich your travels overall.

Buddhism

Buddhism is based on the teachings of Siddhartha Gautama, who was born around 567 BC in present Lumbini, Nepal.

Gautama was born a prince of the Shakya clan, and lived a life of comfort and luxury in an opulent palace. But he still found himself discontent. Deep down, he knew that the rich and powerful were just as susceptible to sickness and death as everyone else.

'Why must everyone suffer?' he wondered. And so eventually he decided to embark on a quest for truth. He snuck out of the palace and began living as an ascetic in the forest, spending much of his time in deep meditation. After several years, he eventually achieved a state of full enlightenment, or *nirvana*, and began teaching his method to a group of disciples.

△ Siddhartha Gautama already had a wife and son when he decided to become an ascetic.

In a scene known as the 'Great Departure,' celestial deities arrive to lift up his horse so that nobody would awaken upon his exit in the dead of night.

The Four Noble Truths

At the core of Buddhism are the 'Four Noble Truths,' which describe the cause of suffering and how to end it:

1. Suffering: All humans, regardless of status, wealth or age, are bound to experience suffering and discontent, or *dukkha*. States of happiness and pleasure are only fleeting.

2. The Cause of Suffering: Indulgence in sensory pleasures does not prevent suffering. On the contrary, attachment to material objects and worldly desires only results in more suffering. Everything is impermanent, and attachments blind us from the true nature of all things. Attachments, along with *karma*, also cause the individual soul to be reborn again and again in this world of the senses (*samsara*).

3. The End of Suffering: The permanent cessation of suffering can be achieved by total non-attachment to the ego and worldly desires. This state of enlightenment, referred to as *nirvana*, is the only way to cease an otherwise endless cycle of death and rebirth.

4. The Path: The means through which one can attain *nirvana*, as taught by the Buddha, is 'the Eightfold Path.'

Background Info

The Eightfold Path

The Buddha's Eightfold Path to enlightenment involves the following principles:

Right understanding (of suffering), right resolve, right speech, right conduct, right livelihood, right effort, right mindfulness, right samadhi (concentration)

Divided into three categories, these eight practices cover the correct approach to understanding the Buddha's teachings, the correct way to live one's life, and also the correct way to meditate.

The Tripitaka

Among the most important scriptures of Buddhism is the Tripitaka, also referred to as the 'Pali Canon.' While the Buddha's teachings were preserved orally for many generations, they weren't written down until 29 BC, four-and-a-half centuries after the Buddha's death.

The Tripitaka, first compiled in Sri Lanka, literally means 'three baskets.' As ancient manuscripts were originally written down on dried palm leaves, the name refers to how they were stored in three different baskets depending on their category. The first, the Vinaya Pitaka, deals with rules and protocols of the *sangha*, or monkhood. The second, the Sutra Pitaka, is comprised of the main teachings of the Buddha on *dharma*. And the Abhidharma Pitaka contains commentary by the Buddha's disciples on how *dharma* relates to daily life.

Dharma

An essential concept of both Buddhist and Hindu philosophy, *dharma* could best be translated as 'natural law.' Not only is there a *dharma* of the cosmos which determines the movement of the planets, but each living creature has its own *dharma* as well.

From the Buddhist perspective, living according to *dharma* is synonymous with leading an ethical and moral life.

Many Buddhists also use the term to refer to the Buddha's teachings in general.

The wheel, or 'dharmachakra,' is one of the most common symbols of Buddhism. It represents both the Eightfold Path and the law of dharma itself ›

The Jataka Tales

Before he was born as Siddhartha Gautama, the Buddha experienced many prior incarnations as both human and animal. Stories of these past lives (*jatakas*), known as the Jataka Tales, are included in the Sutra Pitaka of the Pali Canon. To this day, they remain popular in Buddhist countries as a way to teach moral lessons, and they're often the subject matter of temple mural art.

One of the most popular tales is that of Prince Vessantara, who was so generous that he gave away a rain-making elephant to a neighboring kingdom. This greatly angered his father, who sent him into exile.

While in exile, the prince even gave away his own two children to a Brahmin priest. Fortunately, the priest was really the god Indra in disguise, and he returned the children to Vessantara. Eventually, the prince gets invited back to his kingdom to the joy of all.

Buddhist Kingship

According to Buddhist belief, kings were born into their positions of power thanks to the accumulation of good *karma* in previous lifetimes. And a good king should set a positive example for their subjects and rule righteously as a *dharmaraja*.

Ideal past *dharamarajas* include Rama (of the Ramayana) and King Ashoka of the Indian Maurya Empire. But given human nature, Buddhist kingdoms have also experienced their share of bloody wars like any other. As you'll learn, righteous kingship is a common theme throughout the Emerald Buddha's backstory.

Theravada Buddhism

Theravada, which translates to 'way of the elders,' is currently the most prominent Buddhist sect of Thailand, Laos, Cambodia, Sri Lanka and Myanmar.

The ultimate goal of Theravada Buddhism is to become an *arhat*, or enlightened being. The tradition puts a great emphasis on following Siddhartha Gautama, the historical Buddha, as an example of how to live one's life.

Theravada Buddhist doctrine also teaches that one can't go about achieving enlightenment in just any lifetime. A soul must gradually work its way up over the course of many existences. Ultimately, only ordained monks can attain *nirvana*. And Theravada monastic orders are descended from a lineage of ordination that goes all the way back to the Buddha himself.

With that said, it's very common for people to join the order only temporarily, from a period of weeks to years. It's regarded as a positive learning experience, and as a way to increase the chances of a better future rebirth.

Some see Theravada as the simplest and purest approach to the Buddha's teachings.

A Theravada monk in Myanmar carrying an alms bowl. According to tradition, monastics must rely entirely on alms. ▶

Mahayana Buddhism

While Theravada is only one sect, Mahayana, or the 'Greater Wheel' of Buddhism, is comprised of many sects. Among them are Chan (Zen), Pure Land and Nichiren, to name just a few.

Like Theravada, Mahayana Buddhists revere the Tripitaka, but they also consider texts like the Heart, Lotus and Diamond Sutras to be canonical as well.

In contrast to Theravada, Mahayana Buddhists believe that anybody is capable of attaining *nirvana* in any lifetime. The end goal, however, isn't just to become enlightened, but to become a *bodhisattva*. A *bodhisattva* is an enlightened being who chooses to remain in this world to help others become enlightened as well.

While not technically gods, *bodhisattvas* are sometimes worshipped in a similar manner. And among the most popular is Avalokiteshvara, referred to in China as Guan Yin. Interestingly, images of Mahayana divinities can also sometimes be found at Theravada temples.

A Guan Yin statue stands in front of a multi-armed Avalokiteshvara at a Thai temple. These are merely two forms of the same bodhisattva. ▶

Hinduism

For centuries, Hinduism was practiced alongside Buddhism all over Southeast Asia. But once Theravada Buddhism established itself as the region's dominant religion, Hinduism mostly died out. Or did it?

While very few in Thailand, Laos or Cambodia today identify themselves as Hindu, the religion's lasting influence is evident once you look a little beneath the surface.

A statue of Ganesha at a temple in Chiang Mai, Thailand

Hinduism in Relation to Buddhism

At their core, Hinduism and Buddhism share much in common. Both systems agree on the idea reincarnation and that worldly attachments ultimately lead to suffering. And the ultimate goal of both is the full liberation of said suffering. But contrary to Buddhism, which is largely agnostic, Hinduism strongly emphasizes the concept of union with deity.

Most schools of Hindu thought teach the concept of *Brahman*. *Brahman* is the absolute, highest form of metaphysical reality. The individual's higher self, or *Atman*, is part of, or even one with, *Brahman*. Yet, distracted by the sensory realm of *maya*, we've forgotten this.

Through dedicated spiritual practice (*yoga*), however, we can merge with (or rather, remember our union with) *Brahman* and achieve *moksha*. Many feel that the *nirvana* of Buddhism and the *moksha* of Hinduism are merely different names for the exact same concept.

◁ *Indra is one of the original major Vedic gods. Often associated with rain and storms, he's also the ruler of heaven itself. And he also appears in many Buddhist legends, including the Chronicle of the Emerald Buddha!*

Important Texts

The most sacred texts revered by Hindus are the Vedas, written in ancient Sanskrit. The Vedas consist of four books, with the Rig Veda regarded as the most important. The texts detail how to perform certain rituals as well as practical knowledge for daily life. But more importantly, they also explain the nature of reality and *Brahman*. This part of the Vedas is collectively referred to as the Upanishads.

Other major works include the great epics (the Ramayana and Mahabharata) as well as the Puranas.

Priests & the Caste System

The four castes of Hinduism are Brahmins (priests), Kshatriyas (warriors), Vaishyas (merchants) and Sudras (ordinary workers). Some believe that castes were really supposed to be chosen professions based on one's own nature. Be that as it may, hereditary castes have been a major part of Hindu societies for centuries.

At Angkor, only Brahmin priests could carry out the royal rituals. Therefore, they wielded much influence and power. Interestingly, even the later Buddhist kingdoms of Siam relied on Brahmins for special court rituals.

Many of Angkor's priestly rituals involved a linga, a symbol of Shiva ▷

HINDUISM'S MANY GODS

As mentioned, Hinduism places an emphasis on one ultimate reality called *Brahman*. Yet the human mind in its normal state is incapable of comprehending the infinite.

Therefore, according to many Hindu traditions, *Brahman* manifests itself as various deities with definable characteristics that we can more easily relate to. Ideally, one is not supposed to consider a Hindu deity to be a distinct entity, but as merely one manifestation of the unmanifest.

Though there are many (possibly millions!) of gods in Hindu lore, the trinity of Brahma, Vishnu and Shiva are considered the most important.

Brahma
'The Creator'

Vishnu
'The Preserver'

Shiva
'The Destroyer'

Shiva is known as 'The Destroyer,' which could be interpreted as the destruction of ignorance. Shaivism, or Shiva worship, was the prominent religion of the Khmer Empire for hundreds of years. And the Dvaravati civilization who inhabited much of what makes up modern Thailand built many Shiva shrines in their cities.

Even throughout the modern Buddhist world, you'll often see statues of the elephant god Ganesha, who's actually one of Shiva's sons.

Vishnu, meanwhile, is nicknamed 'The Preserver.' However, he often carries out acts of both creation and destruction to maintain balance and harmony in the world. He typically does this by coming down to earth in human (or animal) form as an avatar, the two most famous of which are Rama and Krishna.

While most Khmer temples were dedicated to Shiva, Angkor Wat was built for Vishnu. And even today, the Ramayana is one of the most popular stories in Indochina. Its scenes are beautifully depicted around Wat Phra Kaew, while Vishnu is present on the gable of 'The Chapel of the Emerald Buddha' *(see p148)*.

Brahma (not to be confused with *Brahman*) is 'The Creator,' but according to Hindu legend, he was actually created by Vishnu! Though he's rarely worshipped directly in India, Brahma remains a popular deity in Thailand. Bangkok's Erawan Shrine and many others throughout the country are all dedicated to this four-faced god.

Animism / Folk Religion

A large percentage of Thais, Laotians and Cambodians believe that spirits are everywhere. And everything from an individual's health to the safety of an entire community can be attributed to these spirits, often referred to as *phi*. And just as the spirits have the capability to protect, they also have the ability to cause harm. Therefore, it's considered imperative to stay on these spirits' good side.

All around the region you can spot what are known as 'spirit houses,' or *san phra phum*. At first glance, they look like miniature Buddhist temples, but they're not related to Buddhism. As the name suggests, they're believed to be homes of spirits themselves and are often found in front of large buildings. But why?

When it comes time to chop down the trees to make room for a new construction project, locals believe that they're essentially destroying a spirit's former dwelling place, forcibly evicting it against its will. To placate the spirit, then, a new home is provided.

But spirit houses are far from being mere decoration. They actually require quite a bit of effort to maintain. The spirits must be regularly 'fed' in the form of offerings. Walking past one, you'll likely notice some lit sticks of incense, in addition to some fruit and a bottle of water. In Thailand, oddly enough, red Fanta is one of the most popular offerings of all!

Aside from spirit houses, 'city pillar shrines' are common in most cities in Thailand and Laos. These shrines house golden pillars which are believed to contain the protector spirit of the city itself. When kings would go about constructing new cities, the pillar is typically the first thing they would erect.

▲ *Sakon Nakhon locals pray for good luck*

Further out in nature, you'll likely encounter small shrines in front of large trees or nearby cave entrances. And on your trips to smaller towns, you may notice statues or figurines unique to that locale.

But can one call themselves a Theravada Buddhist while worshipping spirits at the same time? While some in the *sangha* condemn these ancient practices, the Buddha himself instructed his followers to respect local traditions and pray at the local shrines. Nevertheless, conflicts between Buddhists and animists have been fairly common throughout history. In fact, this is a topic touched upon by the Chronicle of the Emerald Buddha itself.

THE SIGNIFICANCE OF BUDDHA STATUES

Buddha statues can be found nearly everywhere in Indochina. It would be hard to imagine countries like Thailand, Laos or Cambodia without them. But what exactly is their true function and purpose?

According to Theravada Buddhism, the purpose of a Buddha statue is to remind one of the Buddha's teachings as well as their own inner Buddha nature. They're just symbols and not meant to be worshipped directly, a monk might tell you.

'Why such innumerable merit makings to this lifeless statue? Quite true, listeners, the statue cannot move or speak, but the most important point is that our Lord [Buddha], the Omniscient, has placed His cult in it.'

- The Chronicle of the Phra Sihing

And while the Buddha is not supposed to be worshipped as a god, his images can certainly become 'energetically charged,'

Bronze Buddha images are cast with an ancient 'lost wax' method at a foundry in Phitsanulok, Thailand

In years past, education was limited to temples, and most people couldn't read. Therefore, Buddha images and mural art were also useful tools to propagate *dharma*.

Yet, the true role which Buddha images play in society is much deeper and more complex than that of a symbol or educational tool. Upon completion of an image, for example, an all-night consecration ceremony takes place at a temple. Chanting, holy water, and a special thread meant for transfering energy from other sacred objects are all used to 'awaken' the image and 'open its eyes.'

As mentioned earlier, elements of both animism and Hinduism remain deeply ingrained in the hearts and minds of locals. In these systems, physical objects can become imbued with mystical powers, even acting as a vessel for spirits or gods.

according to local belief. The more prayer and offerings an image receives, the more potent its energy becomes. One reason why special reverence is given to older images is that they're considered more powerful - not just in a metaphorical sense, but literally.

So this manmade object, initially crafted as a symbol, can transcend its symbolic status, becoming an object with mystical powers. And the Emerald Buddha is regarded by many as the most powerful of all, capable of protecting entire nations.

As detailed in various chronicles, kings would go to great lengths to obtain such Buddha images. If a sacred statue 'allowed' a king to have it, that king's right to rule was legitimized in the eyes of the public. His possession of the statue was proof enough of his righteousness, or, in other words, that he was a *dharmaraja (see p14)*.

Common Buddha Image Postures

Calling the Earth to Witness

This posture, also called *bhumisparsa*, is common all over the Buddhist world, but especially in Thailand.

According to legend, the Buddha meditated under a Bodhi tree as he was close to reaching *nirvana*. But the demon Mara tried to distract him, sending over his minions to attack and even his beautiful daughters as seductresses.

But the Buddha remained resilient. Mara then challenged him to call upon a witness to decide who was more powerful. The Buddha touched his right hand to the ground, signaling for the earth itself to act as a witness.

Bhumi, the Earth goddess, arrived and wrung out her hair, washing Mara and his minions away. Shortly afterward, Siddhartha Gautama attained enlightenment.

Meditation Posture

This posture, known as *dhyana mudra*, simply depicts the Buddha meditating. While the right hand is always folded over the left hand, the legs may either be in *virasana* position (the right leg folded over the left), or *vajrasana* (each foot resting on the opposite thigh).

Naga Prok

Especially popular in Cambodia, these images represent a scene involving the Buddha meditating in the rain. The benevolent *naga* serpent Mucalinda saw this and generously provided cover.

Dispelling Fear

Known as the *abhaya mudra* gesture, the Buddha's outward-facing palms symbolize reassurance and protection, along with the calming of rough waters. Sometimes only a single hand is raised. Some *abhaya mudra* images are seated, though most are standing, and occasionally even walking.

Vitarka Mudra

These images symbolize Buddha teaching his disciples. The thumb and index finger form a ring, symbolizing the wheel of *dharma*.

Reclining Buddha

Though he appears to be sleeping, these images actually depict the Buddha on his deathbed - his final moments of existence in human form.

Visiting Buddhist Temples

Many of the sites covered in this guide book are temples, or *wats*. While fascinating to most at first, travelers can easily get 'templed out' after just a few days. This can be prevented, however, by taking the time to learn about the various parts which make up a *wat* and the significance of each.

Furthermore, learning about each temple's history, as will be covered throughout this book, will help make your visits much more engrossing experiences.

Chedis

Many larger chedis are divided into three sections which represent the underworld, the Earth and the heavens.
>

Chedis, also known as stupas or pagodas, are tall cone-shaped structures which enshrine important relics. The relics inside may be highly significant Buddha statues, or, in special cases, hairs or bones of the Buddha himself.

Chedis are often the most sacred part of a *wat*. They also commonly determine the placement of the other temple structures. Some temples may feature a multitude of *chedis*, though the most important one will stand out as the tallest.

Prangs

A trademark of Siamese temples, *prangs* were adapted from the *prasats* of Angkor (see p203). The Ayutthaya Kingdom started building *prangs* as taller, narrower *prasats* which can resemble corncobs or cacti. After the founding of Bangkok, *prangs* remained an important architectural feature, but they became even taller and skinnier.

An ancient prang in Ayutthaya

A 19th-century Bangkok prang

Ubosot *(Thailand)* / Sim *(Laos)*

The *ubosot* (sometimes called a *bot*, or in Laos, a *sim*) is often similar in appearance to a *viharn* (opp. page). Its primary function, however, is to host ordinations for new monks. Other important ceremonies for resident monks may take place here as well.

Before the construction of an *ubosot*, nine large metal balls called *luuk nimit* are buried underground. Afterward, special stones called *bai sema* are placed above them at surface level. These help demarcate the sacred space within.

Old bai sema stones >

Viharn

A *viharn*, also known as a *vihana* or *wihan*, is an assembly hall where both monks and lay people gather for Buddhist ceremonies. It often houses a temple's primary Buddha image, though sometimes that honor belongs to the *ubosot*.

Note that while temples only have one *ubosot*, larger complexes may contain multiple *viharns*.

Ho Trai

The *ho trai* is a temple's scripture library. It's where copies of important Buddhist texts, such as the Tripitaka, are kept. Many *ho trai* still contain original copies of ancient palm leaf manuscripts *(see pp6-7)*. Other documents might pertain to local history or the backstories of certain relics.

The *ho trai* is often built on an elevated platform to keep its documents safe from both insects and floods.

Mondop

Generally speaking, *mondops* are structures designed to house sculptures or other sacred objects such as 'Buddha footprints.' Bangkok's Wat Phra Kaew even makes use of small *mondops* to contain the *bai sema* stones around its *ubosot*.

Mondops come in all shapes and sizes and their appearance may vary from region to region.

Outer Gallery

In many larger temples, an outer gallery surrounds the main structures in the center. These typically feature a multitude of similar-looking Buddha statues, oftentimes gold in color. In addition to statues, galleries also commonly feature mural paintings along the walls.

The gallery of Bangkok's Wat Phra Kaew is the region's most famous. It's entirely covered in scenes from the Ramakien, or Thai Ramayana. It contains no statues, however.

Ho Rakang

A *ho rakang* is a bell tower used to summon monks for morning and evening prayer. For that reason, it's often situated near the monks' living quarters, or *kuti*. Depending on the temple, the *ho rakang* can vary greatly in size and style.

Other Temple Elements

Naga Staircases

When visiting a Theravada Buddhist temple, one of the first things you'll likely see will be a pair of ferocious-looking *naga* serpents at either end of a staircase. As intimidating as they might appear, *nagas* are actually beloved creatures throughout the region.

Nagas are considered guardians of the underworld. And in the Buddha's time, a friendly *naga* named Mucalinda helped shield him from rain during a meditation session *(see p19)*.

Nagas actually originated in Hindu mythology, and can therefore also be seen at the temples of Angkor. Placing fierce naga statues outside a temple structure is seen as a way to protect it from harmful spirits.

Chinthe

Chinthes are lion-like creatures that also act as temple guardians. Additionally, other common guardian beings include *yakshas* (giant ogres) and *kinnaras* (human-animal hybrids).

Garuda

In Hinduism, Garuda is a singular being that's half-man, half-eagle and who acts as the vehicle mount of Vishnu. But in Buddhism, *garudas* are more of a general bird-like species. They're very popular motifs at temples, including those of ancient Angkor.

Rooftop Finials

The edges of multitiered temple roofs often feature both *chofas*, which symbolize *garudas*, and *hang hong*, which represent *naga* serpents (both pictured to the right).

In Hindu and Buddhist mythology, *garudas* and *nagas* are commonly portrayed as adversaries. However, the interplay between them could be interpreted as the relationship between the air and water elements, or between the heavens and the underworld. In Buddhism, one is ultimately supposed to transcend such dualities in order to attain *nirvana*.

Beautiful chofas *and* hang hong *adorn the roof of the Chapel of the Emerald Buddha* ⌄

Wat's in a Name?

When visiting *wats*, you may notice that many of them have very similar (if not the exact same) names. The words 'Mahathat' and 'Phra That' for example, are quite common in both Thailand and Laos (though with slightly different spellings). This implies that the holy relics enshrined in the *chedi* are those of the Buddha himself, such as a bone, tooth or a strand of hair. Other major temples founded by royalty often contain words beginning with 'Rat-' or 'Racha-.'

And as you'll notice throughout this book, temples are also frequently named after significant Buddha statues, even if that statue is no longer there. For example, there are multiple 'Wat Phra Kaew's throughout the country, a title which tells us the Emerald Buddha was once, or currently is, kept there. There are also a couple of 'Wat Phra Singh's named after the Sihing Buddha image. On the other hand, not every temple those statues once resided in is named after them.

Oftentimes, a temple may take its name from its most prominent architectural feature, such as Wat Chedi Luang. Or it might just be named after the mountain or town in which it's located.

Temple Etiquette

Buddhist temples in Southeast Asia are accepting of all visitors, though there are a few important points you need to keep in mind before entering a *wat*.

The first is dress code. As a general rule, you should make sure to keep your shoulders and your knees covered. It's not always easy to dress this way in the stifling heat, of course. That's why you might want to bring a pair of light trousers in your bag to put on over your shorts.

Sometimes a temple might have long pants or *sarongs* available for visitors to borrow, but that's not always the case. Men can often get by with shorts that come down to their knees (with the exception of Wat Phra Kaew in Bangkok, where long pants are always required). Generally speaking, the dress code is more often strictly enforced for women than it is for men.

But sometimes, you'll carefully choose your outfit, trek over to the temple on a hot day, and then see both local men and women wearing short shorts with no issues. What gives? The reality is that the rules aren't always enforced, and you can't really know in advance how strict things are going to be. Sometimes the monks or other staff may be too polite to say anything.

Another important point is that when you enter a *viharn* or *ubosot*, you need to remove your shoes. This will be made obvious by the loads of shoes left outside the entrance.

On days when it's not a Buddhist holiday, feel free to show up to a temple whenever you like and relax inside the *viharn* or *ubosot*. When sitting down on the floor, be sure to sit cross-legged and don't point your feet toward the Buddha statue, as this is a sign of disrespect.

Photography in most areas of a temple is generally fine, except when there's a sign specifically telling you not to. Taking selfies is frowned upon, though you might even see locals doing it.

Also note that the rules described above may vary when it comes to ancient ruins. This largely depends on whether or not it's still considered an active temple.

Indochina: 1430s

This portion of the story begins in 1434 upon the Emerald Buddha's emergence in Chiang Rai. Interestingly, the 1430s happened to be a pretty eventful decade for the region as a whole.

At the time, the strongest power in Indochina was the Ayutthaya Kingdom. In 1431, they even managed to sack Angkor, likely occupying it for decades. As a direct result, the Khmer Empire moved its capital to Phnom Penh after having ruled out of Angkor for over five centuries.

And in 1438, Ayutthaya formally absorbed the Sukhothai Kingdom into its territory. Sukhothai, founded in 1238, was the first Siamese kingdom. At its peak, Sukhothai once controlled most of the land that would make up Ayutthaya, and even much of Lan Chang (Laos).

Meanwhile, things were stable for the most part in the Lanna Kingdom, where our story begins. In the early 1400s, Lanna wasn't quite as powerful as it had been a century prior. But as we'll find out, a powerful ruler named Tilokarat would come to power in the 1440s, bringing Lanna to its historical apex.

Eventually, the story will take us to Lan Chang, although not until the mid-1500s. The 1430s were a chaotic time for Lan Chang, with the kingdom switching rulers every few years. But things would eventually settle down once King Chaiyachakkapat took the throne in 1441.

Ultimately, the story ends in the Siamese kingdoms of Thonburi and Rattanakosin - neither of which would form until the 18th century.

- 🟩 **Lanna Kingdom**
- 🟨 **Sukhothai** (Vassal of Ayutthaya)
- 🟧 **Ayutthaya Kingdom**
- 🟧 **Khmer Empire**
- 🟦 **Lan Chang Kingdom**

1431
The Ayutthaya Kingdom invades Angkor, occupying it for decades.

1436
King Sam Fang Kaen orders the delivery of the Emerald Buddha to the capital.

1430s

1434
The Emerald Buddha appears in Chiang Rai. / Phnom Penh gets founded.

1438
Sukhothai is formally absorbed into the Ayutthaya Kingdom.

> By the time the Emerald Buddha arrives in Bangkok in the late 18th century, most of these kingdoms will have ceased to exist - at least as independent entities. Learn how and why as the story unfolds.

1441
King Tilokarat takes the throne of Lanna

1440s

1442 - 3
Ayutthaya attacks Lanna - one of many skirmishes over the following years. The two kingdoms would continue to fight over Sukhothai's former territory in the 1450s.

LANNA

*H*aving once functioned as its own kingdom for centuries, the Lanna region of northern Thailand now encompasses nine provinces. And by following the Emerald Buddha's journey, we'll get to explore three of them, while a side trip to the historical city of Lamphun is well within reach.

Today, Lanna is one of the most visited regions of Thailand, and for good reason. It provides a balanced mix of traditional culture, outdoor activities and modern art. Its cities are also slow-paced and laid back, making for a refreshing change of pace from Thailand's bustling capital.

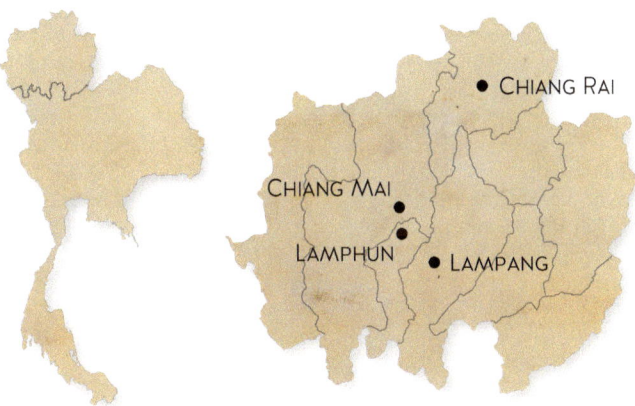

A Brief History of Lanna	28
Chiang Rai	31
Lampang	47
Lamphun	61
Chiang Mai	63

A Brief History of Lanna

While presently, Lanna may just be the name of a region in Northern Thailand, the legacy of the ancient Lanna Kingdom can still be experienced by visitors today. The kingdom, in fact, existed in some form or another for nearly 700 years, only getting formally absorbed into Thailand in 1932.

King Mangrai: Lanna's Founder

The Lanna Kingdom first came to be thanks to an ambitious and charismatic leader named Mangrai. And even following his death, his dynasty would continue to rule Lanna for hundreds of years.

Mangrai's father was the ruler of a small kingdom called Ngoenyang, located in modern-day Chiang Rai Province. The kingdom was comprised of ethnic Tai people - just one of several independent Tai states in the region. Upon succession to the throne, Mangrai sought to unify these states and went about successfully absorbing them into his territory. He hoped to create a strong kingdom that could hold its own against the Mongols who, at the time, were starting to encroach upon the area from the north.

And so the new Kingdom of Lanna (or Lan Na) was formed, which means 'Kingdom of a Million Rice Fields.' King Mangrai soon founded Chiang Rai in 1262, and it remained capital for a little over a decade. He then moved it over to Fang in 1273 - now a small town in Chiang Mai Province.

Lanna grew into a powerful state, but it also bordered some powerful neighbors.

King Mangrai, together with the kings of Sukhothai and Phayao, make up Chiang Mai's Three Kings Monument ▸

Mangrai set out to invade the nearby kingdom of Phayao, but ended up becoming friends with its king, Phaya Ngam Mueang, who was actually his cousin. The two would also form an alliance with King Ram Khamhaeng of Sukhothai, the very first kingdom of Siam *(see p230)*.

With this alliance in place, Mangrai finally felt confident enough to invade the Haripunchai Kingdom to the south. An ethnic Mon kingdom established as far back as the 7th century, Haripunchai had long been a political and cultural powerhouse in the region *(see p61)*. And it's also credited with spreading Theravada Buddhism throughout the area.

With the help of a mole who infiltrated the Haripunchai king's inner circle, Mangrai successfully took their capital (present Lamphun) - something even the mighty Khmer Empire had been unable to do.

Mangrai then hoped to build a new capital more suitable for such an up-and-coming kingdom. He established a city called Wiang Kum Kam *(p77)*, but as the area experienced frequent flooding, Mangrai had to give it another shot. And in 1296, he began constructing Chiang Mai ('New City') near the base of Doi Suthep mountain.

A few years later, the former king of Haripunchai, who'd been exiled to the city of Lampang, decided to have his revenge. He was no match for Mangrai, however, and Lampang would end up getting absorbed into Lanna as well.

But the tireless Mangrai didn't stop there. He even occupied parts of Burma, importing many craftsmen who'd go on to greatly influence Lanna arts and culture.

LANNA AFTER MANGRAI

According to legend, King Mangrai was killed by a lightning strike in 1311. And following his death, the kingdom's strength and influence would remain stagnant for the next hundred years or so. This was in part due to the rise of a powerful new neighbor to the east, the Lan Chang Kingdom (Laos), which formed in 1353 *(see p82)*.

And to the south, following the rise of the Ayutthaya Kingdom, Lanna would engage itself in many bloody battles with the Siamese. The two sides regularly fought over former territories once controlled by Sukhothai. And throughout this period, many Sukhothai monks fled to Lanna, further strengthening Theravada Buddhism in the kingdom.

In 1441, the great king Tilokarat ascended the throne, bringing Lanna to its greatest height of power while expanding its territory to its largest ever size. And it was Tilokarat who'd transfer the Emerald Buddha to Chiang Mai. His reign will be covered more in-depth on p65.

A VASSAL STATE OF BURMA

Interestingly, Lanna would finally lose its independence just a few years after losing the Emerald Buddha. In 1558, the kingdom, already weakened by a lack of an heir to the throne, turned out to be no match for the Burmese Toungoo dynasty.

Lanna would remain a Burmese vassal for more than 200 years. However, other than being led by a puppet ruler and being forced to make annual tributes, local culture was largely left intact. Throughout the 16th and 17th centuries, Lanna culture continued to develop and thrive. And it was even during this time when important manuscripts like the Chronicle of the Emerald Buddha were first written down.

LANNA UNDER SIAM

Eventually, Lanna would be freed from Burmese rule in 1775 with the help of their former arch-rivals, Siam. And one of the main generals in charge of driving out the Burmese was Chao Kawila of Lampang, who's still highly revered as a Lanna hero to this day. Despite their success, however, Chiang Mai was left deserted for a few decades following the turmoil.

At the turn of the 18th century, Kawila was appointed by King Rama I to rebuild and repopulate the region. Lanna then remained a semi-autonomous vassal of Siam until it was officially absorbed into Siamese territory in 1932 - the same year the country transitioned to a constitutional monarchy.

Nowadays, Chiang Mai is Thailand's second-largest city after Bangkok, while the Lanna region as a whole is one of the most popular among tourists.

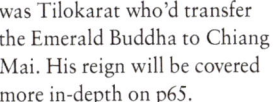

‹ *Chiang Mai's original moat and city walls have largely survived to this day*

Chiang Rai
1434 - 1436

A Chance Discovery in Chiang Rai

One evening, in the year 1434, a great storm began to brew over the glorious city of Chiang Rai. As it picked up in intensity, a sudden flash of lightning struck the golden chedi of Wat Pa Yeah, causing it to crumble to the ground. And once the storm subsided, a resident monk noticed that there was a small Buddha statue buried beneath the rubble.

Though it had been enshrined with other sacred relics in the chedi, it appeared to be much like any other Buddha image. And so the monk placed the statue among the numerous others at the temple. But later on, when the temple's abbot came to take a closer look, he noticed something peculiar.

The Buddha image's nose was starting to disintegrate, revealing a hint of emerald green beneath the outer stucco covering. 'There might be something more to this image than first meets the eye,' the abbot thought. Perhaps there was a valuable stone carving beneath the lime plaster. And maybe, the abbot suspected, it might just be a long-lost Buddha image that people only knew from myths and legends.

Unable to contain his curiosity, he called for the outer stucco layering to be chipped away. And a small crowd gathered, eager to see what was contained underneath. Sure enough, the abbot had been correct.

Beneath the outer covering was a green Buddha image of about one cubit in height. It was carved from a rare gemstone and was completely free of blemishes. There was no mistaking it: this was the revered Emerald Buddha of wondrous powers that had mysteriously disappeared decades prior.

The monks of Wat Pa Yeah celebrated the discovery, and people flocked from all over the region to bring the sacred statue offerings. Many wishes were granted, and a joyous time was had by all. Eventually, however, word got out to the king of Lanna, who demanded that the statue be transported to the capital at once.

---

i While many popular retellings of the Chronicle begin at this point in Chiang Rai, you can start reading about the statue's origin story and early history from p163. However, starting here before approaching the Chronicle's first half as a 'prequel' is probably the easiest way to digest the full tale.

Previous p268

Next p48

The Emerald Buddha in Chiang Rai

The Emerald Buddha's chance discovery at Wat Pa Yeah (current Wat Phra Kaew) is probably the most often retold part of the statue's backstory. While, according to the Chronicle, the image is over 2,000 years old, there's no mention of the Emerald Buddha in historical manuscripts until the 15th century. That's why many summaries of the statue's journeys begin at this moment in 1434 Chiang Rai.

As even now, the Emerald Buddha is revered as the protector of the entire Thai nation, the story of its chance finding in Chiang Rai remains widely celebrated. Most modern versions of the tale detail the dramatic lightning strike and the statue's discovery under layers of stucco. But oddly enough, these details are largely missing from numerous versions of the original Chronicle.

In Camille Notton's English translation of the Chronicle of the Emerald Buddha, the lightning strike is only mentioned in a footnote within the addendum section at the back! Notton notes that the story appears in what's known as the Yonok Chronicle, itself a compilation of various Northern Thai tales.

But in this instance, at least, the Yonok version of the story also seems to be the most historically accurate. It describes the event as having taken place during the reign of Sam Fang Kaen, who was indeed the king of Lanna in 1434.

Other versions, in contrast, date the event to the reign of kings who had already died (such as Kue Na) or who hadn't yet taken the throne. So if the Yonok version of the story managed to nail the right date, then we have reason enough to believe that lightning really did strike the *chedi*.

As mentioned on p20, *chedis* usually contain important relics, even if it means hiding them from public view. Bones or hairs of the Buddha himself are sometimes enshrined in them, while sacred Buddha statues are often concealed within as well. Therefore, had there been no lightning strike at Wat Pa Yeah, the Emerald Buddha might even still be there today!

But who hid the Emerald Buddha in the first place, and why? Those questions will eventually get answered on p268, but it had to do with the tumultuous political situation at the time. In any case, a separate, more recent discovery reveals that concealing statues in stucco was once a fairly common practice.

One day in 1950s Bangkok, a massive 5.5-ton Buddha image was being transported by crane. But the machine could barely hold onto it, and in the process, some of the statue's plaster broke off. Only then did the local monks realize that the image was entirely made of pure solid gold!

The golden image dates back to 13th-century Sukhothai but was later brought to Ayutthaya. To hide it from Burmese looters in 1767, it was concealed beneath thick stucco. And the strategy was so successful that the statue's true nature remained unknown for centuries. Today, the stunning golden image can be visited at Bangkok's Wat Traimit *(see p159)*.

The Emerald Buddha would only stay in Chiang Rai for a few years following its discovery. Nevertheless, Wat Phra Kaew has been inextricably linked with the Emerald Buddha ever since. And even today, it's still considered the city's most important temple.

CHIANG RAI TRAVEL TIPS

First founded in 1262 by King Mangrai, Chiang Rai has remained an important cultural hub ever since. Today, with a population of around 80,000 people, Chiang Rai is Thailand's northernmost major city.

In addition to being a great place to experience traditional Lanna culture, Chiang Rai is also regarded as one of Thailand's most creative towns. It was home to 'National Artist of Thailand' Thawan Duchanee, whose Baan Dam house is a must-visit for all art lovers. Meanwhile, Wat Rong Khun (the White Temple) and the Blue Temple uniquely blend modern art with traditional Theravada Buddhism.

At least two full days in Chiang Rai is ideal, though you could easily fill up three or four.

 ## GETTING THERE

As Chiang Rai has no railway, most people reach the city by **bus**. From Chiang Mai, the ride lasts a little over three hours and buses are operated by a company called Green Bus. A couple of buses leave every hour and there are different classes to choose from, with the most expensive option going for just around 260 baht.

Green Bus tickets can be purchased at the bus station itself or at select travel agents around Chiang Mai. It's also possible to reserve tickets online and pay at a local 7-11 convenience store. Chiang Rai has two bus stations, but be sure to get off at the one located in the center of town (Terminal 1).

Flying is another option. Chiang Rai has its own airport and is well-connected to many other cities in Thailand, including Krabi in the south *(see p196)*. You can expect a taxi from the airport to the city center to cost around 200 baht.

If you're visiting Luang Prabang, Laos first, you can also take a **riverboat** to the border town of Chiang Khong in Chiang Rai Province, about 65 km east of the provincial capital.

 ## GETTING AROUND

If you're based in the city center, you can get to places like Wat Phra Kaew, Wat Phra Singh, the Night Bazaar and the bus station on foot. But to get to the 'colored temples,' Wat Huai Pla Kang or Doi Tung mountain, you'll need motorized transport.

Public buses run from the central bus terminal to the White Temple and Baan Dam, although the dropoff points are some distance away from each. And as the 'colored temples' are located at opposite ends of the city, seeing them all with public transport alone would be a major hassle.

With that in mind, a **ridesharing** app like Grab is the best choice for getting around Chiang Rai. The service is affordable, safe and cheap.

Many visitors also rent their own **motrobikes**, but be sure to understand the safety risks *(see p283)*.

‹ Chiang Rai's Clock Tower is the work of local artist Chalermchai Kositpipat, the man behind the White Temple. Every evening, you can witness a light show at 19:00, 20:00 and 21:00.

CHIANG RAI

WHERE TO STAY

As Chiang Rai's major attractions are spread out all over the area, you're going to be doing a lot of moving around no matter where you stay. But it would be wise to stay within walking distance of the central bus terminal. This would also give you quick and easy access to Wat Phra Kaew, Wat Phra Singh, the Clock Tower and the Night Bazaar.

Chiang Rai is becoming increasingly popular with tourists nowadays, and there are a wide range of accommodation options throughout the city. Depending on your budget, you can find backpacker hostels, cozy inns and luxury hotels all within the city center.

FOOD

During your time in Lanna, don't miss the chance to indulge in Northern Thai cuisine. Lanna's most popular dish is arguably Khao Soi. It consists of soft egg noodles in a coconut-based curry broth. Crispy noodles are then placed on top, while the dish also features an egg and a choice of meat.

Another common noodle dish is Khanom Jeen Nam Ngiao, or rice noodles in a spicy tomato broth. Spicy sausage, or Sai Oua, is also very popular. Many meals in Lanna come with sticky rice, a local staple.

In Chiang Rai, a good place to try local food is the Night Bazaar, while there are a wide variety of restaurants in the city center. Lanna cuisine, of course, can also be enjoyed in Lampang and Chiang Mai.

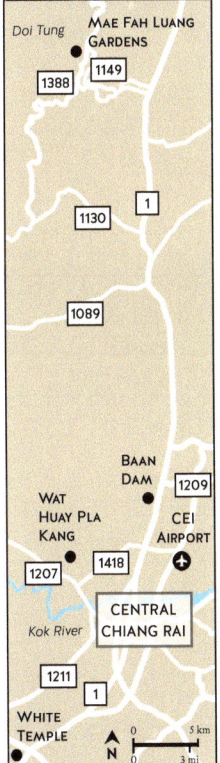

Central Chiang Rai

Wat Phra Kaew • วัดพระแก้ว

The Emerald Buddha was here

As described in the Chronicle, the jade image was found here in 1434. The temple, which likely dates back to the late 14th century, was then known as Wat Pa Yeah ('Golden Bamboo Forest Temple'). But shortly after the amazing discovery, its name was changed to Wat Phra Kaew ('Temple of the Emerald Buddha') - the first of many to be named as such.

- 1 19 Trairat Rd.
- 7:00 - 18:00
- Daily
- Free

Currently, with the exception of the *chedi*, none of the current structures predate the events of the story. Therefore, it's unclear exactly where the Emerald Buddha would've been kept upon its discovery.

Interestingly, the 'Chiang Mai' version of the manuscript implies that the image, while covered in stucco, was never put in the *chedi* to begin with, but on a stand behind the old *viharn*. The existence of the jade statue beneath the stucco, according to this particular version, was revealed to a 9-year-old novice monk in a dream. In it, he saw the Hindu god Indra descending down to Wat Pa Yeah from the heavens.

Though the original statue is long gone, Wat Phra Kaew continues to pay homage to its legacy. As soon as visitors enter the temple, they'll find a brief written history of the Emerald Buddha's journeys. And the temple is also home to the finest Emerald Buddha replica in the country.

In spite of its central location, the temple is surprisingly quiet. While not a huge complex, there's enough here to occupy your time for at least an hour.

‹ *A shrine dedicated to King Mangrai, the founder of the Lanna Kingdom*

The Emerald Buddha Replica

Within a special teak structure called the Haw Phra Yok, you can find one of Thailand's most detailed and accurate Emerald Buddha replicas. The image was completed in 1990 in commemoration of the Princess Mother's 90th birthday. And the following year, it arrived all the way from Bangkok as part of a grand procession.

The statue was carved from a single block of Canadian jade, which is of a noticeably darker hue than that of the original. Furthermore, it was deliberately made to be just .1 cm shorter than the 66 cm-high Emerald Buddha.

The Haw Phra Yok, built specifically to house the replica, opened in 1998. It was built in the traditional style of Chiang Saen, now a town in northern Chiang Rai Province.

Inside, visitors can get an up-close-and-personal view of the image from all angles. This is a real treat considering how the original in Bangkok can only be viewed from a distance.

Around the Haw Phra Yok

Elsewhere inside, scenes from the Chronicle are depicted all around the room. Around the base of the altar, relief carvings show the statue being discovered in the *chedi* and monks chipping away at its stucco covering. The colorful murals along the wall, meanwhile, portray many events from the statue's early adventures, along with the recent grand procession of the replica.

Don't miss the intricate details all around the base of the altar

Jade & its Historic Role in Sacred Art

The Emerald Buddha is just one of many sacred objects around the world to have been carved from jade. The stone, in fact, has been highly revered by numerous cultures for thousands of years. And throughout history, jade objects have been used for everything from rainmaking rituals to burial rites.

What is Jade?

When we use the term 'jade,' we're really talking about either one of two distinct minerals: jadeite or nephrite.

Nephrite, largely comprised of calcium and magnesium, is often found in a greenish hue, but can also come in colors like yellow, white, brown or black. The different shades are dependant upon the amount of other minerals, like titanium or chromium, present in the stone. Nephrite has been used for carvings in China since several thousand years ago, and today it's also sourced from places like Canada.

Jadeite, in contrast, is a silicate of aluminum and sodium, and always comes in varying shades of green. Jadeite can be found in places like Myanmar, Guatemala, the United States, Canada and Russia.

Mesoamerican civilization like the Mayans, Teotihuacanos and Aztecs carved objects from jadeite, valuing it more highly than gold. In addition to nephrite, the Chinese have also used jadeite for carvings as well, but mostly from the 17th century onward.

But which one is the Emerald Buddha? In the 19th century, Thailand's King Mongkut (r.1851-68) proclaimed that the Emerald Buddha was carved from a block of jade sourced from China, but nobody's certain of which variety. As only Thai royalty can touch the image, we're unlikely to find out any time soon. (Some even speculate the statue is made from green jasper.)

Jade's Uses & Significance

In Mesoamerican civilizations, jade was a symbol of life itself. It's been closely associated with agriculture and the material was often used to symbolize the god of corn, Mesoamerica's most important crop.

Mayan royalty adorned themselves with jade jewelry, while the Teotihuacan civilization used it to create expressive burial masks.

A jade mask from Teotihuacan, Mexico

Jade was also used for elite burials in ancient China. During the Han dynasty, for example, the ruling elite even created entire body suits comprised of thousands of jade pieces! And even long before that, round jade discs with holes in the middle were used for millennia, from as far back as 5,000 BC. But for what? To this day, nobody really knows for sure.

Traditionally, jade in China has signified virtues like honesty, integrity, intellect and patience.

And in India, the supposed birthplace of the Emerald Buddha, the most significant jade work belongs to the Jain religion. At the Kolanupake Temple in Telangana is a 1.5 meter-high carving of Lord Mahavira. Not only is it one of the largest jade statues in the world, but it happens to be as old as 2,000 years.

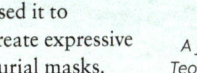

◁ *An 18th-century Chinese nephrite Buddha*

The Saengkaew Museum

Established in 1995, the Saengkaew Museum covers two stories of a structure built in the traditional Lanna style. You'll find all kinds of Buddha images and other relics from the Lanna Kingdom's past, most of which have been donated to the temple over the years.

The museum also contains yet another Emerald Buddha replica made of Canadian jade. It even shares the same dimensions as the one at the temple. And there's also one more green image, but instead of jade, it was carved from a stone found in the Mekong River.

Museum entry is **free** and it closes at 17:00.

A modern statue in the traditional Chiang Saen art style. It's made of locally sourced green stone.

^ From the museum window, you can see the 'golden bamboo' after which the temple was originally named

The Chedi

It was this very *chedi*, that, according to legend, was struck by lightning, revealing the Emerald Buddha inside. Obviously, it's since been repaired!

The Ubosot

The *ubosot* sits at the center of the complex and dates back to 1890. Built in the Chiang Saen architectural style, the structure contains a Buddha image called the Phra Chao Lanthong. The large brass and copper statue is said to be around 700 years old.

And it moved around a couple of times before being brought here in 1961.

Wat Phra Singh • วัดพระสิงห์

📍 Phra Sing Alley
🕐 6:00 - 17:00
📅 Daily
฿ Free

Also in the city center, within easy walking distance of Wat Phra Kaew, is Wat Phra Singh, once home to the Phra Sihing Buddha image. The golden image is believed to have been created in Sri Lanka in the 2nd century AD. And like the Emerald Buddha, the Phra Sihing has done a fair amount of traveling around the region. It's generally regarded as the country's second most important relic.

The temple was established back in 1385 when the golden Buddha statue was first brought to Chiang Rai from Kamphaeng Phet.

As the legend goes, Maha Proma, the prince of Chiang Rai, desired the statue so much that he arrived in Kamphaeng Phet with an army of 80,000 men! Fortunately for everyone involved, the local king parted with it 'voluntarily.'

The Viharn ›

The *viharn*, which houses a small Phra Sihing replica, was built in the typical Lanna style of architecture. Adorning the interior walls are beautiful murals which portray scenes from the statue's long and eventful history.

The Ubosot

The *ubosot*, also of the Lanna style, contains an assortment of different Buddha images, one of them being a purple replica of the Phra Sihing! The doors, meanwhile, were carved by the late Thai National Artist and Chiang Rai native, Thawan Duchanee *(see next page)*.

▲ Before your visit to Wat Phra Singh, be sure to read the statue's full history covered on pp190-193. You'll likely recognize a few scenes along the walls!

The Chedi

The *chedi* is likely one of the temple's oldest structures. It's entirely plated with gold, much like the *chedis* at Wat Phra Singh in Chiang Mai *(see p74)*.

The 'Colored Temples'

Chiang Rai is home to an exciting creative movement which blends modern art and architecture with the philosophy of Buddhism. This is exemplified perfectly by the city's three 'colored temples,' each the brainchild of a different artist.

Black

- 414 Moo 13 Nanglae
- 9:00 - 17:00
- Daily
- ฿ 80

Baan Dam

Once the compound of influential artist Thawan Duchanee, Baan Dam, or the Black House, comprises of roughly 40 structures. You'll encounter animal bones, traditional Lanna architecture, Balinese wood carvings and the artist's trademark monochrome paintings.

‹ *Expressive guardians and divinities can be spotted all over the temple complex*

Outside, countless arms grasp at the air, seemingly from the depths of the underworld. Wat Rong Khun takes visitors through hell before ultimately elevating them to heaven.

The Blue Temple

Like the White Temple, the Blue Temple, or Wat Rong Suea Ten, is also a growing and evolving modern temple. Created by one of Kositpipat's students, the vibrant sapphire blue which covers the temple has a mesmerizing and calming effect.

Chiang Rai

White	Blue
📍 San Sai	📍 306 Rim Kok
🕒 6:30 - 18:00	🕒 6:30 - 19:00
📅 Daily	📅 Daily
฿ 50	฿ Free

TRANSPORT: The temples are located at opposite ends of the city. While a public bus (20 baht) from central Chiang Rai can take you to either the White Temple or Baan Dam, the easiest way to see all three temples would be to use a ridesharing app.

Take a look inside Baan Dam's various chedis - you never quite know what you'll find inside!

^ A crocodile hide forms the shape of a pentagram in front of a row of custom-made chairs

The White Temple

The White Temple, or Wat Rong Khun, is the masterpiece of legendary Thai artist Chalermchai Kositpipat. As an ever-growing work-in-progress, some consider it to be Buddhism's Sagrada Familia. The symbolism, which ranges from hellish to heavenly, will stick with you long after your visit.

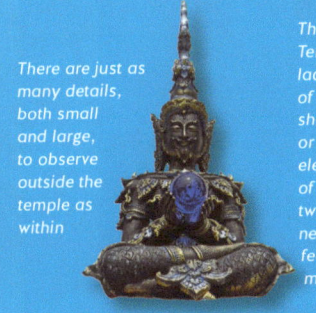

There are just as many details, both small and large, to observe outside the temple as within

The Blue Temple lacks some of the more shocking or darker elements of the other two, but nevertheless feels very modern

Mae Fah Luang Botanical Garden

🕐 6:30 - 18:00
฿ 90 (200 w/Royal Villa)

Overlooking the mountains of neighboring Myanmar, Doi Tung's Mae Fah Luang Botanical Gardens are home to a gorgeous array of plants and flowers from around the world. But while strolling through the peaceful gardens, one would never guess that the area was once ground zero for a thriving opium and weapons trade.

Home to members of the Akha minority hilltribe, the area was once occupied by the Chinese Kuomintang army who used it as their base from which to fight Communist forces. They relied on poppy cultivation to fund their operations, with much of the labor being carried out by the local Akha. But now that that page of history has turned, Thai authorities have been working hard to clean up the region.

Beginning in the late '80s, Princess Srinagarindra started the initiative to create the botanical garden while also providing locals with alternative means to earn an income. Local Akha now put their efforts into coffee production and handicrafts.

Located far from the city center, private transport is required to get to Doi Tung.

Wat Huai Pla Kang · วัดห้วยปลากั้ง

One of Chiang Rai's more recent temples, Wat Huai Pla Kang is located around 6 km northwest of the city. The most striking feature of this mountaintop temple is its gargantuan statue of Guan Yin, the 'Bodhisattva of Compassion,' which stands at 9 stories high. As impressive as it is from the outside, visitors can ride to the top (40 baht) for stunning views of the surrounding countryside. The interior also contains shrines decorated with intricate stucco carvings of Buddhist divinities.

Additionally, the temple features a towering 9-tier Chinese pagoda. Its pyramidal style is especially unique for Thailand. Inside, visitors can leave offerings for a Guan Yin statue made of sandalwood. If the Chinese influence wasn't clear enough, the edge of the temple grounds contains a mini recreation of the Great Wall of China. The Lanna-style *viharn* in the center, meanwhile, almost feels out of place given its surroundings.

The Hilltribes of Thailand

Northern Thailand, along with neighboring Laos, is home to a number of ethnic groups commonly referred to as 'hilltribes.' For hundreds of years, these groups have maintained their distinct culture, dress and spiritual beliefs, in spite of numerous hardships. Most of them, however, aren't native to Thailand. Many trace their roots to Myanmar or southern China, having crossed the border due to various uprisings in those lands.

While each hilltribe has its own distinct culture and language, they generally practice animism. Many of their important rites and rituals involve local shamans, though an increasing number of tribes are also converting to Christianity.

Traditionally, most tribes have been nomadic, relying on slash-and-burn agricultural techniques. And in addition to crops like rice and maize, many have also relied on the opium trade. Fortunately, though, coffee has gradually been replacing opium as a major cash crop.

The main ethnic groups living in Northern Thailand (and many parts of Laos) are the Akha, Hmong, Karen, Lahu, Lisu and Mien.

For those interested, there are a number of ways to experience hilltribe culture. One of the best ways is to combine a trekking excursion with a homestay in a local village.

To learn more information, visit the HillTribe Museum in Chiang Rai, the Hmong village of Chiang Mai's Doi Suthep (*p76*), or the Traditional Arts & Ethnology Center in Luang Prabang (*p104*).

A Hmong house

Traditional Akha dress

- 553 Moo 3, Rim Kok, Chiang Rai
- 8:00 - 17:00
- Daily
- ฿ 40 (for elevator only)

The Chinese pagoda as viewed from the massive Guan Yin statue ▸

TRANSPORT: This is yet another destination accessible via private transport only. A ridesharing app is the most economical choice. As it's relatively close to Baan Dam, consider combining the two in a single outing.

Lampang
1436 - 1468

The Statue and the Stubborn Elephant

Learning of the miraculous discovery of the Emerald Buddha in Chiang Rai, Sam Fang Kaen, the king of Lanna, ordered a hasty delivery to the capital of Chiang Mai.

The statue was placed on top of an elephant, and the procession headed toward the capital as ordered. Near the crossroads between Lampang and Lamphun, however, a problem arose.

Arriving at the intersection, the elephant carrying the Emerald Buddha refused to move toward Chiang Mai. Instead, it began heading in the opposite direction toward the city of Lampang. The king's men began pulling it back the other way, but to no avail. Once again, the elephant slowed down to a halt.

Yet another attempt was made, but the stubborn elephant still refused to proceed toward the capital. The animal seemed to be in pain, the men realized. Bizarrely, the statue would become extremely heavy once it was pulled in the direction of Chiang Mai. So heavy that even all the men combined could hardly lift it.

On the other hand, once the elephant changed course toward Lampang, the sacred Jewel Image would miraculously return to its normal weight.

King Sam Fang Kaen was a devout believer in the spirits and felt that such a sign should not be taken lightly. He decided to send forth a medium to communicate with the statue itself. During the divination ceremony, the medium concluded that it was the Emerald Buddha's will to travel to the splendid city of Lampang.

The king decided that he had no choice but to accept the omen. Canceling his original plan, he told his men to direct the elephant and the statue toward Lampang, where it would remain for the following thirty-two years.

Previous
p32

Next
p64

The Emerald Buddha in Lampang

The case of the stubborn elephant is one of the most whimsical parts of the entire Emerald Buddha story. But it deals with a topic that people took very seriously in those times: the omen.

As discussed on p17, traditional folk beliefs have long played an important role in Thai culture. According to these beliefs, warnings from the spirits can sometimes manifest as peculiar animal behavior. And choosing to ignore such signs could result in potentially serious consequences.

Interestingly enough, King Sam Fang Kaen was known to have favored spirit worship over Buddhism. In fact, numerous Lanna historical texts refer to him as a heretic! Given his mindset, it's not surprising that he'd take the advice of his spirit medium and cancel his plans to bring the statue to Chiang Mai.

In modern summaries of the tale, it's often implied that the elephant itself was the one who willed to go to Lampang. And this would not be out of place within Thai folklore, as elephants are highly venerated creatures that have traditionally been used to make important decisions.

Kings, unsure of where to build new temples, would often leave the decision up to their royal white elephants. The location of Chiang Mai's Wat Phra That Doi Suthep, for example, was chosen by an elephant carrying relics of the Buddha *(see p76)*.

The statue's sudden increase in weight, meanwhile, is emphasized by the Jinakalamali version of the Chronicle. Interestingly, a nearly identical legend comes from the northeastern province of Nong Khai. In the 1800s, King Mongkut (Rama IV) wanted the venerated Luang Phor Phra Sai statue brought to Bangkok. But, seemingly taking on a mind of its own, the statue became so heavy that the cart carrying it wouldn't budge, no matter how many elephants tried pulling it. After the decision was made for it to stay at Wat Pho Chai (where it remains today), the statue returned to its normal weight *(see p120)*.

As discussed on p18, powerful relics are believed to be capable of acting as spirit vessels. As such, they may sometimes express their own wills, likes and dislikes. A king's reign is considered to be legitimized by the mere possession of such a powerful relic. After all, if the relic itself didn't approve of the king's reign, it could express itself through a variety of natural disasters or supernatural phenomena.

While many orthodox Buddhists shun the worship of spirits, this part of the Chronicle is just one example of how in actual practice, animism and Buddhism are deeply intertwined - even in modern times! To this day, Lampang residents even believe their town to be cursed, a story we'll cover on p55.

Today, Lampang is a city of around 60,000 people and acts as the capital of Lampang Province. While largely overlooked by tourists, it features a plethora of grand temples and historical sites - most notably Wat Phra Kaew Don Tao, the Emerald Buddha's former home.

LAMPANG TRAVEL TIPS

Though it may just be a 90-minute drive from Chiang Mai, not a whole lot of foreign visitors have heard of Lampang. Once home to a thriving teak trade in the 19th and 20th centuries, the city has been in a slump ever since the industry fizzled out. Some locals even blame Lampang's decline on a curse *(see p55)*!

Be that as it may, Lampang is still home to some of North Thailand's most impressive architecture. Around town, you can find teak homes from the 1800s, temples built in the Lanna Kingdom's prime, and even remnants of the ancient Haripunchai Kingdom of which Lampang was once part. Two days should be enough to see the main highlights of this hidden gem.

GETTING THERE

There are a number of ways to reach Lampang. The city is situated on the Northern Line of the national railway, making it directly accessible by **train** from Chiang Mai (around 2 hours) and Bangkok (around 11 hours).

When coming from elsewhere in the Lanna region, **bus** is the easiest option. A one-way trip from Chiang Mai takes just around 90 minutes. From the Arcade Bus Terminal, you can take a bus run by the Green Bus company. And you also have the option of riding in a shared minivan. Just ask a staff member and they should direct you to whichever vehicle is leaving next. As they depart often, don't worry about making reservations in advance.

From Bangkok, you can also find direct buses from the Mo Chit Bus Terminal. And Lampang also has its own airport with direct **flights** to and from Bangkok's Don Muang Airport (DMK).

GETTING AROUND

Getting around Lampang can be a bit of a challenge. Lampang has no tuk tuks, few taxis that you can hail down from the street, and at the time of writing, no ridesharing services. One of the only options is a songthaew (converted pickup truck). But aside from the bus station, you won't see too many driving around town.

Fortunately, many of the city's landmarks can be accessed **on foot**. It's imperative, however, that you find a hotel near the Old Town *(see next page)*.

Or, you could try Lampang's trademark travel method: **horse-drawn carriage**. For around 400 baht an hour, enjoy a slow and peaceful ride to the various landmarks around town.

Wat Phra That Lampang Luang *(p56)* is about 15 km southwest of the city, and to get there you'll need to hire a taxi. Your hotel should be able to arrange one for you. If you have the time and cash, a carriage may even take you as well.

Lampang

 ## WHERE TO STAY

Lampang is divided into two main districts on either side of the Wang River: the Old Town (north side) and the New Town (south side). While most of the tourist attractions are in the Old Town, the New Town is where many hotels are located. Given the city's lack of public transport, this can be an issue. Consider staying at Regent Lodge Lampang, located just south of the river and walkable from Wat Phra Kaew Don Tao and other sites.

 ## FOOD & DRINKS

Many of the city's most popular restaurants and bars are located around the Clock Tower, a few kilometers away from the city's main attractions. But you may be able to find food at your hotel, while typical local Thai food is abundant throughout the city (English menus might not be easy to come by, however). If you're visiting over the weekend, be sure to check out the local Night Market *(see p59)*.

 ## SHOPPING

Lampang is famous for its ceramic industry, which dates back to the 1950s. One of its trademark products is a bowl with a rooster painted on it. Originating in China, the design was once popular all over Thailand for years, but few places outside Lampang produce it today.

You can buy your own rooster bowl, or a wide variety of other ceramics, at various outlets and factories around town - especially along Highway 11.

Wat Phra Kaew Don Tao • วัดพระแก้วดอนเต้าสุชาดาราม

This expansive temple complex was constructed around the year 1436 for the purpose of hosting the Emerald Buddha. But an older 7th-century temple previously existed at the same spot.

- Wiang Nuea, Lampang District
- 7:30 - 17:00
- Daily
- ฿ 20

Some attribute the original to the son of Queen Chamathewi, the first ruler of the ancient Haripunchai Kingdom (see p61). The central *chedi*, in fact, dates all the way back to that time. Later, over the span of several centuries, both traditional Lanna and Burmese-style structures would be added around the complex.

Wat Phra Kaew Don Tao is a large temple that contains plenty to explore for at least a couple of hours. And while there, you'll even find signs and sculptures commemorating the Emerald Buddha's time in the city.

The Emerald Buddha was here

THE CHEDI

The 50 m-high central *chedi* is visible from well outside the temple boundaries. It's said to enshrine a hair of the Buddha and it also predates the modern incarnation of the temple. It was first constructed by the Haripunchai Kingdom, but has likely been redesigned sometime since.

THE BURMESE MONDOP

Just next to the *chedi* is a much newer *mondop*, built in 1909 in the Burmese style.

Though the Lanna Kingdom was a vassal of Burma from the 16th-18th centuries, this structure, and many like it around Lampang, are much more recent creations. This is largely due to the presence of wealthy Burmese teak traders in the early 20th century.

‹ The mondop *isn't just pretty from the outside. The interior houses a serene Mandalay-style Buddha image in front of a backdrop of beautifully decorated mosaic glass.*

THE UBOSOT

The temple's current *ubosot* was built in the 1920s. Inside is a large golden Buddha image seated at the center of the altar. But looking closely, you can also see two Emerald Buddha replicas on either side.

Given the building's age, it's probable that an older *ubosot* would've once occupied the same spot. While it's uncertain exactly where the Emerald Buddha was kept for its 32 years at the temple, it was likely in an older structure that's no longer with us.

The Viharn

Like the *ubosot*, the main *viharn* was also constructed in the 1920s. It sports a multitiered roof that's typical of the Lanna architectural style. And inside you'll find a golden reclining Buddha image.

The *viharn* is also home to a small museum containing various Lanna artifacts, though it often seems to be closed.

^ The viharn's glistening Buddha image is often kept behind bars. It represents the Buddha's last moments before departing from this world.

Wat Suchadaram

Wat Suchadaram was built in 1804 as a way to appease the angry spirit of a wrongfully beheaded woman named Mae Suchada *(see opposite page)*. It was once its own separate temple but has since merged with its older and larger neighbor. In fact, the full official name of the temple complex nowadays is 'Wat Phra Kaew Don Tao Suchadaram.'

The small *ubosot* here incorporates elements of Lanna, Burmese and Lao architecture. In front of it is a larger wooden *viharn*. But unfortunately, it's often kept locked up and can only be admired from the outside.

Locals say that the grounds on which this temple stands used to be Mae Suchada's watermelon field. And this is also where she would've acquired her magical fruit.

‹ Mae Suchada figurines like these ones can be spotted all over Lampang these days

‹ Nearby Wat Suchadaram is an old brick chedi. It was originally a round top above a square base. Supposedly, an old local ruler of the town used to keep his elephant here as he went to worship the Buddha's relics at the main central spire.

The Watermelon, the Stone and the Curse

A local Lampang legend has it that a woman called Mae (or sometimes Nan) Suchada once offered a watermelon to a monk. But this was no ordinary watermelon. Opening it up, the monk discovered a large green stone inside. Suspecting some sort of black magic or witchcraft, the locals were so intimidated by Mae Suchada that they went as far as beheading her! (According to another version, however, the townsfolk thought she'd been trying to seduce the monk.)

Before her gruesome death, Mae Suchada made sure to put a curse on the town. And any misfortune or disaster that's befallen Lampang since gets blamed on her hex.

Small statues of Mae Suchada can now be found all over Lampang, from temple grounds to homes to storefronts. In many Southeast Asian cultures, offerings are often made to vengeful spirits in order to keep them at bay, ideally encouraging them to provide protection rather than cause harm.

And in addition to the countless small idols of Mae Suchada around Lampang, Wat Suchadaram was also constructed in her honor.

But what about the green stone? According to legend, the monk hired a sculptor to turn it into a Buddha statue, referred to locally as the 'Watermelon Emerald Buddha.' Supposedly, the two Emerald Buddhas resided at Wat Phra Kaew Don Tao for the exact amount of time: 32 years!

Strangely, the local legend does not seem to acknowledge the original Emerald Buddha directly. And the Chronicle of the Emerald Buddha makes no reference to Mae Suchada whatsoever. It's likely that the watermelon story was concocted later on to help locals cope with the loss of the original image. Mysteriously, though, the true creation date and origins of the 'Watermelon Emerald Buddha' remain unknown.

Mae Suchada and the monk

A poster of the 'Watermelon Emerald Buddha' at Wat Phra That Lampang Luang

Today, both green relics are honored at the Wat Phra Kaew Don Tao, albeit separately. Around the large complex, you'll find both sculptures and informational plaques dedicated to each.

The 'Watermelon' carving now resides at a temple called Wat Phra That Lampang Luang, about a thirty-minute drive away *(see next page)*.

The story of Mae Suchada is just one example of how the Emerald Buddha's backstory has become intertwined with various local legends.

Wat Phra That Lampang Luang • วัดพระธาตุลำปางหลวง

Constructed in the 13th century, Wat Phra That Lampang Luang is widely recognized as one of the country's most important temples. Supposedly, the Buddha himself even visited the site a few thousand years back.

- Ko Kha district
- 7:30 - 17:00
- Daily
- Free

Situated on a hill, the temple was built as a fortified monastery and the complex is surrounded by thick boundary walls. Looking closely, you might even spot some bullet holes from an early 18th-century battle against the Burmese.

The temple remains very well-preserved, and it's one of the best surviving examples of a classical Lanna temple. You'll find sand-covered grounds and open, airy *viharns* - features that were quite common several centuries ago.

Viharn Nam Tam

This early 15th-century *viharn* is considered to be the oldest unrestored wooden structure in all of Thailand! It contains a plethora of Buddha images along with ancient murals.

The Chedi

Though rebuilt in 1449, the central *chedi* is likely even much older. Standing at 45 m high, it's said to contain a hair of the Buddha which he supposedly left during a visit to the area. ⌄

The Soom Phra Baht

One of the most unique features of the temple can be found inside the small Soom Phra Baht chapel. Stepping inside, the light that shines through the hole in the door produces a full reflection of the temple's main *chedi*, albeit upside down.

This is a natural phenomenon referred to as a 'pinhole image' or 'camera obscura.' It has to do with the way light gets reflected when traveling through small openings.

^ Sorry ladies, but this particular structure is restricted to men only

The 'Watermelon Emerald Buddha'

The 'Watermelon Emerald Buddha' *(see p55)* is kept in a museum near the northwestern corner of the complex. The image remains behind bars for most of the year, only getting taken out for special ceremonies. While hard to see, nearby posters offer a clearer picture. The statue is quite similar to the original, but skinnier. It also wears a variation of seasonal costumes like its brother in Bangkok *(see p149)*.

Viharn Luang ^

The largest of the temple's many *viharns*, Viharn Luang dates back to the late 15th century. It has a three-tiered roof and is held up by large pillars adorned with intricate gold patterns.

‹ This massive Bodhi tree requires dozens of sticks to hold up all its branches

The Ubosot ⌄

Compared to many of the *viharns* around the compound, the *ubosot*, which dates back to the late 15th century, is small and humble. The golden-patterns adorning the gable are a fine example of Lanna temple art.

The House of Many Pillars • บ้านเสานัก

Built in 1895, the House of Many Pillars, or Ban Sao Nak as it's locally known, remains one of Lampang's most significant landmarks. Originally the family home of a wealthy Burmese businessman named Mon U San Ong, the house utilizes both traditional Lanna and Burmese architecture. It's entirely built out of teak, and, as the name suggests, is held up by many pillars - 116 of them in total!

In the 19th and 20th centuries, Lampang's teak industry was booming, with the town acting as a hub for traders from both China and Burma. Not only is the House of Many Pillars an architectural marvel, but it's also a symbol of Lampang's bygone heyday.

- 85 Rathwattana Rd.
- 10:00 - 17:00
- Daily
- 50

The house's interior contains all sorts of antiquities, ranging from lacquerware to clothing to old record players. Walking around inside, it's easy to get the sense that the family might return home at any moment.

Wat Chedi Sao Lang • วัดพระเจดีย์ซาวหลัง

- Thon Thong Chai
- 8:00 - 16:30
- Daily
- Free

This unique temple is named after its twenty white *chedis*. Each supposedly contains hairs of Indian monks who came to the region about 2,000 years ago.

Aside from the usual structures you'd expect to find at a Thai temple, Wat Chedi Sao Lang also features a strange museum. In addition to dozens of miniature Buddha images, there's even a gun collection on display, while stacks of old computers and television sets take up much of the first floor!

LAMPANG

Given the laidback atmosphere of Lampang (a vibe which many compare to that of Chiang Mai from twenty years ago), you might want to stick around for awhile. Note that some of the region's main highlights, featured on the following two pages, require full day trips outside the city.

AROUND TOWN

THE PRATU MA WALLS

Pratu Ma, or the Ma Gate, is the northernmost of Lampang's seven original gates. The city walls were first established in the 13th century back when the town was known as Khelanga. This is actually the same name used in the Chronicle of the Emerald Buddha to refer to the city of Lampang.

THE WANG RIVER

Another enjoyable activity is a walk along the Wang River. There aren't many places to sit riverside to enjoy a meal or coffee, but much of the area is walkable nonetheless.

THE NIGHT MARKET

Those visiting over the weekend shouldn't miss the Night Market which takes place along Talat Gao Road on Sat. and Sun. nights. You'll find an array of tasty treats at a market primarily intended for locals rather than tourists.

And at one end is the eye-catching Ratsadapisek Bridge which lights up after dark.

LANNA-STYLE HOUSES

Traditional Northern Thai houses, often made of teak, are typically built on stilts. The bottom space might be used for storage or as a common area.

These houses are also known for their triangular gables, with V-shaped *kalae* extending out from the top. Often intricately decorated, the *kalae* are said to represent water buffalo horns.

They often comprise of multiple cabins which are typically grouped together, sharing a single veranda. The main cabin also usually doubles as a shared sleeping space for the entire family.

In Lanna today, traditional houses are becoming an increasingly rare sight. But as Lampang is among Lanna's least modernized cities, it can be a good place to spot some.

Wat Chalermprakiat · วัดเฉลิมพระเกียรติฯ

Wat Chalermprakiat, a mountain temple located in the north part of Lampang Province, evokes a sense of magic and mystery from ages long past. Surprisingly, though, it's actually one of Lampang's newest attractions. After nearly a decade of work, the unique temple was finally completed in 2015.

Looking out at the dozens of white *chedis* topping the distant mountain crags, it's unclear how the temple builders were able to accomplish such a feat. But it's a jaw-dropping sight nonetheless.

From the base, visitors hike up an 800-meter trail to reach an open *viharn* and several lookout pavilions. They all offer excellent views of the distant *chedis*, with Lampang's lush green countryside as a backdrop.

TRANSPORT:

Wat Chalermprakiat can only be reached by private transport, and it's about equal distance from both Chiang Mai and Lampang. In total, visitors pay 260 baht to access the temple. From the entrance, you'll need to ride up the steep road to the base area via an official songthaew that's included in the ticket price.

Lamphun

Located in between Lampang and Chiang Mai, the small city of Lamphun is one of Thailand's most historically significant cities. Before the emergence of Lanna, the kingdom of Haripunchai had long been the dominant force in North Thailand.

Established in the 7th century by Queen Chamathewi from Lopburi, Haripunchai was a major cultural center where religion and the arts thrived for centuries. It was also Queen Chamathewi's younger son who originally founded Lampang.

Many of Lamphun's original temples are still standing, most of which can be enjoyed in a single day. The town, therefore, is a must-visit for history and temple lovers.

Wat Phra That Haripunchai

A Self-Guided Walking Tour

Start your day off at the **Chamathewi Monument**, where you'll find an overview of Lamphun's history carved in beautiful bas-reliefs. Then head over to **Wat Mahawan**, home to the ancient Phra Rod image, the basis for one of Thailand's most popular amulets.

Further west, **Wat Chamathewi** features the Mahapol Chedi, the finest example of its style in all of Thailand. Back in the town center, the **Haripunchai National Museum** is the place to learn about the town's history, art and architecture.

And just nearby is **Wat Phra That Haripunchai**. The elaborate temple is situated on the site of Queen Chamathewi's royal palace, and its central golden spire enshrines a relic of the Buddha himself.

East of the walled city is **Wat Yuen**, known for its massive Burmese-style *chedi*. Northwest of that is **Ku Chang Ku Ma**, a pair of brick tombs. One enshrines Queen Chamathewi's magical white elephant, while another enshrines her son's horse.

Finally, no visitor to Lamphun should miss **Wat Sanpanyang Luang**. Originally a Hindu shrine, it was converted to a Buddhist temple in 531 AD, making it the oldest temple in all of Northern Thailand! Appropriately, the temple's stunning decoration fuses together Hindu and Buddhist motifs.

‹ *The Mahapol Chedi*

TRANSPORT: From Chiang Mai, take a shared minivan (around 20 baht) from either Bus Terminal 1 (Chang Phueak station) or Warorot Market.

From Lampang, you should also be able to find songthaews and minivans from the main bus station.

On the Northern railway line, Lamphun is the stop in between Lampang and Chiang Mai.

Chiang Mai
1468 - 1551

The Long-Awaited Arrival

Sam Fang Kaen's son, Tilokarat, took over the Lanna throne in the year 1441. As the Emerald Buddha sat in Lampang, King Tilokarat worked hard to complete the spectacular 'Royal Spire' that would come to be known as Wat Chedi Luang.

Enshrined within the chedi were the ashes of Tilokarat's great-grandfather, Kue Na. Though it was started by his grandfather and expanded by his father, the great monarch Tilokarat was the one to finally bring the spire to completion.

It was, by far, the tallest structure in the land. And it would be a worthy home for the magnificent Emerald Buddha statue, King Tilokarat decided. He ordered the Jewel Image to be brought to the Lanna capital from Lampang. And upon its arrival, he placed it in the eastern niche of the giant chedi to the delight and celebration of all.

As the Emerald Buddha resided in Chiang Mai, the city and kingdom of Lanna enjoyed many years of prosperity, and the religion of the Buddha flourished. King Tilokarat eventually passed away at the age of seventy-eight, but his descendants would continue to rule Lanna for the next eight decades.

And they all kept close watch over the sacred jade statue. That is, until, the lack of a proper heir to the throne caused great worry and confusion throughout the land.

A statue of King Tilokarat at Wat Ched Yod, where the king's ashes are enshrined. To learn more about Tilokarat's reign, you can also visit a free museum at Wat Inthakin in the center of Chiang Mai's Old City

Previous
p48

Next
p86

The Emerald Buddha in Chiang Mai

Nearly four decades after its rediscovery, the Emerald Buddha finally made its way to the Lanna capital during the reign of King Tilokarat (a.k.a. Tilokkarat, Tilokaraj, Tilok, Tilaka or a number of other variations). Upon the completion of the massive 'Royal Spire,' or Wat Chedi Luang, Tilokarat had the Emerald Buddha delivered from Lampang, placing it in the *chedi's* eastern niche. This event is widely agreed upon by historians.

After King Mangrai, Lanna's founder, Tilokarat is arguably the kingdom's most important historical figure. It was during his reign that Lanna experienced its 'Golden Age,' reaching its apex both militarily and culturally.

King Tilokarat expanded Lanna to its largest ever size. He captured the neighboring territories of Nan and Phrae, which had previously been controlled by Sukhothai, along with some Shan states to the west. Even parts of present-day Yunnan, China, were absorbed into Lanna during his reign.

Tilokarat also assisted the nearby superpower of Lan Chang (modern-day Laos) in a struggle against the Vietnamese. And throughout his reign, he'd become involved in numerous skirmishes with Lanna's longtime rival, the Ayutthaya Kingdom.

Tilokarat was also adamant about strengthening Lanna on a cultural level. In contrast to his father, Sam Fang Kaen, Tilokarat was a devout Buddhist. He bolstered ties with the Theravada stronghold of Sri Lanka, and in 1477, he hosted the eighth World Buddhist Council in Chiang Mai. In preparation for the event, he built Wat Ched Yod, a replica of Mahabodhi Temple in Bodh Gaya, India. This temple now enshrines his ashes.

As mentioned, Tilokarat also finally completed Wat Chedi Luang. The massive *chedi* contains the ashes of his great-grandfather, Kue Na. Finishing the project was no easy feat, and it had already been undergoing construction throughout the previous two reigns.

King Tilokarat, who took the throne in 1441, waited for 27 years before finally bringing the Emerald Buddha over from Lampang in 1468. And as we'll go over on p69, the *chedi* wasn't even fully complete by that point! But it was at least deemed acceptable enough to host the Emerald Buddha, which would remain there for 83 years.

While not mentioned in the Chronicle, the earthquake that took the top off of the *chedi* likely happened while the Emerald Buddha was sitting in its eastern niche! But somehow, it survived unscathed. This would be just one of many calamities the statue would come out of with hardly a scratch.

Following Tilokarat's death in 1487, the Lanna Kingdom would enter a period of gradual decline. Interestingly enough, Lanna would even lose its independence not long after losing the Emerald Buddha. This wouldn't happen until the mid-16th century, however, and these events will be detailed in the following section on Luang Prabang.

Wat Ched Yod >

CHIANG MAI TRAVEL TIPS

While Chiang Mai, Thailand's second-largest city, has been undergoing rapid development as of late, it still retains much of its old charm. Many of the city's original temples and cultural sites - some as old as King Mangrai himself - still remain in pristine condition.

But modern Chiang Mai is also a great place to check out art galleries, see live music and relax at cozy coffee shops. While a few days are enough to see the main sights, those with flexible schedules may choose to stick around for much longer.

GETTING THERE

Chiang Mai is the transport hub of North Thailand and can be reached in a number of ways. **Flying** is easier than ever nowadays. Thailand has plenty of budget airlines to choose from, and one-way tickets from Bangkok's DMK Airport can sometimes go for as cheap as 1,000 baht (roughly $30).

There are also plenty of direct flights between Chiang Mai and other smaller cities in Thailand. And for those coming from elsewhere in Asia, there are direct flights from cities like Kuala Lumpur, Saigon, Shanghai, Hangzhou and Luang Prabang. Chiang Mai International Airport (CNX) also happens to be a short drive from the city center.

You can also easily reach Chiang Mai by **bus** from virtually any city in Thailand. And Chiang Mai is situated on the Northern Line of the national rail system. That means you can get there directly by **train** from Bangkok, Ayutthaya and other cities (*see more on p279*).

GETTING AROUND

Within areas like the Old City or Nimman, Chiang Mai is easy to explore on foot. But you'll want some kind of motorized transport to get from one district to another.

The easiest and most stress-free option is to download a **ridesharing** app like Grab. The rates are cheap and a driver usually shows up within minutes.

You can also get around by hopping in a **red songthaew**. These converted pickup trucks follow regular yet flexible routes for a flat fee of around 30 baht. Flag one down and tell the driver where you're going. Then, hop in the back with the other passengers. The driver will then make slight detours to drop everyone off at their destination. With that in mind, songthaews aren't ideal if you're in a rush.

Tuk tuks are generally best avoided, as they often quote foreigners outrageous rates. And regular taxis are seldom even seen aside from at the airport.

At the time of writing, the city has just revamped its bus system. For around 15 baht per ride, you can take a **public bus** to the railway station, bus terminal, Thaphae Gate and the zoo.

Renting your own **motorbike or scooter** is also an option. Be sure to have the proper license, as there are many police checkpoints throughout the city. Read more about road safety on p283.

CHIANG MAI

🛌 WHERE TO STAY

The two most convenient places to stay in Chiang Mai are the Old City and Nimman. Staying anywhere within or just outside of the moat (*see map*) would be fine, as you can easily get around the Old City on foot. As covered in the following sections, many of Chiang Mai's prominent temples are located here, and it's also home to the famous Sunday Night Market.

West of the Old City, the trendy Nimman district comprises of the general area around Nimmanhaemin Road, its various *sois* and the MAYA shopping mall.

The Old City and Nimman areas are both among the best places in Chiang Mai for dining options, and there's a near limitless number of restaurants to choose from. Learn more about Lanna cuisine on p35.

Wherever you choose to stay, you can find both hotels and vacation rental apartments at a wide range of budgets. If you're looking for luxury, there are also high-rise hotels in the eastern part of the city, in between the Old City and Ping River.

The Old City ⌄

Wat Chedi Luang • วัดเจดีย์หลวง

The Emerald Buddha was here

The construction of the gargantuan Wat Chedi Luang was a long, arduous task that spanned the reigns of three different kings. And it was all so that their ancestor could finally ascend to heaven.

📍 103 Prapokkloa Rd.
🕕 6:00 - 18:00
📅 Daily
฿ 40

According to legend, King Kue Na (r.1355-1385) did not go straight to heaven when he died. Instead, he became the spirit of a banyan tree, located somewhere in between Chiang Mai and Pagan, Burma. One day, during the reign of Kue Na's son, Saen Muang Ma, the spirit spoke to some traveling merchants that were passing by.

'Instead of being reborn in *devaloka*, the realm of the gods, I ended up as this tree spirit! Please, I implore you, tell my son that he needs to build a large *chedi* in the middle of the capital to enshrine my ashes! One that can be seen from at least 4 kilometers away. Only then can I enter heaven.'

And so work began on the *chedi*. But by the time King Saen Muang Ma died in 1401, it was no more than 24 m high. King Sam Fang Kaen then worked on it all throughout his reign, but he also died before its completion. It was finally finished by King Tilokarat in 1481. The Emerald Buddha, however, had already been placed in the *chedi's* eastern niche in 1468.

Located in the center of the Old City district, Wat Chedi Luang remains one of Chiang Mai's most significant temples. Presently, the large complex is actually a composite of three former neighboring temples. And though you couldn't tell by looking at it today, the area around the *chedi* remained a deserted ruin for decades until it was finally restored in the 1990s.

The Chedi

According to some ancient sources, Tilokarat brought the *chedi* up to 96 meters in height, though we'll never know for sure if this was true. Much later, in 1545, an earthquake struck Chiang Mai which caused the *chedi* to collapse. As the Emerald Buddha remained there until 1551, it somehow survived the catastrophe with hardly a mark on it!

Some, however, say that the damage occurred much later in the 18th century during King Taksin's effort to liberate Lanna from the Burmese. Instead of an earthquake, the *chedi* was possibly damaged by cannon fire. Incidentally, Taksin happens to be a major figure in our story, as we'll go over in future sections.

Even with its top missing, the *chedi*, or 'Royal Spire' as it's referred to in the Chronicle, remained the tallest structure in Chiang Mai well into the 20th century.

Aside from its imposing dimensions, the *chedi* is also unique in style, as it pays homage to the Sinhalese, or Sri Lankan style of architecture.

In the 1990s, when the temple was being restored, city officials originally intended to rebuild the missing top. But with no surviving illustrations, no one could fully agree on how it would've originally looked. And so the plan was nixed. The *chedi's* base, however, which had been covered in overgrowth, was cleaned up and redecorated.

The multiheaded naga serpents at the base of the staircases were not part of the original design. They caused quite a stir when they were added in 1992, as locals complained that the Khmer style of the serpents did not mesh well with the Sri Lankan-style chedi.

In 1995, in celebration of the chedi's 600th anniversary, a small Emerald Buddha replica made of black jade was placed in the eastern niche - the same spot where the original once sat. Locals call it the Phra Yok.

Of the 5 elephants in the middle of the chedi, all except the one closest to the southern staircase are recent recreations.

THE CITY PILLAR SHRINE

Just inside the temple entrance, you'll come across what's known as the Chiang Mai City Pillar Shrine. In Indochina, most towns have city pillars which are believed to contain protective spirits. From ancient times until now, local residents have come to pray and bring offerings to these pillars. They hope that their prayers will bring safety and prosperity to their towns.

As is the case with the nearby *chedi*, Chiang Mai's city pillar is also the focus of a popular local legend.

As the story goes, Chiang Mai's original pillar was gifted by none other than Indra himself *(see p15)* long before the city's founding. At the time, the land was a forested area that was rife with demons. After a local hermit prayed to Indra for help, the god sent two giants to carry the protective pillar down from the heavens. They then buried it beneath the earth on the condition that it receive regular offerings. Over time, though, the pillar was neglected and the demons returned.

Years later, when King Mangrai was planning his new capital, he discovered the old pillar underneath the ground. He enshrined it at a temple called Wat Sadue Muang (now Wat Inthakin) and built his new capital with the pillar at the very center. In 1800, while revitalizing the city, Chao Kawila established a new city pillar at Wat Chedi Luang. But the original location can still be visited at Wat Inthakin nearby.

Inside the shrine, beautiful murals depicting Lanna historical events cover the walls, while the top of the pillar is adorned with a standing Buddha image. ⌄

* This shrine is restricted to men only

The Inthakin Festival

Candles and Buddha images surround the large *chedi*, while hundreds of gatherers flood the city pillar shrine. They flow in and out of the structure in a constant stream. And by the time the sky grows dark, the temple grounds are entirely covered in garland flowers and incense sticks. This is no ordinary evening at Wat Chedi Luang, but one of the six-night long Inthakin Festival.

Each year in the sixth month of the lunar calendar (either May or June), a special festival is held in honor of the local city pillar. As the legend goes, Indra gifted it to Chiang Mai on the condition that it receive regular offerings. And the festival is one way to ensure that the people of Chiang Mai uphold their end of the agreement.

But the city pillar isn't considered the only protector of Chiang Mai. Just outside the shrine is a massive *yang* tree which is believed to be the home of yet another protective spirit. When Chao Kawila refurbished Wat Chedi Luang following years of conflict with Burma, he planted three such trees throughout the temple grounds. Should anything ever happen to the trees, locals believe, disaster is bound to strike the city. Additionally, the trees are also symbolic of Chiang Mai's 19th-century rebirth.

Aside from the pillar itself, the focal point of the Inthakin Festival is an image called the Phra Fon Saen Ha. This Buddha statue also contains - you guessed it - a protective guardian spirit! Each night, the image gets paraded around the city before being brought back to Wat Chedi Luang to sit in front of the *viharn*. There, locals ritually pour cups of water over it as part of a rain-making ritual. Meanwhile, replicas placed all around the *chedi* receive similar honors.

During the festival, the pillar, the Buddha image and the tree are all connected by a special white thread, believed to be a way of transferring and sharing potent spiritual energy.

In spite of the Buddhist imagery, the Inthakin Festival is more rooted in animism and Hinduism than in Theravada Buddhism. Supposedly, back in the festival's early days, spirit mediums and even animal sacrifices were involved!

There are still some Buddhist elements to the festival, however. Stepping inside the main *viharn*, you'll see 108 alms bowls (a highly significant number in Buddhism) laid out for people to leave donations and offerings.

To witness the event, simply show up at Wat Chedi Luang as it takes place. You'll likely find yourself as one of the only tourists in attendance.

The Viharn

The main *viharn* was constructed in 1926 and contains a large standing Buddha image known as the Phra Chao Attarot. The image dates all the way back to the reign of King Saen Muang Ma (r.1385-1401). The golden statue stands with one palm facing outward, which is one form of the *abhaya mudra*, or 'dispelling fear' posture.

The Acharn Mun Bhuridatto Viharn

The *viharn* was built in honor of Isaan-born Acharn Mun (1870-1949), a highly revered monk who founded the Thai

Forest Tradition. Though he'd go on to spend his final years in Sakon Nakhon (*p224*), he was the abbot of Wat Chedi Luang from 1932-34. Built in the traditional Lanna style, the *viharn* only dates back to 2003, despite appearing to be much older.

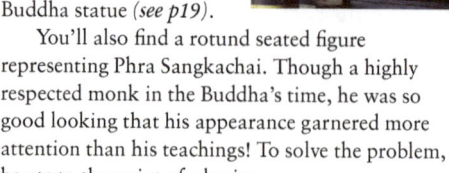

Western Viharns

There are a number of noteworthy images in the western *viharns*, such as a large golden reclining Buddha and a *naga prok* Buddha statue (*see p19*).

You'll also find a rotund seated figure representing Phra Sangkachai. Though a highly respected monk in the Buddha's time, he was so good looking that his appearance garnered more attention than his teachings! To solve the problem, he ate to the point of obesity.

Manuscript Library

Built in 2010, this two-story building contains not only Buddhist scriptures but also information about the temple's history.

Another popular activity for visitors is the **monk chat**. Between 9:00 and 18:00 on most days, temple visitors have the opportunity to speak with monks in English about their religion and lifestyle.

WAT CHIANG MAN • วัดเชียงมั่น

Situated in the northeast corner of the Old City, Wat Chiang Man was the first temple established by King Mangrai in 1297. It's mainly known for its beautiful 'elephant *chedi*' built in the Sri Lankan style.

📍 171 Ratchapakhinai Rd.
🕒 6:00 - 17:00
📅 Daily
฿ 40

Regrettably, both images are normally kept behind bars except on special occasions ˅

The temple contains two *viharns*, the larger of which was renovated in the 1920s by the highly respected Lanna monk Khruba Siwichai. The smaller one, meanwhile, contains two of Lanna's most cherished relics.

THE CRYSTAL BUDDHA

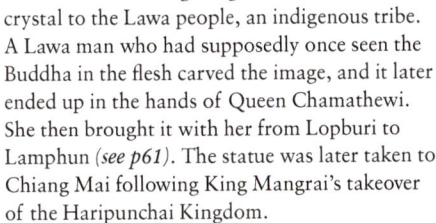

The Crystal Buddha, or the Phra Kaeo Setangkha Mani, is a small image (only 10 cm high) made of quartz crystal. It even has its own chronicle, which tells of Indra gifting the crystal to the Lawa people, an indigenous tribe. A Lawa man who had supposedly once seen the Buddha in the flesh carved the image, and it later ended up in the hands of Queen Chamathewi. She then brought it with her from Lopburi to Lamphun *(see p61)*. The statue was later taken to Chiang Mai following King Mangrai's takeover of the Haripunchai Kingdom.

THE PHRA SILA

The Phra Sila is not a statue but a stele. It depicts the Buddha subduing the wild elephant Nalagiri, a famous Buddhist fable. Interestingly, its chronicle bears similarities to that of the Emerald Buddha. It was supposedly made in Bihar, India a couple of thousand years ago before it traveled to Sri Lanka. It later wound up in Burma, Sawankhalok Province, Lampang and now Chiang Mai. The story, however, was not written down until 1785.

Wat Phra Singh • วัดพระสิงห์

As is the case with Wat Phra Singh in Chiang Rai *(see p41)*, this temple is also named after the famous golden Buddha image. It's also one of Chiang Mai's most significant and eye-catching temples.

📍 2 Samlan Rd. (end of Ratchadamnoen Rd.)
🕒 6:00 - 17:00
📅 Daily
฿ 50 (for viharn)

The Phra Sihing gets paraded around Chiang Mai for Songkran every April. Locals splash it with water as a merit-making gesture. ⌄

It wasn't originally built to house the statue, however. The *chedi* was constructed in 1345 to enshrine the ashes of a former king. The Phra Sihing image was then brought here decades later in 1407.

As the story goes, Maha Proma, the prince of Chiang Rai who'd obtained the Phra Sihing from Kamphaeng Phet, attempted to usurp the Lanna throne. At the time, the teenage Saen Muang Ma had just succeeded

Murals in the viharn ▶

Maha Proma's older brother, Kue Na (whose ashes are at Wat Chedi Luang). Maha Proma figured he could easily defeat his inexperienced nephew, but his attack on Chiang Mai was repelled.

According to one version of the story, Saen Muang Ma took the image during a counterattack. Another version has it that Maha Proma offered it as an apology. Whatever the case may be, the Phra Sihing ended up in Chiang Mai and remained in the city for over 250 years. While the original statue is said to be the one now in Bangkok, some argue that the one still in Chiang Mai could be the real thing. See p190 for the full story.

Viharn Lai Kham

This *viharn* was built to house the Phra Sihing upon its arrival in the city. 'Lai Kham' refers to the intricate red and gold patterns which adorn the interior pillars. And the murals on the walls, which date back to the 1820s, depict various Jataka Tales.

In 1922, thieves broke into the *viharn*, stealing the Phra Sihing's head! Though it was never recovered, it's since been replaced.

Viharn Luang

The largest *viharn* in the center of the complex houses a massive golden Buddha statue that's over 500 years old. The current structure dates from 1925, and it was built by Khruba Siwichai, one of Lanna's most highly revered monks. It replaced the original *viharn* constructed in the 14th century.

The Ubosot

The *ubosot* was built in 1806. In its center is a tall structure specifically built for holding Buddha images. The *ubosot* also contains smaller replicas of both the Phra Sihing and the Emerald Buddha. But the latter, for some reason, is not always present.

The Ho Trai

Another architectural highlight of Wat Phra Singh is its *ho trai*, or manuscript library. It dates back to 1477 and sits on a high platform which helps protect the manuscripts from insects and flooding. Some even consider it to be the finest *ho trai* in Lanna.

The Golden Chedis

Just like its statues, Wat Phra Singh's *chedis* glisten with gold. The central *chedi* is the oldest structure of the entire temple. Constructed in 1345, it contains the ashes of King Kham Fu. It was later enlarged in the early 19th century.

Doi Suthep • ดอยสุเทพ

Roughly 15 km west of central Chiang Mai, Doi Suthep is without a doubt Lanna's most important mountain. It's even said to be inhabited by some of the city's guardian spirits. Ecologically speaking, Doi Suthep is home to thousands of different plant and hundreds of different animal species, all protected by the Doi Suthep-Pui National Park.

The mountain's most famous landmark is **Wat Phra That Doi Suthep**. According to legend, a monk from Sukhothai took a shoulder bone relic of the Buddha to King Kue Na. The king placed the relic on a white elephant, intending to build a temple wherever the elephant chose to go. The elephant proceeded to climb all the way up the mountain, and in 1368, Kue Na enshrined the relic in a large golden *chedi* there.

Around the temple complex, you'll find an *ubosot*, concentric gallery and an open-air terrace with panoramic views of the Chiang Mai area. The temple remains an important pilgrimage spot and can easily be reached by red songthaew *(see p67)*.

Halfway up the mountain is **Wat Pha Lat**, built on the spot where the same elephant from the legend eventually perished (or just rested, according to another version). The scenic temple doubles as a meditation retreat and is known for its unique and evocative sculptures (pictured left). It's accessible by car or on foot via the Monk's Trail which begins near the back entrance of the Chiang Mai Zoo.

Doi Suthep is also home to the botanical gardens of **Bhubing Palace** along with the colorful **Hmong Village** *(see p45)*. The mountain also has no shortage of **waterfalls** and **hiking trails**.

Wiang Kum Kam • เวียงกุมกาม

Wiang Kum Kam, some 6 km southeast of the Old City, was King Mangrai's first attempt at building a new capital for his kingdom. The area was settled in the 1290s but was prone to frequent flooding. Mangrai went on to choose a new location (present Chiang Mai) for his capital, but people continued living in Wiang Kum Kam for hundreds of years. Eventually abandoned during Burmese rule, it wouldn't be discovered again until the 1980s.

Spread throughout a quiet residential area, the free-to-visit archaeological site consists of at least 20 or so ancient temples.

You can get around via horse-drawn carriage (departing from the Information Center), or even on foot.

Outdoor Chiang Mai

Chiang Mai Province has plenty to offer nature lovers. The region is home to countless **elephant sanctuaries** which make for great day trips with friends, family or solo. When choosing among the seemingly endless options, be sure to research whether that place treats their animals humanely. Checking reviews online would be the best way to get an idea. Baan Chang Elephant Park is one good choice among many.

Doi Inthanon National Park is home to Thailand's highest mountain which stands at 2,565 m tall. The park is popular for its hiking trails, wildlife and the Mae Ya Waterfall, Thailand's highest. At the top of the mountain are a pair of twin *chedis* built in honor of King Rama IX and Queen Sirikit for their sixtieth birthdays. You can also buy goods produced by the Karen or Hmong. Group tours to the mountain are very popular.

For those looking to cool off, **bamboo rafting** excursions are popular in both the Mae Taeng and Mae Wang rivers - an activity you could also combine with some elephant interaction (pictured below).

Southwest of the city center is Chiang Mai's own **Grand Canyon**, a former quarry from which visitors can cliff dive into the water from 20 m high.

North of the city, Bua Tong, or the **Sticky Waterfalls**, is a unique site where visitors climb up a series of rocks against the current of the cascading water.

Further afield, **Pai** in Mae Hong Son Province is famous for its caves and gorgeous waterfalls.

Around Town

Those sticking around in Chiang Mai for awhile won't run out of things to do. The city is home to street markets, Muay Thai stadiums, great restaurants and a local zoo. And there's still even plenty more for temple lovers, like Wat Ched Yod, Wat Suan Dok, Wat Umong and the Silver Temple *(see below)*.

The Silver Temple

100 Wua Lai Rd. ฿ 50

Also called Wat Sri Suphan, this is Chiang Mai's answer to Chiang Rai's 'colored temples' *(p42)*. Located just south of the Old City, the *wat* is centuries old. But the stunning *ubosot*, completely covered in silver, was erected by the local silversmith community in 2008. (**Only men are allowed inside the* ubosot.)

Chiang Mai Contemporary Art

Chiang Mai has long been a major creative hub, appealing to artists of all types. **Street art** is abundant throughout the Old City and Nimman districts, while Nimman also hosts some of the city's best art spaces. There, don't miss **Gallery Seescape** or the **CMU Art Center**. Further afield, check out **MAIIAM** in the San Kamphaeng district. West of town, there's the **Wattana Art Gallery** and the **Baan Kang Wat Artist Village** near Wat Umong.

Shopping & Nightlife

The Old City's **Night Market** is worth checking out at least once. Every Sunday evening, it takes up nearly the entire eastern half of the district. Also in the Old City, music lovers can visit the **North Gate Jazz Coop** for nightly free jazz and fusion sessions. The district is also filled with nightclubs and bars. **Nimman** is where to go for modern shopping malls, while there's a bar or restaurant just about everywhere you look.

Muay thai

Those wishing to see some live Muay Thai, Thailand's national sport, have the choice between three venues. **Chiang Mai Boxing Stadium** is the largest, while **Thapae Stadium** is notable for having live musicians play traditional Sarama music during the fights. **Loi Kroh Stadium**, meanwhile, is located in the hub of a lively (yet seedy) bar scene. Check web sites or flyers around town for schedules and costs.

Beginners looking to learn the basics, or *nak muays* wishing to hone their skills, should visit the **Chiangmai Muay Thai Gym** in the Old City or **Lanna Muay Thai** west of Nimman. In the northern part of the province, meanwhile, legendary fighter Buakaw runs the **Banchamek Gym**.

CHIANG MAI FESTIVALS

There's no place to experience traditional Thai festivals quite like Chiang Mai. Even Thais from other regions gather here during major holidays to take part. If your travel plans are flexible, consider visiting Chiang Mai in April or November.

SONGKRAN

Songkran, or Buddhist New Years, is celebrated every April. For three full days, the entire city becomes a battleground for action-packed water fights. Squirt guns are the most popular weapon of choice, with buckets a close second. Things get especially lively around the Old City moat, with some revelers even entering the grotty water to stock up on 'ammo.'

But Songkran is, after all, a religious festival. Water is traditionally poured over Buddha images as a means of purification and making merit. Near the Old City's Tha Phae gate, images like the Phra Sihing get paraded through the busy streets *(see p74)*.

The only way to avoid getting soaked during Songkran is to stay indoors. Anything goes as far as water is concerned, so be sure to keep your phone and wallet safe in sealed plastic bags before going out.

YI PENG & LOI KRATHONG

Every year in November, hundreds of thousands of people flock to Chiang Mai to take part in the dual celebrations of **Yi Peng** and **Loi Krathong**. Over the course of three days, both the waters and skies of Chiang Mai are illuminated with innumerable lanterns, candles and floats. Meanwhile, parades and ceremonies also take place on land. The end result is one of the most magical weekends one can experience in Thailand.

As part of Yi Peng, participants release countless numbers of cylindrical *khom loi* lanterns up into the sky, both at temple courtyards and along the Ping River.

Some say the tradition is related to the story of the Buddha's top knot, now kept in a special crystal *chedi* up in the heavens. The lanterns, then, are a way to send offerings to that mythical relic in the sky.

Loi Krathong, meanwhile involves sending special floats made of folded banana leaves and bamboo down the river. The release of both the lanterns and the floats could be symbolic of letting go of one's anger and negative attachments.

LAOS

The landlocked nation of Laos doesn't get quite as much attention as its neighbors. But that's gradually changing, as an increasing number of savvy travelers are beginning to catch on.

In this chapter, we'll be examining Laos's two largest cities: Luang Prabang and Vientiane. At the time of our story, they were both controlled by the mighty Lan Chang Kingdom. And to this day, awe-inspiring landmarks from the Lan Chang era remain in abundance. Meanwhile, the scenic Mekong River, or 'The Mother of Rivers' as it's known locally, flows through both destinations.

A BRIEF HISTORY OF LAOS 82

LUANG PRABANG 85

    THE JOURNEYS OF THE PHRA BANG 98

VIENTIANE 107

    ONWARD TO NORTHEAST THAILAND 121

A Brief History of Laos

Today, Laos is among the least developed nations in Southeast Asia, and the country spent much of its recent history under foreign occupation. But from the 14th-18th centuries, the kingdom of Lan Chang, the precursor to modern-day Laos, was one of the most dominant and influential superpowers in the region.

The Founding of Lan Chang

Lan Chang (also spelled Lan Xang) was founded in 1353 when a ruler named Fa Ngum united many of the area's smaller territories. But he couldn't have done so without assistance from the Khmer Empire. Though born in Luang Prabang, Fa Ngum actually grew up in Angkor. And that was all because of his father's scandalous behavior.

Fa Ngum's father, Phi Fa, was the son of the king of Luang Prabang. Phi Fa had a penchant for women, and even ended up having an affair with his father's concubine! Upon getting caught, he was exiled to Angkor and so he took his young son with him.

Years prior, the territories around Luang Prabang, Vientiane and the present-day Isaan region of Thailand, had all been controlled by the Khmer Empire. But by the 14th century, Angkor's power and influence were greatly on the decline.

Many former Khmer frontier territories were conquered by the Sukhothai Kingdom. But later, due to Sukhothai's waning influence, they largely reverted back into the hands of local rulers, such as Fa Ngum's grandfather. Eager to reestablish influence over the region (albeit this time covertly), the king of Angkor granted Fa Ngum with 10,000 soldiers to go and take back his hometown.

Fa Ngum then marched up the Mekong with his army, snatching up all the *muang* (local municipalities) that he could. And after finally taking Luang Prabang, he declared himself the new king of Lan Chang, or 'A Million Elephants and White Parasols,' a name which suggests great military prowess.

Later, Fa Ngum headed back south to conquer Vientiane in 1356. And from there, he launched a campaign to take over the Khorat Plateau (now Northeast Thailand). At this time, much of that region was being swallowed up by the newly-formed Ayutthaya Kingdom *(see p230)*, and Fa Ngum agreed to go no further than Roi Et. Finally, he returned to Luang Prabang to govern his kingdom.

But Fa Ngum, encouraged by the diminishing power of the Sukhothai and Lanna kingdoms (at least at the time), continued conquering more and more territory, making Lan Chang one of Indochina's largest and mightiest kingdoms.

The king was also a major patron of Theravada Buddhism, and he invited his mentor from Angkor, Maha Pasaman, to come live in his kingdom. Upon his arrival, the monk brought along a sacred statue called the Phra Bang after which the capital would eventually name itself *(see p98)*.

Following the death of his wife, however, Fa Ngum's behavior grew more and more erratic, and he ultimately had to be banished by his own people.

Mosaics at Wat Xieng Thong depict traditional life in Laos

AFTER FA NGUM

The next few kings had peaceful and relatively uneventful reigns. Then came a period of instability, during which seven kings ruled over the course of ten years! Fortunately, though, King Chaiyachakkapat (r.1441-1479) and his descendants would maintain order throughout the 15th and 16th centuries.

King Visoun, the son of Chaiyachakkapat, took the throne in 1500. A patron of Buddhism, he had many important texts translated to Lao. And he finally brought the Phra Bang image to Luang Prabang after a series of mishaps interrupted its prior journeys.

Visoun's son was Photisarath, another influential king and the father of Setthathirath. King Setthathirath, who would move the capital to Vientiane, is one of the most important kings in all of Lan Chang's history. And his reign is also a major focus of the Emerald Buddha's story.

Though Setthathirath was successful at keeping Burma's Toungoo dynasty at bay (who by then had conquered Lanna), the Burmese would occupy Lan Chang for 18 years after his death. They installed Setthathirath's son, No Muong, on the throne, expecting him to rule as their puppet. But he turned against them and declared independence in 1593. No Muong died without an heir, however, and decades of instability ensued until Suriya Vongsa came to power in 1637.

Lan Chang experienced its 'Golden Age' during Suriya Vongsa's 57-year reign. He promoted Buddhism and the arts, constructed many new temples and maintained friendly relations with King Narai of Ayutthaya. He was even the first Lan Chang ruler to receive Dutch dignitaries. However, he too would die without an heir. And following his death in 1690, Lan Chang was rife with chaos.

Vongsa had expelled his elder brothers and cousins early on in his reign, leaving many claimants to the throne after he died. This infighting caused Lan Chang to split into three kingdoms: Luang Prabang, Vientiane and Champasak. Luang Prabang and Champasak would align themselves with Siam, while Vientiane would become an ally of Burma.

Later on in Siam, after the Burmese obliterated Ayutthaya in 1767, a general named Taksin managed to unite his country and kick Burma out. He then went on to conquer his neighbors to the north. Luang Prabang even aided the Siamese in their takeover of Vientiane, during which the Emerald Buddha was also captured. But Taksin later demanded that Luang Prabang become a Siamese vassal. Thus, each Lao kingdom lost its independence in 1778.

The Patuxai Monument, a symbol of modern Laos

OCCUPATION & REVOLUTION

Siam (Thailand) maintained control over Laos until 1893 when colonial France seized power over all Laotian territory east of the Mekong. And Laos would not regain independence until shortly after World War II.

A few decades later, during the Vietnam War, Laos provided safe passage for North Vietnamese troops. As a result, the United States launched a massive (but largely unpublicized) bombing campaign on Laos, making it the most bombed country in world history.

And in 1975, Laos experienced a Communist revolution of its own, with the Lao royal family being ousted for good. The Lao People's Revolutionary Party controls the country to this day, but Laos is gradually becoming more open as of late.

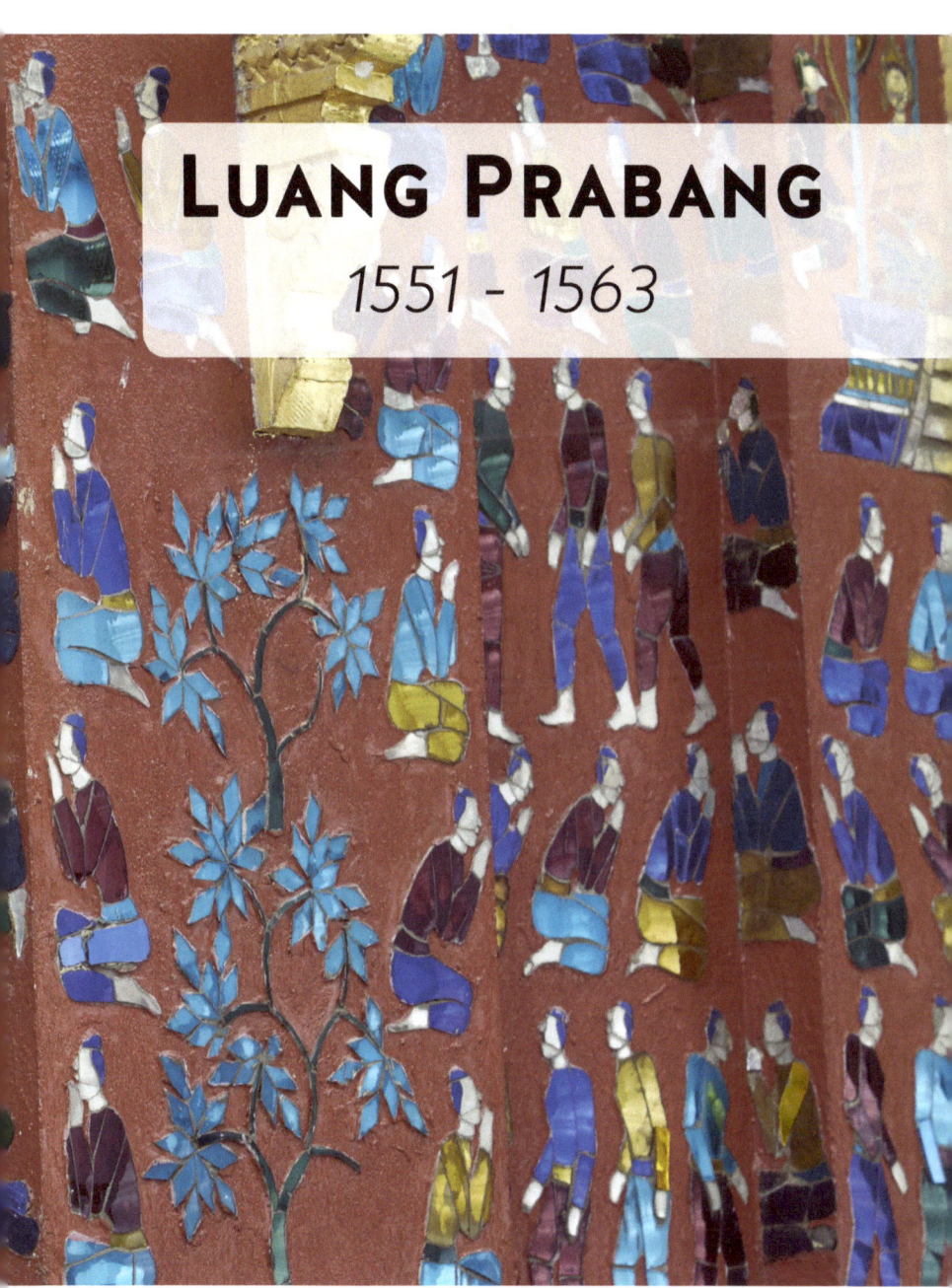

Luang Prabang
1551 - 1563

The Dual Monarch

In the year 1520, in the prosperous kingdom of Lan Chang, a young king named Photisarath ascended the throne upon the death of his father, King Visoun. Photisarath was a devout and righteous ruler. During his reign, he destroyed the heretical altars of the phi spirits that were in such favor among the residents of Luang Prabang. He deposed of the shrines in the Mekong River, and under his reign, Buddhism flourished.

Photisarath's pious character impressed King Ketklao of Lanna so much that Ketklao offered one of his daughters in marriage. And before long, King Photisarath and his queen had a son who'd become known as Setthathirath. Subsequently, he bore two more sons with his other consorts.

After some time had passed, King Ketklao departed from this world, leaving no male heir to the Lanna throne. Such an event was unprecedented in the kingdom's history, and the Lanna nobles were unsure of what to do. After a meeting at Chiang Mai's Wat Phra Singh, they finally came to a decision. They determined that Ketklao's grandson, the prince of Lan Chang, should be the one to rule over Lanna.

But it was a move of considerable risk. Not only was Setthathirath Lan Chang royalty, but he was no more than a young teenager. Nevertheless, there was no better option at the time. Setthathirath, with Photisarath's blessing, accepted the invitation in the year 1546. And the two headed to Chiang Mai for the coronation ceremony with a humongous procession of countless elephants, cavalry and infantry.

But soon into Setthathirath's reign, Photisarath was tragically killed when he fell from an elephant during a hunting expedition. Following the incident, his other two sons, both Setthathirath's junior, each claimed half of Lan Chang.

When the news reached Setthathirath, he could not keep himself from weeping. He needed to return to Luang Prabang to console his family, he told the Lanna nobles. And surely, they would be comforted by the Emerald Buddha and the golden Phra Sihing image, which he promised to bring back upon his return to Lanna.

King Setthathirath, however, would never return to Chiang Mai. For upon his arrival in Luang Prabang, he was recognized as the rightful heir and ruler of the Lan Chang Kingdom.

Previous
p64

Next
p108

The Emerald Buddha in Luang Prabang

This portion of the Chronicle, which takes us from Lanna to Lan Chang, largely corroborates with the accepted version of historical events. The Chronicle, however, leaves out a few interesting bits of information. First, let's take a look at the reign of Ketklao, Tilokarat's grandson.

King Ketklao actually had two reigns: from 1525-35 and again from 1543-45. The first reign ended when his son, Saikham, usurped the throne and exiled him to the Shan States at the edge of Lanna's territory. But Saikham was not a popular ruler. After several years, the nobles had finally had enough, and even went as far as putting Saikham to death! Ketklao was then invited back to the throne, but he was in no state to rule given all the traumatic events that had transpired. The frustrated nobles then put Ketklao to death as well!

Aside from Saikham, Ketklao also had two daughters. One of them, as mentioned in the Chronicle, was married off to Photisarath, the king of Lan Chang. His other daughter, Chiraprabha, actually acted as interim ruler for a couple of years as the nobles were figuring things out.

After the teenage Setthathirath accepted the invitation to rule over Lanna, he and King Photisarath, a renowned elephant tamer, made quite the entrance to the coronation ceremony. Their procession consisted of 2,000 elephants and 300,000 men!

But Setthathirath would only be in power for a brief time before learning of the death of his father (ironically, at the hands of an elephant). While it could be said that he returned to Luang Prabang to console his family, he couldn't have been pleased with the idea of his younger brothers ruling Lan Chang instead of him.

And so, upon Setthathirath's return to Luang Prabang, he managed to take control of the kingdom himself. That meant that both Lanna and Lan Chang actually shared the same king for a time!

On his trip to Luang Prabang, Setthathirath took not only the Emerald Buddha, but also the Phra Sihing and several other significant relics. (Oddly, one version of the Chronicle states that the Phra Sihing had 'flown' to Luang Prabang beforehand.)

As the palladium of Laos, the Phra Bang image *(see p98)*, was already in the city, Luang Prabang was briefly home to all three of Indochina's most important Buddha statues. But where was the Emerald Buddha kept?

While it would only remain in the city for 12 years, the Chronicle doesn't mention the name of the temple. While we may never know for sure, Wat Visounnarath, home to the Phra Bang at the time, is the most probable answer.

King Setthathirath would go on to become one of Lan Chang's most important rulers, and we'll continue examining his reign in the following section on Vientiane. Not only was he the one to bring the Emerald Buddha to Luang Prabang, but he'd also be the one to take it away.

‹ A statue of King Setthathirath on display in Vientiane

LUANG PRABANG TRAVEL TIPS

Despite being the second-largest city in Laos, Luang Prabang is a tranquil riverside town that makes for a great place to unwind. But the historical capital is by no means boring, and you'll find plenty to see and do within a relatively small area.

The main part of the city is a peninsula surrounded by the Mekong and Nam Khan rivers on three sides.

Given its size and layout, navigation couldn't be easier. Designated a UNESCO World Heritage Site in 1995 (yes, the entire town!) the old architecture of Luang Prabang remains remarkably well preserved.

The main sites can all be visited in just a couple days, but taking things slow is recommended if you have the time.

GETTING THERE

Those coming from Thailand can reach Luang Prabang via **riverboat**, which takes two days with a one-night stopover in between.

First, head to the Chiang Khong border crossing, 65 km east of Chiang Rai. It's accessible by bus from Chiang Rai in about 2.5 hours, with buses departing hourly from Terminal 1 *(see p35)*. After crossing the bridge and getting your visa on arrival *(see p281)*, you'll enter the town of Huay Xai, from where most boats depart. It's possible to buy a slow boat ticket at the jetty, and boats usually depart around 10:00 or 11:00.

There are also numerous package tours and 'river cruises' available, some of which will arrange all overland transport for you. Just be sure to research if the company is reputable, as scams are not unheard of.

Those coming from elsewhere can also **fly**. Luang Prabang has an international airport with direct flights from Bangkok, Chiang Mai, Hanoi, Siem Reap and Kuala Lumpur.

At the airport, you can get a visa on arrival for $35 USD. To save yourself some hassle, it's best to have the cash on hand in advance, as the ATMs are actually outside the airport. Shared van taxis into town cost around 5,000 kip per person.

Traveling from within Laos, you can take a domestic flight. Bear in mind, however, that flights within Laos tend to be considerably pricier than domestic flights in Thailand.

People coming from Vientiane often take the **bus**, but many complain of the poor roads and an overall uncomfortable ride. Breaking up the long journey with a stopover in Vang Vieng would be ideal.

GETTING AROUND

Getting around Luang Prabang is incredibly easy. The city is very small and compact and nearly all the main sites can be reached **on foot**. Some people also rent **bicycles** or **motorbikes**.

When going on excursions out of town, such as to the Kuang Si Falls or the Pak Ou Caves, transport can be arranged at your hotel or tour offices *(more on pp101-103)*.

LUANG PRABANG

WHERE TO STAY

Staying on the peninsula gives you easy access to the main sites, all sorts of restaurants and also the night market. The peninsula contains a wide range of accommodation options, from budget hostels to fancy hotels with views of the river.

There are also some hotels and guest houses a little bit south of the peninsula, right by Wat Visounnarath.

The city's colonial architecture mostly dates from the 1890s to 1910s. Many buildings are a unique fusion of French, Lao and even Vietnamese styles.

FOOD

Luang Prabang has plenty of restaurants to choose from, especially along the riverside and Sisavang Vong Rd. Like its neighbors, Laos has no shortage of noodle dishes, with rice noodles being among the most popular. Many Lao dishes include *padaek*, or fermented fish sauce. Buffalo steaks are another local favorite you can try in town. And one of Lao cuisine's staple food products is sticky rice, which can be eaten by hand *(see p101)*.

Furthermore, you'll find plenty of cafes to grab a French baguette with your coffee. And don't miss the chance to try to freshly squeezed mango juice.

Luang Prabang isn't known for its nightlife, but alcoholic beverages are easy to find at restaurants and bars around the city.

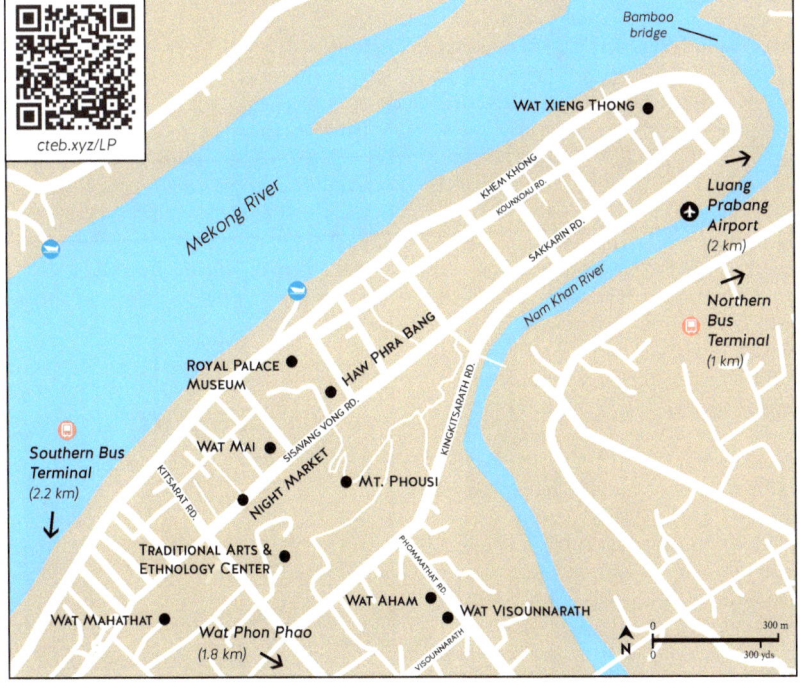

Wat Visounnarath • ວັດວິຊຸນ

Wat Visounnarath was built in 1513 by King Visoun to host the Phra Bang image, the palladium of Laos. Visoun was the father of Photisarath and the grandfather of Setthathirath. Photisarath even spent time at the temple as a monk before taking the throne. But did the Emerald Buddha spend time here as well?

- Visounnarath Rd.
- 8:00 - 17:00
- Daily
- 20,000

Wat Visounnarath is widely regarded as the city's oldest temple. Interestingly, before the temple even existed, a 15th-century battle between Lan Chang and Vietnam took place at the same spot, in which hundreds of thousands were killed.

Later in the 19th century, the temple managed to survive an invasion by Chinese Black Flag rebels. The *sim* was badly damaged, however.

The Phra Bang image remained at the temple from 1513 up until the early 18th century, and it was brought back again in the 1800s *(see p98)*.

During the Emerald Buddha's twelve-year stint in Luang Prabang, could it have stayed here together with the Phra Bang? If so, it would not be the last time the two statues would share a temple together. It's also possible, of course, that the Emerald Buddha's former home in the city no longer exists.

Most visitors to Luang Prabang overlook Wat Visounnarath, as it's just outside of the main peninsula area that contains most of the town's landmarks. With that said, the temple is no more than a 15-minute walk from the Royal Palace, making it easily accessible from most hotels and guest houses.

The Black Flag Attack

In 1887, most of Luang Prabang was ravaged by Haw Chinese invaders known as the Black Flag Army. As a result, only a handful of the city's original structures remain. These include Wat Visounnarath, Wat Mai, Wat Mahathat and Wat Xieng Thong.

THE SIM

The temple's main structure is its *sim* (or *ubosot*). The timber and brick building features a double roof decorated with multiple *naga* serpents.

Stepping up to the porch, you'll find ornately carved golden doors which depict the Hindu deities Vishnu, Brahma and Shiva *(see p16)*. And all around the building are windows that were clearly inspired by the typical 'baluster windows' of classical Khmer architecture.

In the 19th century, France, who desired to control all Indochinese territory east of the Mekong River, sent a team of researchers to survey the land. The group reached Luang Prabang in 1867. And there, the team's artist Louis Delaporte made a sketch of Wat Visounnarath, which is now the only depiction we have of it before the Black Flag attack.

According to legend, the *sim* required over 4,000 trees when it was built in the 16th century. Unfortunately, the 1896 reconstruction by King Zakarine doesn't quite do the original justice.

The sim's central Buddha image is the largest in the city

The Museum

The *sim* also doubles as a museum, which is really just a collection of old relics kept behind the massive central Buddha image.

The collection largely comprises of standing Buddha statues, many of which date back to the 14th century. They're mostly either Lao or Khmer in origin. Many of the objects once found at Wat Visounnarath, however, are now on display at the Royal Palace Museum (*p97*).

‹ *One of many wooden standing Buddha images at the museum*

The Watermelon Chedi

Wat Visounnarath is perhaps best known for its 35 m-high *chedi*, situated just across from the *sim*. It was commissioned by King Visoun's wife in the Sinhalese, or Sri Lankan style of architecture.

It's known as either That Pathum or That Mak Mo. 'Mak Mo' translates to watermelon, which is a reference to the *chedi's* shape. This wouldn't be the first time a watermelon has appeared in our story (*see p55*)! Coincidence?

Notably, this is the only Sri Lankan-style *chedi* in all of Laos. The Emerald Buddha's home in Chiang Mai was at Wat Chedi Luang, a temple also known for its large Sinhalese *chedi*. Could King Setthathirath have seen this temple as the Emerald Buddha's logical new home?

In any case, at some point in its history, someone placed a large collection of Buddha images inside of it. The *chedi* collapsed in 1917, revealing all sorts of ancient relics, many of which are now on display at the Royal Palace Museum. The *chedi* was later repaired and renovated in 1932.

WAT AHAM · ອັດອາຮາມ

🕐 8:00 - 17:00
₭ 20,000

Just next to Wat Visounnarath is Wat Aham, a site closely associated with the city's guardian spirits, Pu No and Na No. During his reign, King Photisarath (Setthathirath's father) felt that the shrine

was a heresy against the teachings of Buddhism, and had its contents thrown into the river. These events are mentioned (and in fact, praised by) the Chronicle of the Emerald Buddha.

What's not mentioned in the Chronicle, however, is that following the shrine's destruction, all sorts of natural disasters and diseases befell Luang Prabang. Locals believed that the angry spirits were to blame, and so the shrine was eventually rebuilt. Today, though, the spirit shrine is gone again and only a Buddhist temple stands at the spot. Pu No and Na No are now believed to reside in the two large banyan trees out front and they're honored annually during the Lao New Year festival.

THE PHI

Phi is a term used in both Laos and Thailand to refer to a wide array of spirits, such as nature spirits, personal guardians and wandering ghosts. To this day, *phi* play a major role in Lao folklore and local ceremonies. They're generally considered as powerful yet neutral forces, with the potential to either cause harm or provide protection *(see p17)*.

One popular ceremony still practiced in Laos is that of the Phi Fa, performed for patients recovering from an illness. From dusk until dawn, participants dance around a sacrificial altar to the sounds of hand drums and a mouth organ called the *khaen*. The ceremony is directed by a local shaman, who also acts as a spirit medium.

Many Lao believe that each person has 32 guardian spirits called *khwan*. But as they're prone to wandering off, special rituals are required to bring them back to their owner - especially before that person is to embark on a long journey.

Malicious spirits may also sometimes possess a person, with cleansing and exorcism rituals necessary for healing. In rural Lao, people accused of having been possessed by the demonic Phi Rob spirit are sometimes exiled from their village. Such accusations, however, may also be convenient ways to banish those who disagree with the village elders.

As a visitor, you're unlikely to stumble upon a local *phi* ritual by accident. But you will encounter all sorts of shrines set up in the local spirits' honor.

A roadside shrine ›

The multitiered roof of the sim

WAT XIENG THONG · ວັດຊຽງທອງ

Wat Xieng Thong, at the eastern edge of Luang Prabang's central peninsula, is one of the city's most visited landmarks. Depending on the source, the temple was either completed in 1559 or 1560. And it was commissioned by none other than King Setthathirath himself.

📍 Edge of the peninsula
🕒 8:00 - 17:00
📅 Daily
₭ 20,000

Wat Xieng Thong is another one of the few temples to have survived the 1887 sacking of Luang Prabang by Black Flag rebels. The rebel leader, in fact, had spent time here as a monk when he was a young boy. Rather than destroy it, the invading militants used the temple as a base from which to pillage the rest of the city.

And for that we should be thankful, as Wat Xieng Thong is truly one of the most beautiful temples in all of Laos.

While purely speculative, the Emerald Buddha had already been in the city from 1551, meaning that it could've possibly stayed here for its last few years in town.

Major restorations took place at the temple throughout the 20th century. And up until the 1975 Communist revolution, Wat Xieng Thong remained a royal temple managed by the Lao monarchy.

THE CHAPEL OF THE STANDING BUDDHA

Inside this small chapel, you'll find a shiny golden Buddha image reminiscent of the Phra Bang, which was a gift from the king of Thailand. Meanwhile, the interior walls are intricately decorated with gold leaf.

This is one of the more recent structures of the temple complex, having been added in the 20th century.

The Sim

The *sim* is worthy of close inspection, both inside and out. The back wall features a beautiful mosaic image of the universal symbol of the 'Tree of Life.' It's flanked on either side by large peacocks.

Inside, the altar contains a wide assortment of Buddha images of various sizes, poses and colors. But the real highlights, perhaps, are the eight large black pillars which have been entirely adorned with intricate golden patterns.

◁ *In numerous Southeast Asian countries, the peacock has long been a symbol of royalty*

Chapelle Rouge

One of Wat Xieng Thong's most significant relics is a graceful reclining Buddha image that dates all the way back to the temple's establishment. Throughout the 20th century, the statue spent time in Paris and Vientiane before eventually returning to its original home. The structure's exterior features more eye-catching mosaics, this time of scenes from daily local life *(also pictured on pp84-5)*.

The Chariot Hall

The Chariot Hall, built in 1962, is another fairly recent addition. The funeral carriage at the center is that of King Sisavang Vong, who died in 1959. The elaborate chariot appears to be floating on top of a multi-headed *naga* serpent.

Meanwhile, don't miss the rows of old Buddha statues lined up against the wall, many of them in the *abhaya mudra* posture.

WAT MAI · ວັດໃໝ່

Built in 1780 as a royal temple, Wat Mai Suwannaphumaham is another structure to have survived the Black Flag attack of 1887. It's mainly known for having hosted the Phra Bang palladium throughout most of the 1900s.

The *sim* is completely decorated in lacquer and gold leaf. In addition to a replica of the Phra Bang image, the temple also contains a number of detailed Emerald Buddha replicas *(see opposite page)*.

📍 Sisavang Vong Rd.
🕐 8:00 - 17:00
₭ 10,000

THE ROYAL PALACE MUSEUM · ຫໍຄຳ

The Royal Palace Musem was once home to Luang Prabang's royal family who maintained power until the Communist revolution of 1975.

It was constructed in the early 20th century, shortly after the original was destroyed by Black Flag rebels. Built during France's occupation of Laos, the palace is a blend of French and Lao architectural styles.

Inside the museum are the royal family's former living quarters in addition to numerous artworks and Buddhist relics. Many of them were discovered in various temples throughout the city *(see p92)*.

📍 Sisavang Vong Rd.
🕐 8:30 - 11:00, 13:30 - 16:00
📅 Daily
₭ 30,000

HAW PHA BANG · ຫໍພະບາງ

It's hard to believe that this ornate golden structure, situated within the Royal Palace complex, was finished as recently as 2006.

It was constructed for the sole purpose of housing the Phra Bang image, which was moved here in 2016.

Though the Phra Bang has moved around quite a few times over the centuries - including stints in Vientiane and Bangkok - Luang Prabang has always been considered its true home. In fact, the city was named after it!

Access is free, but photographing the

image inside is not allowed. The Haw Pha Bang is also beautiful to look at at night. You can learn all about the Phra Bang's storied history on the following few pages.

The Journeys of the Phra Bang

Just as the Emerald Buddha is revered as the protector of Thailand, the Phra Bang is regarded as the palladium of Laos. And like the Emerald Buddha and Phra Sihing images, the Phra Bang also has its own chronicle. It's one of the few to have not been fully translated into English, however. Nevertheless, we know the full details of the statue's journeys thanks to historical records.

Standing at 83 cm high in the *abhaya mudra* posture, the statue is said to be Sri Lankan in origin, dating back to sometime between the 1st and 9th centuries. Some people believe, though, that the Khmers made it much later.

In either case, it was the Khmer Empire that gave the Phra Bang as a gift to Lan Chang's founder, Fa Ngum. Fa Ngum had hoped to promote Theravada Buddhism in his kingdom and requested a sacred image to aid in his task. While the image was supposed to go straight to the capital of Luang Prabang, then called, Muang Saw, things wouldn't quite turn out as planned.

Fa Ngum's wife was a Khmer princess, and following a visit to her hometown, she and her caravan returned to Lan Chang with the Tripitaka scriptures, a Bodhi tree sapling, the Phra Bang image and Maha Pasaman, her husband's spiritual mentor. When the queen became ill, however, the caravan stopped at a place called Phainam.

Eventually, they moved on to the towns of Muong Kae and then Vieng Kam. It was there that due to a series of supernatural omens, the crew concluded that the Phra Bang (or spirit inside of it!) didn't want to leave that town. And so they moved on without it.

It wasn't until the reign of King Chaiyachakkapat, who took the throne in

1441, that there was another attempt at bringing the image to the capital. Tragically, however, the boat carrying the Phra Bang capsized at the Keng Chan Rapids! The survivors then took it to Vientiane instead.

Finally, during the reign of King Visoun, Setthathirath's grandfather, the Phra Bang was brought to the capital, and the town was renamed Luang Prabang after it.

Wat Visounnarath (see p90) was specifically built to house the image, which stayed there from 1513–1707. In 1707, the kingdom of Lan Chang dissolved, and the statue was taken to the newly formed Kingdom of Vientiane.

From there, the Phra Bang would travel together with the Emerald Buddha to Thonburi following the Siamese invasion of 1778-79. Both images were kept at Wat Arun (p130), but after a series of disasters struck the city, many suspected that they 'didn't get along.'

‹ *Phra Bang replicas are a common sight all over Laos*

Two years later in 1781, the king of Vientiane, then a Siamese vassal, passed away. His son, Nanthasen, was living in Thailand, having been abducted during the prior invasion. Assigned to return to Vientiane and take the throne as a puppet ruler, he requested to bring the Phra Bang with him. And authorities willfully agreed.

A few decades later, however, the Siamese captured the Phra Bang a second time after sacking Vientiane in 1827. This time it was housed in Wat Chakrawatrachawat Woramahawihan in Bangkok's Chinatown district (p159). But they returned the statue to Laos again after 39 years, sensing the same incompatibility issues with the Emerald Buddha as before.

In 1867 the statue finally returned 'home' to Luang Prabang. It was kept once again at Wat Visounnarath until 1887, the year that most of the city was ravaged by Black Flag invaders. Following the incident, the Phra Bang was moved to the nearby temple of Wat Mai.

Wat Mai housed the Phra Bang image throughout most of the 1900s. Then, from around the year 2006, the statue was kept in Luang Prabang's Royal Palace Museum, just a short walk away. The Laotian government then decided to move the image to a brand new structure within the same compound.

Known as the Haw Pha Bang, construction actually began as far back as 1963, but it wasn't completed until 2006. After a several-year delay, the Phra Bang was finally transferred to its new home in 2016. Notably, it's the first temple to have been built specifically for the Phra Bang since Wat Visounnarath 500 years earlier!

Despite being so new, most visitors to Luang Prabang would never guess that the Haw Pha Bang was not another well-preserved historical temple like the others. The gorgeous golden structure was built in the traditional Lao style and fits in perfectly with its surroundings in the UNESCO World Heritage town.

To this day, special Lao New Year ceremonies still take place during which the Phra Bang is paraded around the city and ritually cleansed at nearby Wat Mai.

According to a number of Lao citizens, though, that's not quite where the story ends. A couple of conspiracy theories regarding the Phra Bang continue to circulate the internet. Some people are convinced that the current Phra Bang statue in the Haw Pha Bang is a fake and that the *real* Phra Bang was removed from the city decades ago.

Some theories claim that the statue is locked in an underground vault of the Laos National Bank in Vientiane. A number of others, meanwhile, swear that the Phra Bang is located in, of all places, Moscow, Russia! If true, this would likely have something to do with the former USSR's relationship with Laos, which remains a Communist-run state to this day.

But let's consider the fact that possession of the Phra Bang has long been regarded as a symbol of the government's legitimacy. These alternate theories, then, may reveal less about where the Phra Bang actually is, and more about people's attitude toward the current administration.

Mt. Phousi · ວັດພູສີ

One of the most popular gathering spots for the evening sunset, Mt. Phousi's entrance can be found just across from the Royal Palace Museum. Before your ascent up the steps, you'll encounter a ticket gate where they'll ask you for a payment of 20,000 kip. After that, the climb to the top only takes about ten minutes.

Once there, you'll come across a little temple called Wat Chomsi. And the platform around it provides fantastic panoramic views of the city and the distant green mountains.

If you're coming for the sunset, be forewarned that you'll be far from alone, as just about everybody else in town will have the same idea. Out of all the famous landmarks in Luang Prabang, this is the only one that ever really gets overcrowded. You might want to consider visiting in the afternoon instead.

While at the top, you'll likely be approached by local students who want to practice their English. And they may even give you helpful tips on some other places to check out in the city.

Heading back, you can try an alternate route which will take you down the opposite side of the mountain. At various levels, you'll encounter shrines and statues which make for a somewhat eerie sight in the darkness. Fortunately, Luang Prabang is so small and safe that even getting lost at night comes with little risk.

- 5:30 - 18:00
- Daily
- 20,000

WAT PHON PHAO · ອັດໂພນເຜົາ

Wat Phon Phao is a rather obscure temple about a 30-40 minute walk southeast of

the central peninsula. Sadly, the temple is nearly always closed, and the opening hours posted on the door outside mean little. Yet, it nonetheless makes for an interesting visit. Built in the 1990s, this is a one-of-a-kind temple structure that's fascinating from the outside, even if you can't go in.

The area also provides excellent views of the city and mountains in the distance. So much so that the temple remains a popular meeting spot for local youth to gather and chat with friends.

THE LIVING LAND FARM

Visitors looking for a more hands-on type of experience might want to take a day trip to the Living Land Farm. A guide will walk you through the 14 steps required to produce one of the region's staple food products: sticky rice.

You can both observe and try various procedures like soaking the seeds, walking a water buffalo to soften the mud, planting the seeds and then cutting the stalks.

After smashing the dry stalks to release the grains, you'll eventually get to eat a delicious sticky rice-based meal.

The cost is around $40 USD, a percentage of which goes to local schoolchildren. A visit can be arranged at tourist offices around town.

Kuang Si Falls

An easy day trip from Luang Prabang, the mesmerizing turquoise pools of the Kuang Si Falls are perfect for cooling off on a hot day.

Though you're free to take a dip in the first pools you see at the bottom, adventurous travelers can also hike up to the very top of the waterfall. There, surrounded by jungle, is a tranquil (albeit brown) pool of water that also offers amazing views of the rolling green hills in the distance.

Heading back down, admire the waterfall from the viewing platform before hopping in the turquoise water.

The beautiful aqua color of the cascading pools is a result of light reflecting off the white calcium carbonate at the bottom, and then back up again through the mineral-rich water.

Kuang Si is also home to a bear rescue center.

GETTING THERE: Round-trip tickets generally cost 500,000 kip while it's another 20,000 kip to enter the site. Transport can be arranged at travel agents or at your hotel, and you'll have the choice between morning or afternoon excursions.

Pak Ou Caves · ถ้ำติ่ง

₭ 20,000 + around 75,000 for transport

The Pak Ou Caves have long been considered a sacred spot. In ages past, they were used to worship the *phi*, or local nature spirits *(see p93)*, especially that of the river.

But in the 16th century, King Setthathirath converted the caves into a Buddhist holy place. To this day, locals regularly bring Buddha images to the caves to either donate or purify in holy water.

In total, the caves now contain over 5,000 Buddha images. And most of them are small – not much bigger than toy action figures!

The caves also remain an important pilgrimage spot for locals during the Buddhist New Year in April.

Over time, the caves have also become one of the region's top tourist attractions. What makes the day trip especially unique is that Pak Ou can only be reached by boat.

The journey there is a long one, but the scenic limestone cliffs which line the Mekong River make up for it.

Overall, the Pak Ou Caves aren't very big, which may be anticlimactic for some. The caves, however, have a lot in store for those with a keen eye for small details. While some simply walk in and then out again a few minutes later, the real magic of Pak Ou is revealed to those who take their time inside.

‹ The main cave visitors first encounter, named Tham Ting, has a deeper and darker sibling, called Tham Teung. Accessible by a steep cliffside pathway, it's best explored with your own torch.

Around Town

The sites covered on the previous pages can all be visited within the span of a few days. But taking things slow in attune with Luang Prabang's relaxed pace of life is the best way to experience the town. Here are a few other things to see and do around the area if you have extra time.

The Night Market

The local night market takes place every evening, and you'll be able to find all sorts of trinkets and t-shirts for sale (though many of the vendors sell identical items). There are also plenty of options for dinner and dessert. Enjoy some local Lao or Thai food, and try not to get addicted to those round coconut pancake balls (*khao nom kok*)!

Crossing the Bamboo Bridge

Central Luang Prabang has two bamboo bridges connecting the peninsula with the other side of the river, though you'll only find them during low tide. Aside from some temples, there's not a whole lot on the other side, but you can get some great views of the peninsula and the river itself. Crossing each bridge costs 5,000 kip.

Phra Lak Phra Ram Performance

One of the most popular stories in Laos is Phra Lak Phra Ram, a local adaptation of the Indian Ramayana epic *(see p153)*. In Luang Prabang, you can witness a performance at the **Royal Palace Theatre**, just across from the Haw Pha Bang. Considering the length of the entire story, only certain scenes are portrayed on any given night. Tickets are relatively pricey, ranging from 100,000 to 150,000 kip. But fans of the Ramayana story will likely enjoy it.

The demon Ravana about to abduct Rama's wife Sita

Traditional Arts & Ethnology Center

Laos is home to a large number of hilltribes, such as the Akha, Hmong and Khmu, to name just a few *(see p45)*. And to learn more about their customs, rituals and agricultural practices, this well laid-out museum is a great way to spend an afternoon.

- 📍 By Dara Market
- 🕘 9:00 - 18:00
- 📅 Closed Mon.
- 💰 25,000 kip

VIENTIANE
1563 - 1779

A New Beginning in Vientiane

The Lanna nobles, sensing that King Setthathirath's loyalties lie with Lan Chang, were once again tasked with electing a new ruler. They chose a monk named Mekuti, a distant relative of the royal bloodline of King Mangrai. And so Mekuti left the order and began ruling as Lanna's king in the year 1551.

Setthathirath, however, was very displeased upon hearing the news, as he still considered himself the rightful ruler of Lanna. And so he decided to take back Lanna by force. First, he took Chiang Saen, a convenient base from which to rule both the Lanna and Lan Chang kingdoms.

From there, he intended to conquer Chiang Mai, but was faced with great difficulties and could not complete the task. Though he would remain in Chiang Saen for three years, he was ultimately unable to follow through with his plan. Dejected, he finally returned to Luang Prabang to focus on governing Lan Chang.

Before long, Setthathirath decided to shift the Lan Chang capital further south to the city of Vientiane. Taking the Emerald Buddha with him, he established a beautiful new temple for the miraculous Jewel Image. He worshipped the image day and night, presenting it with offerings of gold, silver and various precious gems.

Buddhism flourished under Setthathirath's reign, and he built the splendid Pha That Luang chedi on the site first established by King Ashoka. Upon its completion, all sorts of offerings were made to the chedi, including rice fields and even a great number of slaves. Finally, after decades on the throne, King Setthathirath left this world at the age of thirty-eight.

At the moment of his death, Setthathirath had both the Emerald Buddha and the beautiful golden chedi of Pha That Luang on his mind, and he was reborn into heaven. The Emerald Buddha remained in Vientiane for a long time afterward. And for many years, the town greatly prospered thanks to the wondrous Jewel Image's powers.

> *ⓘ* This is where the most 'recent' version of the Chronicle comes to an end. Fortunately, though, we have detailed historical accounts of exactly how the Emerald Buddha would later leave Vientiane in the 18th century. Find out how in the following section.

Previous
p86

Next
p126

The Emerald Buddha In Vientiane

This portion of the Chronicle deals with Setthathirath's failed attempt to retake Lanna, as well as his decision to move the Lan Chang capital to Vientiane. A couple of noteworthy historical details are missing from the manuscript, however.

As mentioned on p87, Setthathirath successfully solidified his rule over Lan Chang upon returning to Luang Prabang. But he fully intended to remain the king of Lanna as well. In his absence, he asked Chiraprabha (his aunt) to rule in his place, but she declined his offer.

As the Chronicle states, Setthathirath then took over Chiang Saen after learning that the Lanna nobles had elected Mekuti as their new king. Interestingly, Chiang Saen, and not Chiang Mai, was actually the city from which Setthathirath ruled during his brief reign over Lanna. Rulers preferring to live in cities other than the capital was not unheard of in those times.

In any case, Chiang Saen was also a convenient base from which Setthathirath could rule both kingdoms. And from there, he also intended to stage an invasion of Chiang Mai which remained the Lanna capital. He first tried in 1555 but came up short for a number of reasons - one of them being uncooperative allies who interfered with his plans.

The biggest obstacle in Setthathirath's way, however, was the Toungoo dynasty of Burma, then based at Pegu (current Bago, Myanmar). King Bayinnaung, who'd ascended the throne in 1555, had goals to control the entire region. (In fact, his empire would become the largest ever in Southeast Asian history.) He invaded Chiang Mai, taking over and keeping Setthathirath out. This also meant that King Mekuti would be the last ever ruler of an independent Lanna Kingdom.

As for Luang Prabang, it too was extremely vulnerable, Setthathirath felt. And that's the main reason he moved the capital south to Vientiane in 1563.

But why is there no mention of the Burmese invasion in the Chronicle of the Emerald Buddha? While we can't say for sure, it's probably due to the fact that many versions were written down in Lanna while it was a Burmese vassal. Perhaps the monks who transcribed the story wanted to avoid controversy by leaving out mention of the Toungoo dynasty altogether.

Let's return our attention to Vientiane, which had already long been an established city by that point. The area had been controlled by the Khmer Empire for hundreds of years before being absorbed into Lan Chang by Fa Ngum in 1356. But it was Setthathirath who would go on to make it one of the finest capitals in the region. (Sadly, due to later sackings, this is not so apparent today.)

One of his major projects, as mentioned in the Chronicle, was the beautiful golden *chedi* of Pha That Luang. And he also built a brand new temple, the Haw Phra Kaew, specifically for the Emerald Buddha. In total, the statue would remain there for 216 years.

As for the other major relics, Setthathirath decided to leave the Phra Bang image in Luang Prabang. And while one version of the Chronicle erroneously states that he took the Phra Sihing to Vientiane as well, he actually returned it to Lanna after several years.

Following Setthathirath's death, the Toungoo dynasty managed to take control of Lan Chang for 18 years. But for whatever reason, they'd never take the Emerald Buddha.

VIENTIANE TRAVEL TIPS

Vientiane is sometimes called Asia's 'forgotten capital.' At one point in time, it would've been one of Indochina's most stunning cities. But after being laid to waste by the Siamese in the 1820s, Vientiane was left abandoned for decades.

The French later helped bring it back to life, but the city then hosted fighting during the Laotian Civil War.

While things are back to normal now, Vientiane presently lacks either the charm of Luang Prabang or the energy of Bangkok. Nevertheless, the city is home to some stunning and well-preserved temples that no visitors to Laos should miss. The main temples can be seen within one full day, while you'll also want an extra day to visit the Buddha Park.

 ## GETTING THERE

The cheapest way to reach the capital from elsewhere in Laos is by **bus**. Buses from the north often arrive at the Northern Bus Terminal. Meanwhile, routes linking Vientiane with nearby cities drop passengers off at the Khua Din Bus Station outside Talat Sao Mall.

If you're coming from Luang Prabang, prices can range from 150,000–200,000 kip. Keep in mind, though, that some dub this the 'bus ride from hell.' The roads in Laos are bad, and 10 hours on a bumpy, cramped bus is often too much for people to bear.

You can break up the journey by staying a few nights in scenic Vang Vieng, which also has a reputation for being a backpacker party town.

Flying is by far the easiest but also the most expensive option. Flights within Laos are operated by just a couple of different airlines and are considerably more expensive than flying within Thailand. Expect to pay around $100 USD for a domestic flight.

Coming from abroad, Vientiane can be reached from Bangkok, Chiang Mai, Phnom Penh, Siem Reap, Kuala Lumpur, Singapore, Hanoi and more.

Vientiane is also easily accessible **overland from Thailand**. First, you'll need to get to Nong Khai, accessible by train from Bangkok or by bus from Udon Thani. Then take a bus over the Friendship Bridge. You will, of course, need to go through immigration and apply for your 'visa on arrival' if you didn't get one in advance *(see p281)*.

 ## FOOD

If noodles are your thing, you'll have no trouble finding them all throughout Vientiane. A popular local dish is *fue*, which is reminiscent of Vietnamese *pho*.

Talat Sao features both a market and a food court that has a couple of vegetarian options to choose from. And the Ban Anou Night Market is also worth a visit. Additionally, Vientiane is home to French, Italian, Chinese and Indian restaurants, while Beer Lao is served just about everywhere.

 ## WHERE TO STAY

Vientiane has no clearly defined city center. It would be ideal, however, to base yourself somewhere near the Talat Sao Mall. From there you'll have easy access to most of the city's landmarks by bike or on foot. And the adjacent bus station can also take you to the Buddha Park or even across the river to Thailand.

GETTING AROUND

While Vientiane is much larger than Luang Prabang, it's by no means a huge city. Most of the sites mentioned in the following section can be reached **on foot**, provided you're staying in a relatively central location. Pha That Luang (*p116*) is best accessed by vehicle, however.

Vientiane has regular **taxis**, **tuk tuks** and **bicycle rickshaws**. Whichever option you choose, it's best to haggle and agree on a price before getting in.

At the time of writing, there are no Uber or Grab services in Laos. But there is a local **ridesharing** alternative called LOCA which works in much the same way. As technology can change at any moment, be sure to check for updates online before your trip.

You can also rent a **bicycle**.

Vientiane's traffic isn't nearly as hectic as other cities in Southeast Asia and it's much more pleasant to ride around.

To get to places like the Buddha Park (*p119*) and the Friendship Bridge (to Thailand), buses depart from the Khua Din Bus Station outside Talat Sao Mall.

View from the Patuxai Monument

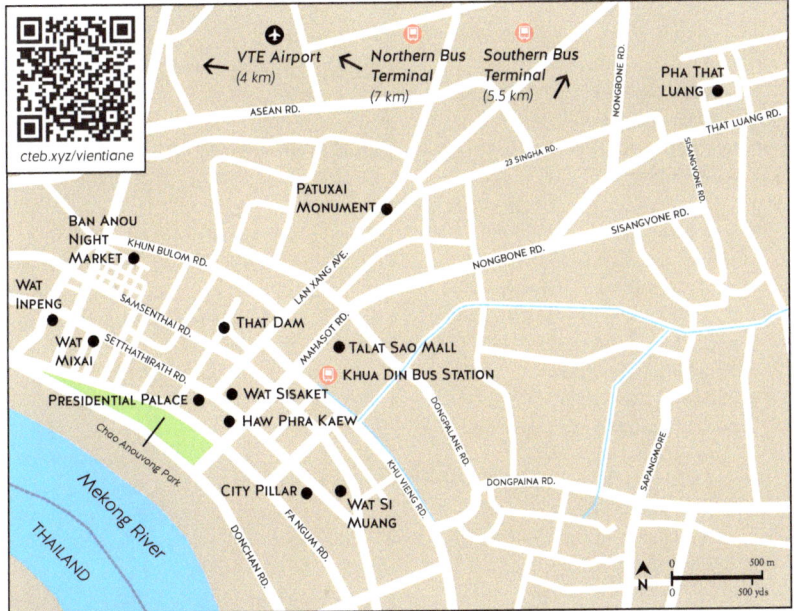

cteb.xyz/vientiane

Haw Phra Kaew

• ຫໍພຣະແກ້ວ

The Emerald Buddha was here

Haw Phra Kaew (also spelled Ho Pha Kaeo) was built in the 1560s by King Setthathirath specifically for housing the Emerald Buddha. A part of his royal palace complex, it was his first major construction project upon moving the Lan Chang capital to Vientiane.

📍 Setthathirath Rd.
🕗 8:00 - 16:00
📅 Daily
₭ 5,000

The Emerald Buddha remained at the temple for over 200 years before its eventual capture by Siam. And even after the statue's departure, the temple was renovated and expanded by King Anouvong in 1816.

But the Siamese would sack Vientiane again in 1827 and 1828 *(see p114)*. Haw Phra Kaew was left badly damaged and remained deserted for decades.

We largely have the French to thank for the temple's survival. The colonial rulers carried out a major reconstruction project between 1936-1942. And the project was supervised by Prince Souvanna Phouma, a future prime minister of Laos who'd studied engineering and architecture in Paris. The architects even made sure to leave a few surviving remnants of Setthathirath's original temple intact.

Compared to other temples built for the Emerald Buddha, Haw Phra Kaew is rather modest, consisting of just a single building. But it would remain Lan Chang's main royal temple for the remainder of the kingdom's existence. And from 1707, it would be administered by the Kingdom of Vientiane. Appropriately, it's now one of the city's most popular tourist attractions.

THE SIM

After walking through a well-manicured garden you'll reach the *sim*. Look up at the gable to see Indra riding his animal mount Erawan (or Airavata), a three-headed elephant.

The open gallery around the *sim* is home to a myriad of bronze Buddha statues, both in seated and standing positions. There are also a number of old steles, some in a better state of preservation than others. In the back of the temple, you'll find an old wooden box that once contained the Tripitaka scriptures.

While the *sim* was repainted in red and gold, a few surviving parts of the original temple have been preserved as they were found. Protected behind glass is an old doorway that's been there since Setthathirath's time. According to a nearby sign, it's been restored as recently as 2016. And the same goes for one of the original posts located near the *sim's* entrance.

The interior of the *sim* is now a museum for old Buddhist relics. Though the Emerald Buddha is long gone, you can find a replica of the *busabok*, or gilded processional throne that it once sat on. Other objects include ancient Khmer artifacts and palm leaf manuscripts, much like the ones on which the Chronicle was first written (*see p6*). Unfortunately, no photography is allowed inside.

An original pillar and wooden door, carved with scenes from the Buddha's life

▲ The front doors have since been redecorated with golden guardian divinities and colorful mosaics

Many of Vientiane's significant Buddha images were looted over the years, but the ones here are centuries old ▾

A collection of old stone slabs and a Tripitaka storage box ▾

DOK SO FAA

On display just outside the *sim* is an old *dok so faa*. Could it have once adorned the roof of the temple? In Laos, many temple roofs are topped with these decorative elements which consist of a set of spires pointing up to the sky. The tallest and central one is said to represent Mt. Meru, the center of the universe in Buddhist cosmology. The style, decoration and even number of spires of a *dok so faa* may vary from temple to temple.

HAW PHRA KAEW IN THE 19TH CENTURY

In 1828, the Siamese sacked Vientiane for the second time in two years, not even sparing the Emerald Buddha's former home. But why?

At the time, the Kingdom of Vientiane was a vassal of Thailand. Its king, Anouvong, had taken the throne in 1805. Early on in his reign, he helped the Siamese with numerous military campaigns, forging a good relationship with King Rama II.

At home, he took a great interest in Haw Phra Kaew. He renovated and expanded the temple in 1816, even having a new Emerald Buddha replica carved. Later on, when visiting Bangkok for Rama II's funeral, Anouvong requested the return of Laotians who'd been forcibly relocated to Thailand during the prior invasion. But his request was denied.

In 1827, when the British were approaching Thailand, Anouvong saw his chance to rebel. But he greatly miscalculated the situation. The British were only coming to talk, not invade.

Anouvong rallied a large army and marched all the way to Nakhon Ratchasima. His Chief Minister, however, betrayed him. Siamese troops soon put an end to the rebellion and attacked Vientiane in 1827.

Despite promising peace, Anouvong then staged not one but two more ambush attacks on Siamese forces. In response, Siamese troops laid waste to the entire city in 1828, not even sparing Haw Phra Kaew.

When the French Mekong Expedition (*see p91*) arrived in 1867, Vientiane was largely a deserted jungle ruin. And Louis Delaporte sketched Haw Phra Kaew as he found it then. The temple was eventually rebuilt by the French in the 1930s.

Louis Delaporte's 1867 sketch of Haw Phra Kaew in ruin

◀ *A statue of Anouvong at Chao Anouvong Park*

Wat Si Saket · ວັດສີສະເກດ

Commissioned by King Anouvong in 1824, Wat Si Saket is one of Vientiane's most beautiful temples. Just across the street from Haw Phra Kaew, Anouvong often used it for important political meetings.

Its gallery contains over 6,800 Buddha images made from the 16th-19th centuries.

And its south-facing *sim* is a cross between Lao and Thai architecture. In 1828, Siamese troops used the temple as their base from which to sack the rest of the city. Wat Si Saket, therefore, was the only temple left untouched.

🕐 8:00 - 16:00
📅 Daily
₭ 5,000

Patuxai Monument · ປະຕູໄຊ

An icon of modern Laos, this concrete arch was designed by architect Tham Sayasthsena and built between 1957-68. It's dedicated to Lao soldiers who perished during the 20th century, including the war of independence from France. Largely modeled after the Arc de Triomphe in Paris, it's since become a symbol of the capital.

By climbing up seven floors, you can access a platform with panoramic views of the entire city. The spacious park in front is also a popular gathering spot for locals.

📍 Lan Xang Ave.
🕐 8:00 - 17:00
📅 Daily
₭ 3,000

Pha That Luang · ພະທາດຫຼວງ

Pha That Luang is widely regarded as Laos's national symbol. It's as to Laos as Angkor Wat is to Cambodia or Wat Phra Kaew is to Thailand. It was built in 1566 by one of the main characters of our story, King Setthathirath. The area on which the temple stands, however, has been considered sacred ground for a very long time.

- That Luang Rd.
- 8:00 - 16:00
- Daily
- 5,000 (for chedi)

Legend has it that during the reign of the great Indian Buddhist monarch King Ashoka (c.268-232 BC), monks from the Maurya Empire *(see p166)* visited the site and possibly even brought one of the Buddha's bones.

And then in the late 12th century, when the region was part of the Khmer Empire, King Jayavarman VII *(see p210)* established a temple at the same spot. Statues of both Jayavarman VII and Setthathirath *(pictured p87)* can be seen at the temple today.

Like many other landmarks in the city, Pha That Luang was damaged and looted by the Thais in 1827-28. Later 20th-century reconstruction attempts were interrupted by conflicts such as the Franco-Thai War and World War II. The temple was finally rebuilt after the war's end, and the project was largely based off of 19th-century sketches by Louis Delaporte *(see pp91, 114)*.

The Golden Chedi

Standing at 45 m high, the main *chedi* was built in a lotus-bud shape known as a *that*, which is typical of Lao temple architecture. It's surrounded by an outer gallery, which, at the time of writing, is mostly empty. At each of the four cardinal points, you'll find shrines flanked by *naga* staircases and statues.

Wat That Luang Neua

Wat That Luang Neua, to the north of the golden *chedi*, is one of the four original temples of the complex. Compared to the surrounding structures, its design is rather simple and modest. But its resident happens to be the Supreme Patriarch of Laotian Buddhism. As you approach the structure, notice the intricate patterns adorning the large gable.

Supposedly, somewhere deep within the *chedi* is one of the Buddha's breastbones brought millennia ago by Ashoka's monks.

Note that while it costs 5,000 kip to get up close to the *chedi*, most of it is clearly visible from all around the complex.

Wat That Luang Tai

This spacious collection of structures and courtyards acts as a temple within a temple. It's most famous for its massive golden reclining Buddha statue. But don't miss the airy main hall, which is completely covered in colorful murals portraying various Buddhist legends.

Haw Dhammasabha

Among the newer structures at the complex, the Haw Dhammasabha was completed in 2010 in honor of the city's 450th anniversary. Built for hosting religious ceremonies and conventions, the beautiful structure is notable for its multi-tiered roofing, which appears to be a modern take on classical Lao architecture.

> **Boun That Luang Festival**
>
> Boun That Luang takes place every November and lasts for three days. A procession begins at Wat Si Muang (p118) and ends at Pha That Luang, where people walk around the *chedi* three times in the manner of *pradakshina*. Numerous food stalls are set up during the festivities.

(i) **Pradakshina** *is a Buddhist and Hindu tradition which involves circling a holy site three times in a clockwise direction. It's thought to help participants connect with the sacred space within. The gap between the chedi and gallery at Pha That Luang was added with* pradakshina *in mind.*

WAT SI MUANG • ວັດສີເມືອງ

Wat Si Muang is a highly significant temple for locals, yet seldom visited by foreign tourists. The temple is yet another to have been built by King Setthathirath in the 1500s.

📍 Rue Thadeua
🕐 6:00 - 19:00
📅 Daily
💰 Free

Legend has it that around that time, angry spirits were causing trouble throughout Vientiane. And in an attempt to appease them, a pregnant woman named Si Muang sacrificed herself to protect the city.

The temple was then built on the same spot where Si Muang died. Although it was destroyed by the Siamese in the 1820s, it was rebuilt again in 1915. Walking around the courtyard, you'll find a pile of bricks that are believed to have been there from Si Muang's time.

THE CITY PILLAR SHRINE

Just nearby Wat Si Muang is a more recent structure built to house Vientiane's city pillar. As mentioned on p17, most cities in Indochina have city pillars which are believed to protect and provide good fortune for their cities.

This impressive building was built as recently as 2012. And when you consider the history of Wat Si Muang, which functions as the city's protective temple, the location is very appropriate.

And on the subject of guardian deities, yet another one is said to reside in the That Dam *chedi (see p120)*!

This stunning structure can be appreciated from many angles

Buddha Park • ສວນພະພຸດທະເຈົ້າ

Buddha Park, or Xieng Khuan, may be an easy bus ride from central Vientiane, but it feels like a completely different world. It contains hundreds of sculptures, all constructed by Bunleua Sulilat and his followers from the 1950s to 1975.

The concrete sculptures, some of them of monumental proportions, represent beings from both Buddhist and Hindu lore. You can even step inside a three-story dome with an entrance in the shape of a *kala*, a fierce god which represents time.

After encountering the demonic statues at the bottom, climb up to the very top where you'll be rewarded with a fantastic view of the entire park.

To get there, take a #14 bus from Khua Din Bus Station. Buses leave every half hour, with the ride lasting around 45 minutes.

📍 Thanon Tha Deua
🕒 8:00 - 17:00
📅 Daily
₭ 5,000

Who was Bunleua Sulilat?

Bunleua Sulilat was born in 1932 in Nong Khai, Thailand, and later moved across the river to Laos. As he was taking a walk one day, he suddenly fell into a cave. And there he met Keoku, the man who would become his guru.

Keoku taught Sulilat a philosophy which fuses Buddhist and Hindu ideas. And Sulilat would then go on to lead numerous devotees of his own, who followed his every instruction up until his passing in 1996.

Sulilat saw producing monolithic sculptures of the Buddha and Hindu deities as his life's work. Remarkably, he started Buddha Park with zero prior artistic experience.

Returning to Nong Khai in 1975, he built yet another park which he continued working on until his death. It's also where he's entombed (*see p121*).

Around Town

Vientiane may not be the prettiest capital city in Asia, but its top-class temples more than make up for that. While we've already covered the essentials, here are some additional things to do and see around town. Nature lovers may also want to visit the Phu Khao Khuay National Protected Area around 40 km northeast of the city.

The Presidential Palace

Though this palace was built in 1986, it stands on the grounds of the former royal palace of Lan Chang. Located nearby Haw Phra Kaew, at the junction of Lan Xang Ave and Setthathirath Rd, this is the area where rulers like Setthathirath and Anouvong once lived. The building, a unique blend of Eastern and Western architectural styles, can only be appreciated from the outside.

The Riverside

Regrettably, Vientiane's riverside area can't hold a candle to the scenic riverside promenade of Luang Prabang. The large concrete walkway isn't very easy on the eyes. But you can, at least, find a small night market and even some song and dance performances.

Nearby is **Chao Anouvong Park**, built in dedication to the final monarch of an independent Kingdom of Vientiane (*see p114*).

That Dam  140 Rue Samsenthai

This large brick *chedi* is said to be the former home of a seven-headed *naga* serpent tasked with protecting the gold that once covered it. The *naga* failed to do its job, however, as the gold was looted by the Thais during the 1827-28 invasions. Now situated in the middle of a roundabout near the Patuxai Monument, the ancient *chedi* has largely been left neglected.

Local Temples

▲ *Wat Inpeng's naga staircase*

Nearby the river, further down the western end of Setthathirath Rd, are a number of lesser-known temples that are worth exploring. Among the more impressive ones are the large and elaborate **Wat Inpeng**, as well as the unique bright yellow temple of **Wat Mixai**.

Onward to Northeast Thailand

Just across the river from Vientiane is Thailand's northeastern region, commonly referred to as Isaan. Previously part of the Lan Chang Kingdom, Isaan shares much in common with Laos, including dialect.

A simple bus ride over the Friendship Bridge is all that separates the two. But you will, of course, need to go through immigration (see p281). The places below are all within easy traveling distance of Vientiane, but we'll also cover Isaan more in-depth from p223.

^ Every year on Buddhist lent, mysterious lights appear over the Mekong. Locals say that they come from nagas who inhabit the river.

Wat Pho Chai

📍 600m E of Bus Sta.
🕐 8:00 - 17:00

This Nong Khai temple is home to the venerated Luang Phor Phra Sai image. Lao in origin, the Siamese brought it across the river after the 1828 sacking of Vientiane.

King Mongkut then ordered the statue's delivery to Bangkok, but, as detailed on p49, things didn't quite turn out as planned.

Sala Keoku

📅 Daily
฿ 50

Nong Khai is home to Bunleua Sulilat's other park that he created after fleeing Laos. Sala Keoku is larger and more refined than the original, and Sulilat is even entombed here! It's an easy bike ride from the city.

Phu Phra Bat

Udon Thani's Phu Phra Bat Historical Park is a must for nature lovers. You'll find ancient cave paintings, bizarre rock formations, and stunning cliff-side views.

BANGKOK

*J*ust about every traveler visiting Indochina will pass through the Emerald Buddha's current home of Bangkok, a city whose founding also coincides with the statue's arrival.

In addition to being Thailand's capital and largest city, Bangkok is also counted as one of the country's 76 provinces (or more specifically, a 'special administrative area'). And in this chapter, we'll be looking at two districts in the heart of Bangkok's urban core: Thonburi and Rattanakosin.

Thonburi, situated on the west bank of the Chao Phraya River, predates the founding of Bangkok proper by fifteen years. And when Bangkok was officially established across the river in 1782, it all began on Rattanakosin Island, bordered by the river on one side and canals on the others.

While Bangkok's more ancient attractions are the main focus of this guide, we'll also cover some of the best things to do and see in the bustling metropolis's downtown districts.

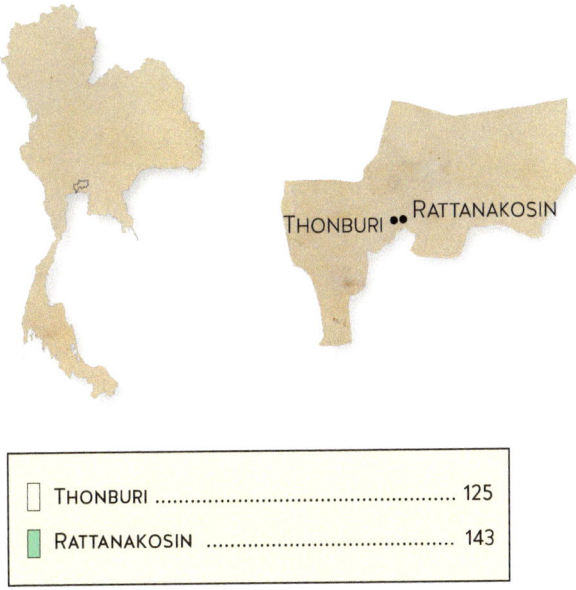

| ☐ Thonburi .... 125 |
| 🟩 Rattanakosin .... 143 |

Thonburi
1779 - 1784

The Return to Siam

The Holy Emerald Jewel remained in Vientiane for more than two hundred years. And during that time, civil war split the Lan Chang Kingdom into pieces. The newly-formed Kingdom of Vientiane allied itself with Burma, while its rival to the north, Luang Prabang, formed an alliance with Ayutthaya.

And over in the golden city of Ayutthaya, the Burmese persisted in their relentless attacks. For many years, the Siamese were able to defend their capital. But finally, in 1767, the Burmese breached Ayutthaya's defenses, making their way onto the opulent island city.

They destroyed Ayutthaya's great temples and monuments, taking any gold, silver or precious gemstones they could find. And even the king of Ayutthaya, Ekkathat, died of starvation while in hiding. But the Burmese military had matters at home to attend to, and many soldiers left Ayutthaya shortly after the sacking.

Following Ayutthaya's fall, Siam split into five parts. But one man aspired to reunite them. The great general known as Taksin, who had served under King Ekkathat, managed to drive out the remaining Burmese soldiers from Ayutthaya. And then he retook territories such as Phimai, Phitsanulok and Nakhon Si Thammarat. But as Ayutthaya was beyond redemption, Taksin established a new capital at Thonburi on the west bank of the Chao Phraya River.

And then, with the help of another great general, Chao Phraya Chakri, Taksin succeeded in taking Cambodia and the Lanna Kingdom. And in 1778, along with 20,000 men, Taksin sent General Chakri to take one of their last great rivals, the Kingdom of Vientiane. After a siege which lasted four months, Siamese troops successfully conquered Vientiane and they returned to the capital of Thonburi with numerous riches.

None so great, however, as the miraculous Emerald Buddha image. And together with it, they also brought the sacred statue known as the Phra Bang. Taksin the Great then placed these holy relics at the royal temple of Wat Arun, and he prayed in front of the statues day and night. Taksin became a devout follower of the faith, meditating constantly on Lord Buddha's sacred teachings.

> *i* As mentioned on p108, the Chronicle of the Emerald Buddha had already been written down by this point. This chapter and the next, therefore, are attempts at imagining how the original author(s) might've described these historical events.

Previous
p108

Next
p142

The Emerald Buddha In Thonburi

While most versions of the Chronicle of the Emerald Buddha were written down before the statue left Vientiane, a whole new chapter could've been written on all that transpired in the 18th century.

As mentioned on p83, by the 1700s, the once-mighty Kingdom of Lan Chang was no more. Infighting among the late Suriya Vongsa's relatives caused the kingdom to split into three. While Luang Prabang and Champasak allied themselves with Ayutthaya, the Kingdom of Vientiane sided with Burma.

The Burmese, who still controlled the Lanna Kingdom, were dead set on occupying Siam as well. And throughout the 1760s, Burma, then controlled by the Ava-based Konbaung dynasty (1752-1885), launched repeated attacks on Ayutthaya. In 1767, they finally breached the island city's defenses, destroying its temples and looting all its valuables.

While the last king of Ayutthaya, Ekkathat, starved to death while in hiding, his skilled general and advisor Taksin managed to escape. He fled to the southeastern province of Chanthaburi where he gathered numerous soldiers. From there, they sailed up the Chao Phraya River where they took over the town of Thonburi in November 1767. Next, Taksin even managed to expel the last Burmese troops from Ayutthaya.

Luckily for Siam, Burma itself was being invaded by China at the same time. Distracted and in desperate need of troops, few Burmese soldiers were left in Ayutthaya by the time Taksin arrived. But the city was so badly damaged that he opted to make Thonburi his new capital instead. (What we now know as Bangkok did not yet exist.)

While not having any connection to the royal bloodline, the charismatic Taksin was well-liked by the surviving Siamese nobility. And there was no question that he was an outstanding general. And so, King Taksin was officially coronated on December 28, 1768, at Wang Derm Palace.

At first, not all of Siam was on Taksin's side, as several regions had already declared themselves independent. With the help of his main general (and childhood friend) Chao Phraya Chakri, Taksin conquered the rebel states of Phimai, Phitsanulok, Uttaradit and Nakhon Si Thammarat. But Taksin didn't stop there.

By 1771, Thonburi was in control over much of Cambodia. And in 1776, the kingdom went on to take Lanna, a longtime vassal of Burma and former rival of Ayutthaya.

Then in November 1778, they invaded the last Burmese stronghold in the region, the Kingdom of Vientiane. After a four-month siege led by Chao Phraya Chakri, the Emerald Buddha, along with the Phra Bang, were taken to Thonburi and kept at the magnificent Wat Arun.

But the Kingdom of Thonburi would only last from 1767 to 1782. Learn more about what led to its demise in the following section.

‹ *Statues of Taksin the Great remain a common sight throughout Thonburi*

THONBURI TRAVEL TIPS

In between the destruction of Ayutthaya and the founding of Bangkok, the city of Thonburi functioned for a short time as the Siamese capital. And even after Bangkok's establishment, Thonburi operated as its own city all the way up until 1971.

Today, the term 'Thonburi' refers to the general area of Bangkok on the west bank of the Chao Phraya River. But while technically part of the capital, Thonburi maintains a distinct atmosphere. Few tourists, however, bother to explore the historical district beyond Wat Arun.

GETTING THERE

As mentioned above, Thonburi is just one of modern Bangkok's many districts. Check p144 to learn how to get to and from Bangkok itself.

Getting to Thonburi can be done in a number of ways. From either airport, you can take a **taxi** (roughly 400 baht) or use a **ridesharing** app.

And as a day trip from central Bangkok, you can take a **river ferry** to get back and forth between the two sides. The **MRT Blue Line** now extends into Thonburi, with Itsaraphap and Tha Phra stations accessible directly from central Bangkok (see p144). Thonburi can also be reached by **public bus**, while there are **BTS Silom Line** stations in the district's southern area.

WHERE TO STAY

Most visitors to the Bangkok area base themselves on the eastern side of the river. From there, Thonburi can easily be visited as a day trip. More than a single day, however, is required to visit all the locations mentioned in this section.

Depending on your schedule and level of interest, you may choose to spend a few nights in Thonburi to get to know the ancient capital better. But if you don't have time to spend a couple of nights on each side of the river, it's best to stay somewhere on the eastern bank, within easy reach of the Grand Palace (see p144).

If you do stay in Thonburi, look for a hotel that's near Wat Arun, an MRT station (such as Itsaraphap), or close to the river, which would allow you to take advantage of Bangkok's express boat system.

Also note that since few tourists come to Thonburi other than to see Wat Arun, the language barrier might be a bit of an issue at some hotels or local restaurants.

GETTING AROUND

Thonburi is a large area overall, but many of the sites in this section are situated along the Chao Phraya River within **walking** distance of one another. To get to some of the more distant locations, take advantage of the newly expanded MRT Blue Line or use a **ridesharing** app like Grab.

◀ A King Taksin the Great memorial near the Wongwian Yai BTS Station

CHAO PHRAYA RIVER BOATS

Note: the following info is also relevant for the next section on Rattanakosin.

One of the best ways to get around Bangkok is with a Chao Phraya River boat. There are five different 'lines,' each with its own color flag. But most popular sites can be accessed with either the orange or blue boats.

Orange flag boats stop at most piers and run from 6:00-19:00 every day. They run every 20 minutes and cost 15 baht per person, regardless of distance.

Blue flag boats are 'Chao Phraya Tourist Boats,' running from 9:00 - 19:00. They stop exclusively at the major tourist attractions (minus Wat Arun). They cost 50 baht per ride, regardless of distance. Full day **'hop-on, hop-off' passes** are also available for around 180 baht and work with any color boat.

Most piers have both names and numbers. Major stops include N5 Rajchawongse for Chinatown (along with the next few), N8 Tha Thien for Wat Pho, N9 Tha Chang for the Grand Palace, N12 Phra Pin Klao Bridge for Thonburi's Royal Barge Museum, and N13 Phra Arthit for Khao San Rd.

To get to Wat Arun from the other side, you'll need to take a special cross-river boat which runs between Wat Arun Pier and N8 for just a few baht.

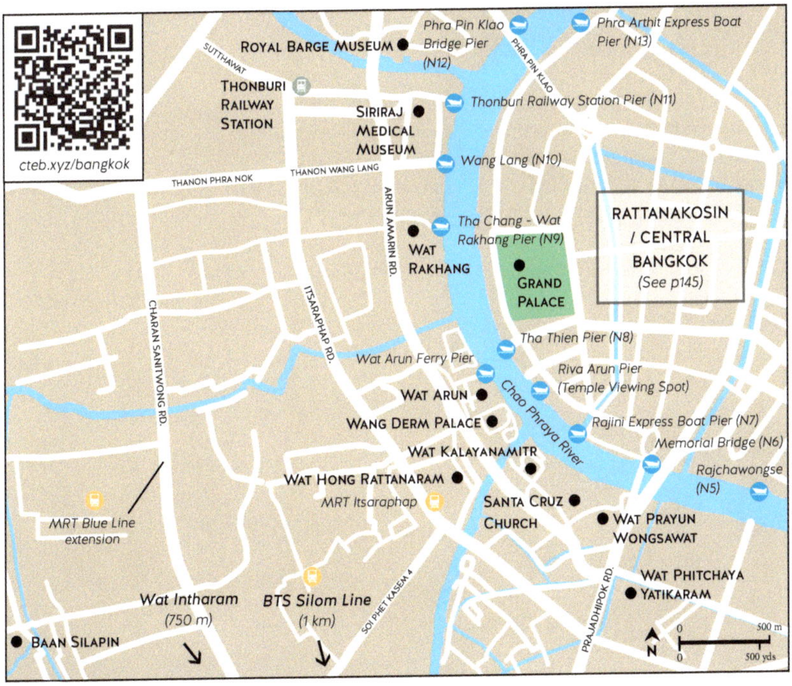

Wat Arun • วัดอรุณราชวราราม ราชวรมหาวิหาร

The Emerald Buddha was here

Established in 1768, Wat Arun is easily one of Bangkok's most impressive temples. The *wat* served as the main royal temple of the short-lived Thonburi Kingdom, though King Taksin didn't build it from scratch. Historical records indicate that there was a temple there for at least a hundred years before his reign.

📍 158 Thanon Wang Doem
🕐 8:00 - 17:30
📅 Daily
฿ 100

Legend has it that Taksin vowed to restore the temple while cruising along the Chao Phraya River at dawn. Wat Arun, in fact, translates to 'Temple of the Dawn.' It's associated with Aruna, the charioteer of Surya, the Hindu Sun god. During Taksin's reign, however, it was called Wat Chaeng. And the earlier temple at the same spot was named Wat Makok, or 'Olive Temple.'

Later kings of the Chakri dynasty, such as Rama II, III and IV, continued expanding Wat Arun throughout the 1800s until it took on its current form.

The Emerald Buddha was placed here after it was brought from Vientiane in early 1779. And it would even share a space with the Phra Bang (*see p98*)!

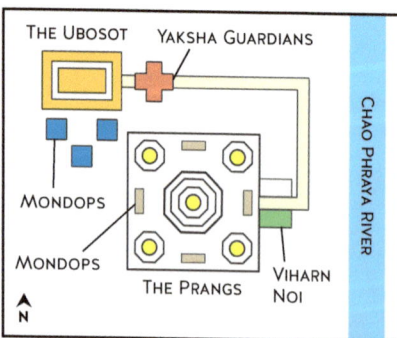

THE PRANGS

The five *prangs* of Wat Arun, each adorned with colorful Chinese porcelain, are arranged in a quincunx. The tallest tower in the center represents Mt. Meru, the abode of the gods in both Buddhist and Hindu cosmology. The mythological mountain is said to be surrounded by four peaks, symbolized here by the four smaller *prangs*.

Wat Arun's layout was largely influenced by the 1630 Ayutthaya temple Wat Chai Watthanaram *(p243)*. And that temple was a Siamese adaptation of the Khmer 'temple-mountain,' the most famous example of which is Angkor Wat *(p208)*. The *prangs* of Wat Arun, however, are much taller and narrower than those of its predecessors.

CENTRAL PRANG
The 67 m-high *prang* was extended to its current height by King Rama II. It's topped with a *vajra*, the weapon of Indra.

INDRA
The middle section of the central *prang* represents Indra's abode of Tavatimsa (heaven). The four niches contain images of Indra riding his three-headed elephant Erawan (or Airavata). In Thailand, Indra is revered as the protector of Bangkok.

VAYU
The smaller *prangs* are dedicated to the wind god Vayu and feature images of him on his horse.

YAKSHAS & KINNARAS
Various levels of the central *prang* are flanked by guardian beings who appear to be holding up the massive structure.

The Viharn Noi

At the entrance to the temple (at least for those coming by boat) are two *viharns* which most visitors skip on their way to see the *prangs*. The *viharn* to the left, however, known as the Viharn Noi, was home to the Emerald Buddha during its stay at Wat Arun.

Inside, the *viharn* contains English information about King Taksin's life. But oddly, there's no mention of the Emerald Buddha. You will, however, find a replica that's been placed at the center of one of the altars. Elsewhere, you'll also notice a few statues reminiscent of the Phra Bang.

The *viharn* also contains a shrine dedicated to King Taksin in addition to a colorful array of Chinese ornaments, most likely in honor of Taksin's Chinese heritage.

‹ A shrine for Taksin

King Taksin & China

Taksin's mother was Siamese but his father was a Teochew Chinese from Guangdong Province. Taksin spoke Chinese fluently, and during his reign, he actively promoted Teochew merchants to settle in his kingdom. A large community even formed across the river where the Grand Palace now stands.

The former Ayutthaya nobility in Thonburi, however, began to question Taksin's loyalty. These doubts, among other factors, may have led to the king's eventual deposition.

Be that as it may, close trade relations with China flourished well beyond Taksin's reign. All around Thonburi, even many of the temples sponsored by later kings demonstrate a clear Chinese influence.

‹ Wat Arun's prangs are decorated entirely with broken Chinese porcelain, sourced from ceramics used as ballast. And the Chinese statues found around both Wat Arun and Wat Phra Kaew were also once ballast on Chinese trading ships.

The Ubosot

The *ubosot* is home to the current principal Buddha image of the temple, designed by none other than King Rama II *(see below)*. The murals were later added by King Chulalongkorn (Rama V, r.1853-1910). They depict scenes from the Jataka Tales, or the Buddha's past lives.

Also outside, don't miss the beautiful *bai sema*, or boundary stones, that are housed in their own little *mondops*. This is a rare example of *bai sema*, which demarcate the sacred space within, having been carved entirely out of marble.

King Rama II

In front of Wat Arun stands a statue of King Rama II, and for good reason. Following King Taksin's reign and the demise of the Thonburi Kingdom, Wat Arun was largely left abandoned. Phra Phutthaloetla Naphalai, or King Rama II, (r.1809-1824) is credited with taking the initiative to restore and expand the temple. He even raised the central *prang* up to nearly seventy meters.

What's more is that the *ubosot's* main Buddha image was designed by Rama II, while the base of said image even contains some of his ashes! Considered a patron of the arts, Rama II was nicknamed the 'Poet King.' As crown prince, he liked to spend time at Taksin's former royal palace in Thonburi. And he even started planning Wat Arun's restoration before becoming king. But the project was so ambitious that much of it had to be completed by his son, Rama III.

Around the Complex

Exploring Wat Arun, you'll come across various *mondops* and pavilions housing everything from Ganesha statues to King Taksin shrines. One of the more noteworthy structures houses an elaborate copy of the Buddha's footprint.

And over by the entrance to the *ubosot* are two tall statues of *yaksha* guardian giants. Similar ones can also be found around Wat Phra Kaew (*see p152*).

Out in front, there's ample room to enjoy the view of the Chao Phraya River. You can also clearly see the rooftops of Wat Phra Kaew, the Emerald Buddha's current home, over on the opposite side.

Just south of Wat Arun is **Wang Derm Palace,** King Taksin's former royal residence. Now the site of the Royal Thai Naval Academy, it's normally closed to the public except for a few days each December.

The Sunset View

One of the best ways to appreciate Wat Arun is to view it from across the river in Bangkok's Rattanakosin district. All along the riverside are rooftop restaurants and bars, ideal for those who want to appreciate the sunset with food or wine. And river cruises are another option to consider.

But if you just want to see the temple with no strings attached, there's at least one special spot where you can do so for free.

Head south of the Grand Palace and Wat Pho and find Maha Rat Rd, which runs parallel to the river. When you see a high school, turn down one of the small side streets, heading toward the water. Just next to the Supanniga Eating Room restaurant is the **Riva Arun Pier,** from which you can get a clear view of Wat Arun on the other side. Don't expect to find yourself completely alone, but not more than a dozen or so people typically turn up on an average night.

Wat Phitchaya Yatikaram • วัดพิชยญาติการาม วรวิหาร

This ornate temple was abandoned for years before King Rama III's administration restored it in 1841. As trade with China continued to flourish throughout the 1800s, many of the materials used in the temple's reconstruction were sourced from there. Even the *ubosot* is adorned with a Chinese-style roof rather than a Thai one.

Entering the temple area, visitors will encounter a pathway lined with numerous *mondops* on either side, each housing a Buddha image.

A tall *prang*, meanwhile, stands at the center of the complex. Climbing up to its inner sanctuary, you'll find a mesmerizing trio of golden Buddhas inside (pictured above). And turning around, take in the panoramic view of the entire complex and even some of Thonburi's skyline in the distance.

Despite the temple's size and splendor, very few tourists come here. You'll likely be able to explore at your own pace far away from the crowds.

- Somdet Chao Phraya Rd
- 8:00 - 20:00
- Daily
- Free

Beyond Wat Arun, Thonburi has plenty more in store for those with time to explore the area. All the locations mentioned below are free and open daily. Additionally, you may want to check out the Royal Barge Museum and the Siriraj Hospital Museum.

AROUND TOWN

WAT PRAYUN WONGSAWAT WARAVIHARN

📍 *Phrachathipok Rd.*
🕒 *8:00 - 17:30*

A fusion of Theravada Buddhist and Chinese styles, this temple dates back to the reign of King Rama III. Aside from an impressive white *chedi*, the main attraction is a Chinese-style garden complete with turtle pond.

CHURCH OF SANTA CRUZ   📍 *112 Thesaban 1 Rd*

As one of the largest foreign settlements in Ayutthaya, the Portuguese assisted Siam in their resistance against Burma. And in exchange for their efforts, King Taksin granted them with this plot of land in his new capital of Thonburi. The original church was built in 1770, but after a large fire, it had to be rebuilt in the 1830s.

WAT INTHARAM   📍 *256 Thoet Thai*
🕒 *8:00 - 16:00*

One of King Taksin's favorite temples during his reign, he was later cremated and enshrined here. Still widely regarded as the savior of Siam, locals regularly visit to pay their respects. The temple is some 3 km south of Wat Arun, accessible via the Pho Nimit bus station or Wat Intharam Pier.

WAT HONG RATTANARAM

Established during the Ayutthaya era by a rich Chinese merchant, the temple later came under the patronage of King Taksin. Today, the *ubosot* impresses visitors with its stunning artwork and dazzling colors. And be sure to check out the murals behind glass, which depict scenes from various parts of the Chronicle of the Emerald Buddha.

📍 *102 Wang Derm Rd.*
🕒 *8:00 - 18:00*

WAT KALAYANAMITR   📍 *371 Soi Arun Amarin 6*
🕒 *8:30 - 16:30*

Wat Kalayanamitr is yet another Chinese-inspired temple built during the reign of Rama III. As mentioned, even after Taksin's death, trade with China continued to boom throughout the 19th century. In front of the temple are two tall Chinese-style pagodas. Inside the Thai-style *viharn*, meanwhile, is a massive seated golden Buddha.

Exploring the Canals

Thonburi is perhaps most known for its canals. And one of the best places to relax while looking out at the water is the **Khlong Bang Luang Artist House**.

The Artist House (or 'Baan Silapin') was established in 2010, but the structure itself is over 200 years old. In addition to quirky contemporary art sculptures, the house also features a coffee shop. And be sure to visit by 14:00 for a daily puppet show rendition of the Ramakien, or Thai Ramayana *(see p153)*.

As many of Thonburi and central Bangkok's canals have been filled in to make way for new development projects, Khlong Bang Luang and its surrounding area are among the few places left to get a feel for old Bangkok.

Along the wooden boardwalk, local entrepreneurs have taken advantage of the area's popularity, setting up numerous cafes and gift shops. Sit back, relax and look out at the water, enjoying a rare moment of peace in one of Asia's most hectic metropolises.

On the way back to the main road, you may want to stop by a small rustic temple called **Wat Kamphaeng**.

> *Bangkok was once entirely comprised of canals, with most residents living in floating houses. In fact, the first major road, Charoen Krung, wasn't even paved until 1861!*

Baan Silapin a 20-minute walk from MRT Tha Phra Station. It's also a popular stop on Bangkok canal tours.

- 📍 Soi Wat Thong Sala Ngarm
- 🕘 9:00 – 18:00
- 📅 Daily
- ฿ Free

Floating Markets

One of Thonburi's most famous floating markets is **Khlong Lad Mayom**, accessible via taxi from BTS/MRT Bang Wa Station. Far from the city center, this is very much a market by and for locals. It's a great place to try authentic Thai food on weekends until around 17:00.

In the Taling Chan district of Thonburi is the **Taling Chan Floating Market**. Only open on weekends until 18:00, this is a good place to come for a meal or even a massage. To get there, first ride the BTS to Wongwian Yai Station and then hail a cab.

Though well outside Bangkok and Thonburi, **Amphawa Floating Market** is nevertheless one of the most popular. It's frequented by both tourists and locals for eating as well as shopping. Open from Friday to Sunday, this market is often included on tours.

Rattanakosin

1784 - Present

The City of Angels

As the Thonburi Kingdom's power expanded, King Taksin grew increasingly religious. He spent his days in deep meditation, and he even started lecturing the monks themselves. 'Bow down to me,' Taksin told the sangha, 'for I have entered the sacred stream of dharma. The attainment of total enlightenment is within my reach.' Those monks who refused to bow were shamed and demoted.

The sangha, together with the nobles of Thonburi, became increasingly concerned. Taksin the Great had clearly gone mad, they concluded. His blasphemous behavior could not be overlooked, and it was decided that the king must be executed for his crimes. Taksin did not resist, but only begged that his life be spared so that he could live out his days as a humble monk. His request, however, was denied.

Taksin's best general, Chao Phraya Chakri, who was on a mission in Cambodia, quickly returned to Thonburi upon hearing the news. And as the highest-ranked general in the kingdom, Chakri was deemed as Taksin's most suitable replacement.

This had been prophesied years prior, in fact, by the great general Azaewunky of Burma. So impressed with Chakri's military prowess, he told him, 'You shall become a great king someday.' And in 1782, Chakri was coronated as the new king of Siam. Often referred to as King Rama I, he'd found the long-lasting Chakri dynasty.

Rather than stay in Thonburi, he moved his capital to the other side of the river, to the island of Rattanakosin. His first task was constructing a magnificent temple for the holy Jewel Image. And after much labor, the beautiful Wat Phra Sri Rattana Satsadaram, or Wat Phra Kaew, was completed to house the Emerald Buddha. From there, the resplendent image of miraculous powers could keep watch over the new capital and Siam as a whole.

This new city was named as follows: 'The city of angels, the great city that is home to the Jewel Image, endowed with nine precious gems and centered around the Grand Palace, which mirrors the heavenly abode where the gods reside, a city gifted by Indra and built by his divine architect, Vishwakarman.'

Or, more simply, Krung Tep for short. This magnificent city would widely become known around the world as Bangkok, and it remains home to the holy Emerald Buddha to this day.

Previous p126

The Emerald Buddha In Rattanakosin

Over the course of his reign, King Taksin's behavior grew increasingly erratic. He declared himself a *sotapanna*, or a 'future Buddha,' and demanded to be worshipped as such. Earlier in his reign, he'd also made significant reforms to the local *sangha* which had grown corrupt and decadent after the fall of Ayutthaya. These earlier reforms, combined with his egotistical 'Buddha complex,' meant that he had no shortage of enemies within the monkhood.

And as mentioned on p132, members of the nobility were also suspicious of his close ties with the Chinese merchant community. So despite Taksin's earlier accomplishments, it was decided that he had to go.

The exact circumstances surrounding his death remain a mystery. Many sources indicate that Chao Phraya Chakri ordered the execution himself. Alternate versions of the story, on the other hand, suggest that Taksin was already dead by the time Chakri returned to Thonburi. But according to yet another theory, Taksin faked his death and fled to Nakhon Si Thammarat, possibly to escape debt repayment to China (see p189).

In any case, Chakri would take the throne, founding the Chakri dynasty which persists to this day. Though the tradition of Chakri kings being nicknamed Rama (of the Ramayana) wouldn't be implemented until the reign of King Vajiravudh (Rama VI, r.1910-1925), Chao Phraya Chakri is now commonly referred to as King Rama I.

And King Rama I felt that Thonburi, situated on the western bank of the Chao Phraya River, might be vulnerable to future Burmese attacks. Therefore, he decided to construct a brand new capital on the opposite side.

He chose the 'island' of Rattanakosin as his new capital, which was bordered by the river on one side and canals on the others. At the time, it was home to the Chinese merchant community, but they were relocated further south to Bangkok's current Chinatown district.

Rattanakosin means 'Repository of the Gem Image' which is a clear reference to the Emerald Buddha. And the Rattanakosin Kingdom would rule Siam until the constitutional reforms of 1932.

As for Wat Phra Kaew and the Grand Palace, Rama I followed the tradition of building a royal temple and royal residence within the same compound. At the recommendation of royal astrologers, construction officially began on May 6th, 1782, lasting a couple of years. Bangkok's City Pillar Shrine, however, erected on April 21st of the same year, was the very first thing built.

^ *Garuda has long symbolized the Chakri dynasty*

Clearly, Rama I had a special relationship with the Emerald Buddha. He was, after all, the one to take it from Vientiane. And he even went as far as including it in the city's official name! (Which, by the way, is the longest official city name in the world.) Ever since, the Emerald Buddha has been considered the palladium of Thailand.

Modern Bangkok is now a sprawling city of millions and is one of Southeast Asia's premier economic hubs. Not many people realize, however, that it all started with the construction of an opulent home for a small green statue.

CENTRAL BANGKOK TRAVEL TIPS

Bangkok, Thailand's capital and largest city, is a huge metropolis that spreads out to over 1000 km². Now home to around 15 million inhabitants, modern Bangkok has no shortage of skyscrapers, nightlife, or traffic jams!

Though the east bank of the Chao Phraya River was just a small merchant settlement before the arrival of the Emerald Buddha, Wat Phra Kaew is now Thailand's most sacred spot. Elsewhere on Rattanakosin Island, you can find numerous other constructions from the early Bangkok period.

GETTING THERE

Because the city is so well connected, Bangkok is where many people begin their travels in Southeast Asia. The city has two airports: **Suvarnabhumi** (BKK), the main international airport, and **Don Mueang** (DMK), which mostly serves domestic and budget airlines.

From within Thailand, domestic flights with airlines like Nok Air or AirAsia are very affordable. If you book far enough in advance, you can reach Bangkok from places like Chiang Mai for roughly 1,000 baht one-way.

To get into town, you can take the Airport Rail Link from Suvarnabhumi or the SRT Dark Red Line from DMK (from 2020). You can also hire a metered taxi from either airport, while direct buses to Khao San Road are another option.

Most long-distance **buses** arrive and depart from Mo Chit Bus Terminal, while Ekkamai and Sai Tai Mai are other major terminals.

As for **train** travel, nearly every rail line in the country directly connects with Hua Lamphong Railway Station.

GETTING AROUND

Bangkok has two main **rapid transit** systems, both of which run until midnight. The elevated **BTS Skytrain** runs through much of downtown, including the lively Sukhumvit area. Ticket prices vary depending on the distance.

The **MRT** runs underground and requires separate tickets from the BTS. The BTS and MRT converge at only a few stations, such as Saladaeng, Asok and Bang Wa.

For a long time, Rattanakosin had no direct metro access. But that changed in 2019 with the extension of the MRT Blue Line. Visitors can now reach the Grand Palace and Wat Pho via Sanam Chai Station, or Wat Suthat via Sam Yot. The line also extends westward to Thonburi (*see p128*). At the time of writing, Bangkok's transit system is being expanded, so be sure to check online for a current map.

Public bus is another convenient option, with rides only costing 10-20 baht. Your smartphone's GPS application can tell you the right bus to take.

Ridesharing apps like Grab are another great way to get around. **Metered taxis** are ubiquitous throughout Bangkok, but be wary of drivers taking extra long routes. **Motorbike taxis** are another option for when you're really in a rush. But you'd best save yourself a headache by avoiding **tuk tuks** nearby tourist sites. See p129 for info on **boat travel**.

> **SCAM ALERT:** *If a stranger tells you the place you're going to is closed, it likely really isn't*

WHERE TO STAY

Staying in or nearby Rattanakosin (also called the Old City) is ideal. This would give you easy access to most of the sites mentioned in this section. Given the popularity of the Grand Palace and Wat Phra Kaew, it's highly recommended that you arrive right when the temple opens at 8:30 am.

Khao San Road, the budget accommodation district known for being a backpacker party spot, is actually located within Rattanakosin and is even within walking distance of the Emerald Buddha. While Khao San might not be the atmosphere you're looking for, you could find accommodation on a quieter adjacent street instead of the noisy main road. Also consider staying nearby an MRT Blue Line station such as Sam Yot or Sanam Chai.

Outside Rattanakosin, Chinatown or the area around Hua Lamphong Station would make for a convenient base, as you'd have access to both the MRT and the national railway. Alernatively, a hotel near the bustling downtown area would give you access to numerous landmarks and a plethora of shopping and dining options. BTS Siam Station is where the Sukhumvit and Silom lines converge.

While a bit of a trek from central Bangkok, staying near MRT Mo Chit Station or BTS Chatuchak Park would make it easy to reach DMK Airport and the main bus terminal, not to mention the lively Chatuchak Market.

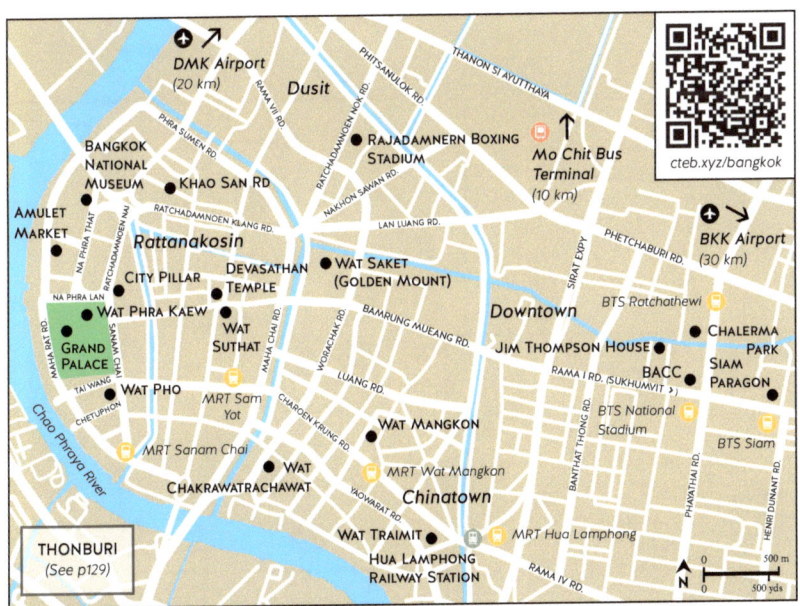

Wat Phra Kaew · วัดพระแก้ว

Home of the Emerald Buddha

Also known as Wat Phra Sri Rattana Satsadaram, Wat Phra Kaew is Thailand's most important temple. Its construction, which began in 1782, coincided with the founding of Bangkok itself. The Emerald Buddha was then placed here in 1784.

The temple is part of the larger Grand Palace complex *(see p154)*, which was the royal residence and administrative headquarters for the Rattanakosin Kingdom. In its entirety, the massive complex covers an area of 218,000 square meters.

Following the reign of King Rama I, later kings continued to expand and renovate Wat Phra Kaew. The magnificent temple is teeming with so much detail that one could spend hours taking everything in.

- Na Phra Lan Rd.
- 8:30 - 16:30
- Daily
- ฿ 500 (includes Grand Palace & museums)

^ Unlike at other temples, these yakshas face inward, always watching the Emerald Buddha

ⓘ Wat Phra Kaew is by far the most crowded destination in Thailand. To fully enjoy the temple, be sure to arrive when it opens at 8:30 am.

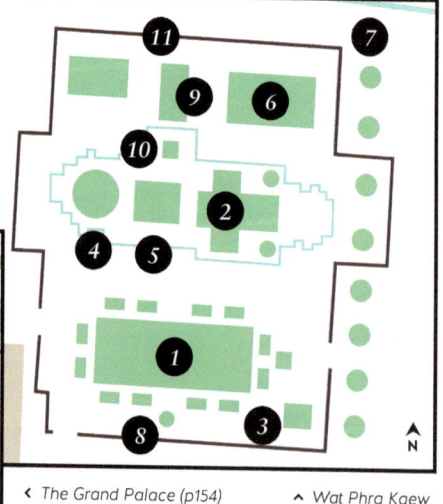

< The Grand Palace (p154)   ^ Wat Phra Kaew

① The Chapel of the Emerald Buddha

The Emerald Buddha is kept in Wat Phra Kaew's *ubosot*, which dates back to the temple's founding. The structure, appropriately, is also referred to as the Chapel of the Emerald Buddha.

Before stepping inside, don't miss the 112 carvings of *garudas* holding *naga* serpents placed all around the building. The doors are inlaid with mother of pearl, while colorful mosaics adorn the pillars. The gable decoration, meanwhile, consists of a golden carving of the Hindu god Vishnu riding Garuda.

No photography is allowed inside, though you're allowed to take pictures of the interior from the terrace. Bring a zoom lens if you have one.

A Khmer lion statue taken from Cambodia

Over a hundred golden garudas surround the exterior

The surrounding bai sema are housed in their own mondops

The Costume Changing Ritual

The Emerald Buddha has three different outfits according to the three Thai seasons: summer, winter and the rainy season. Three times a year, the king acts as master of ceremonies for a special ritual that marks the transition from one season to the next. Before applying the new outfit, the king will carefully wipe the image. He'll also sprinkle water over the statue as part of a special cleansing rite.

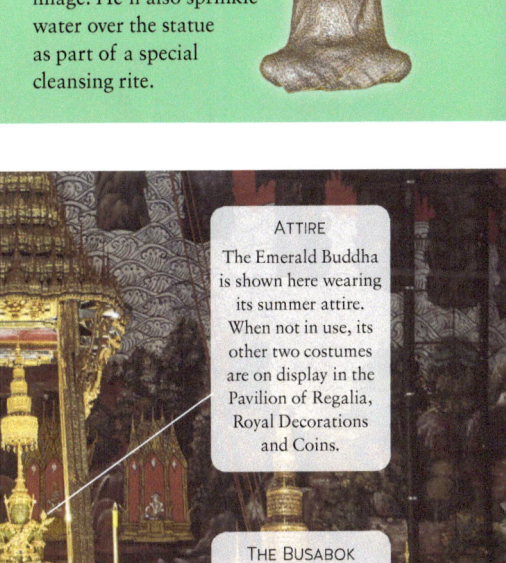

Murals
These murals, which represent the past lives of the Buddha, were added in the 19th century by artist Khrua In Khong, a close friend of King Mongkut (Rama IV).

Attire
The Emerald Buddha is shown here wearing its summer attire. When not in use, its other two costumes are on display in the Pavilion of Regalia, Royal Decorations and Coins.

Standing Buddhas
The various golden standing Buddha images contain ashes of kings and other royal family members. Rama I and Rama II's ashes are inside the two images at the very front.

The Busabok
The *busabok*, or miniature processional throne, dates back to the reign of King Rama I. Its base was added by Rama III, and the statue now towers over the room at around 9 m high.

Before entering the Chapel of the Emerald Buddha, you'll need to remove your shoes. Once inside, sit down cross-legged on the floor as you take in the beauty of the jade image.

② The Royal Pantheon

Also known as the Prasat Phra Dhepbidorn, this is one of the most elaborate structures of the complex. It was first constructed in 1856 by King Rama IV, who intended to move the Emerald Buddha here.

Yet upon completion, the interior was deemed too small, and the Emerald Buddha never left the *ubosot*. The structure now contains statues of former kings of the Chakri dynasty, first placed there by King Rama VI following additional renovations. It's accessible to the public on only one day each year: April 6th, or Chakri Day.

In front are two large golden spires which appear to be supported by monkeys from the Ramakien *(see p153)*. The two *chedis* stand on the same site as older ones placed by Rama I in honor of his parents.

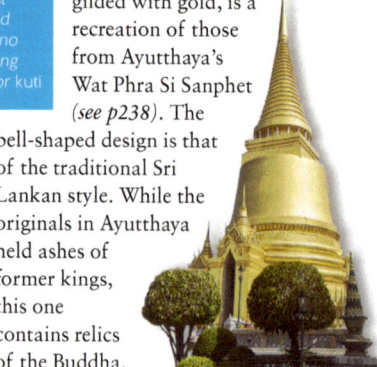

③ Ho Phra Kanthara Rat

This ornate tiled structure erected by King Rama IV contains an ancient Buddha statue from the Gandhara region (encompassing current Pakistan and Afghanistan, *see p166*). The image cannot be seen from the outside, but it's occasionally taken out for special rainmaking rituals.

Being a royal temple, Wat Phra Kaew has no resident monks, and therefore, no monks' living quarters, or kuti

④ Phra Si Rattana Chedi

This imposing *chedi*, gilded with gold, is a recreation of those from Ayutthaya's Wat Phra Si Sanphet *(see p238)*. The bell-shaped design is that of the traditional Sri Lankan style. While the originals in Ayutthaya held ashes of former kings, this one contains relics of the Buddha.

5 Phra Mondop

Most Thai temples have a single structure in which to keep important manuscripts, called the *ho trai (see p21)*. But Wat Phra Kaew has two, as the original was destroyed by

fire. One is the Phra Mondop, built in 1789, which is one of the most beautiful structures of the complex. Its design is based on a particular *mondop* containing the Buddha's footprint in Saraburi Province. And it's recognizable from all over the complex due to its tall spired roof. The walls, meanwhile, are decorated with intricate green tiles.

Surrounding the structure are four ancient Javanese Buddha images that were gifted to King Rama V.

6 Ho Phra Monthian Tham

Built by King Rama I's younger brother, the structure's doors are inlaid with mother of pearl. Like the Phra Mondop, it also holds important texts.

7 Eight Prangs

Rama I built eight *prangs* on the eastern side of the temple. Each represents a virtue of Buddhism, such as the Buddha, *dharma*, *sangha* and *bodhisattvas*.

8 The Belfry

The belfry installed by King Rama III is one of the finest examples of a *ho rakang* in Thailand. It replaced the original one built by Rama I.

9 Phra Wihan Yot

A unique and elegant building decorated with Chinese porcelain, this *viharn* currently houses the Phra Nak Buddha. The 4 m-high standing image comes from Ayutthaya and is made of copper alloy. The statue was originally kept in the adjacent **Ho Phra Nak**, which never changed its name following the move. Neither structure is currently open to the public.

Various Statues

1: *Kinnaras*, who inhabit the mythological Himavanta forest, are half-human, half-horse beings. *Kinnaris*, their female counterparts, are half-woman, half-bird.

2: A shrine in front of the *ubosot* contains a calf and various divinities from Chinese Mahayana Buddhism.

3: The temple is guarded by six pairs of towering *yaksha* giants. Meanwhile, Cheewok Komaraphat, the father of Thai herbal medicine, greets visitors at the temple entrance.

4: The Tantima bird also lives in the Himavanta forest. According to Buddhist lore, it's a cousin of Garuda.

5: The Asura Paksi is another hybrid creature with the head of a *yaksha* and the body of a bird.

6: Elephants are prevalent throughout the complex. In Indochina, they've long been symbols of royalty.

Was the Emerald Buddha once at Angkor Wat? Maybe. Read more on p208

11 The Outer Gallery

The gallery surrounding the temple is entirely covered in vivid murals of scenes from the Ramakien, the Thai version of the Ramayana *(see next page)*. The story is depicted throughout 178 sections, and to see them in order, start opposite the Phra Wihan Yot and then proceed clockwise.

10 Angkor Wat Replica

During Rama IV's reign, Thailand controlled much of Cambodia and the king was an admirer of Khmer architecture. According to one story, in 1860, he even sent men to go and bring back Angkor Wat - as in disassemble it piece by piece!

Ultimately, the king came to realize the implausibility of the plan (or according to another version, his men were ambushed) and opted for this miniature replica instead.

THE RAMAYANA

The Ramakien, presented across gorgeous murals adorning Wat Phra Kaew's long galleries, is the Thai version of the Ramayana. The Ramayana, along with the Mahabharata *(see p217)*, is one of the great epic poems of India. And even outside of the Indian subcontinent the story remains incredibly popular in countries like Thailand, Laos, Cambodia and Indonesia.

The story is about the adventures of Rama, an avatar of Vishnu *(see p16)*. Though Rama, the heir apparent of the Kosala Kingdom, was next in line to the throne, things didn't quite go as planned. When the mother of one of his half-brothers convinced the king to let her son rule and send Rama into exile, Rama left town with his wife Sita and his brother Lakshmana.

While in exile, they rescued a number of villages from *rakshasa* monsters, thus angering the king of all the *rakshasas*, Ravana (or Tosakan in the Ramakien).

This devious king, who ruled the island of Lanka (Sri Lanka), traveled north, where he was able to trick Rama and abduct Sita. The rest of the epic details Rama trying to figure out where Sita was taken. And when he eventually does, a great war ensues at Lanka.

While Rama is a very powerful archer, he doesn't act alone. He makes friends with the monkey king Sugriva by helping him take back the throne from his brother, Valin. Sugriva's subordinate Hanuman then becomes one of Rama's closest allies, and he plays a major role in bringing Sita back.

As Rama represents the archetypal virtuous king *(see p14)*, the Chakri dynasty monarchs named themselves after the hero, as did some earlier kings of Ayutthaya. (Ayutthaya, in fact, was named after Rama's hometown of Ayodhya, India).

While the Ramakien and Ramayana are very similar, the Ramakien is always depicted in a typical Thai style of art. Around Wat Phra Kaew, many of the sculptures resembling monkeys or demons are in fact characters from the epic.

The Grand Palace

The Grand Palace is a massive complex as old as the city itself. While the royal family now lives in Chitralada Palace in Dusit, several buildings here are still used for royal ceremonies. *(See map on p146)*

The entire complex is made up of three sections. The **Outer Palace** is home to Wat Phra Kaew and some administrative offices. The **Middle Palace** (featured on this page) is home to numerous throne halls, reception rooms, and pavilions.

Finally, the **Inner Palace**, which functioned as a city within a city, forbade access to all men other than the king himself. Today, daughters of elite Thai families still attend etiquette courses there.

Chakri Throne Hall

Built by Rama V in 1882 to celebrate a hundred years of the Chakri dynasty, this throne hall features a unique fusion of Western and Thai architecture. It was designed by British architect John Chinitz, who'd originally planned to top the building with three domes. It was eventually decided, however, that spires would be more fitting. The interior houses ashes of former monarchs and it also contains reception rooms.

Phra Maha Monthien Group

Shortly after exiting Wat Phra Kaew, you'll encounter the ornate Amarin Winitchai Throne Hall. The king would meet state and foreign ambassadors here, and the hall contains two lavish thrones. The throne hall is one of the only buildings of the palace to be open to the public (weekdays only).

But the hall is just one part of seven interconnected buildings that make up the Phra Maha Monthien Group. Constructed mainly for residential purposes by Rama I in 1782, these are among the oldest buildings in the Grand Palace.

Dusit Throne Hall

The cross-shaped hall was built by Rama I as a replica of Ayutthaya'a Sanphet Prasat Palace.

The current structure is a smaller reconstruction of the original, which was destroyed by lightning strike. Home to a beautiful teak throne, the hall is still used for the annual Coronation Day.

Aphonphimok Pavilion

Built as Rama IV's changing room before descending onto his palanquin, this pavilion's design was so popular that its replica was displayed at the 1958 World's Fair.

Wat Pho · วัดโพธิ์

Located just nearby Wat Phra Kaew, Wat Pho is one of Thailand's most important temples. While an earlier temple had existed on the site since the 16th century, King Rama I renovated and expanded it in the 1780s. It was then further developed by his grandson, Rama III, who installed the massive reclining Buddha image that Wat Pho is mainly known for.

📍 *Thanon Chetuphon*
🕐 *8:00 - 18:30*
📅 *Daily*
฿ *100*

The vast temple complex covers over 80,000 square meters. You'll find nearly 100 *chedis* in total, in addition to numerous *viharns* and an *ubosot*.

Wat Pho is also home to nearly 700 Buddha images which were rescued from Ayutthaya during the Burmese sacking. You can find some of the more notable ones in the various *viharns* around the complex, while hundreds more can be seen in the gallery surrounding the *ubosot*.

Also of note is a Bodhi tree grown from the sapling of the very tree under which the Buddha attained enlightenment.

The massive 46 m-long reclining Buddha, meanwhile, rests in its own *viharn*. It was first created with brick and stucco before finally being gilded with gold.

> ⓘ *Wat Pho has long been an important center for Thai massage. Rama III established a massage school here to prevent the ancient art from dying out. Come for a massage during your visit, or even become accredited yourself!*

Bangkok National Museum • พิพิธภัณฑสถานแห่งชาติ พระนคร

Thailand's premier National Museum is where you'll find some of the most prized artifacts from all over the country. It should not be missed during your time in Bangkok.

Among the vast collection are relics like the Ram Khamhaeng stele *(pictured p230)* and the Dvaravati Wheel of Law (left). Also on display are sculptures from Lanna, Isaan and the Malay Peninsula, in addition to classical Lopburi and Khmer art.

📍 4 Na Phra That Rd.
🕐 9:00 - 16:00
📅 Closed Mon., Tue.
฿ 200

The museum is located on the grounds of the original Front Palace, the residence of the heir apparent. As such, this is another good place to appreciate architecture from the Rattanakosin Period.

The Buddhaisawan Chapel

Also located on the museum grounds is the Buddhaisawan Chapel, the home of the Phra Sihing image. It's Thailand's second most significant image after the Emerald Buddha. And while three different statues could potentially be the real Phra Sihing, the one here is widely believed to be the original. Like the Emerald Buddha, the Phra Sihing has its own chronicle which details its history and travels. It's also crossed paths with the Emerald Buddha many times, and you can find a summary of its entire backstory from p190.

In front of the chapel is a statue of Vishnu holding a bow and arrow, reminiscent of his avatar Rama. Created by Italian artist Alfonso Tornarelli, it was originally meant for Petchaburi Province. Rama VI, however, decided to place it here instead. The platform on which it stands was originally used for elephant mounting.

Murals dating back to 1795 ❤

Around Rattanakosin

There's still plenty more to see around the Rattanakosin district. Just in front of the Grand Palace, you'll find the **Bangkok City Pillar Shrine**, the very first structure that Rama I built in his new capital. Like all city pillars, it's meant to act as a spiritual protector for the city itself, and Bangkok locals regularly bring it offerings.

For those interested in the growing amulet craze, or for people simply wanting to get a glimpse of a unique Thai subculture, the country's biggest **amulet market** is located along the Chao Phraya River. Spread amongst dozens of narrow alleys, you'll encounter countless shops selling amulets and figurines of all shapes and sizes. Rather than being purely decorative, they're meant to grant special protection for the wearer. Think of them as personal, pocket-sized versions of the protective pillars!

Wat Suthat, a temple started by Rama I, is another highlight of the area. It's home to the Phra Si Sakyamuni, an important Buddha image from Sukhothai. It also features the tallest *viharn* in all of Bangkok. Its interior has been entirely covered in gorgeous, minutely detailed murals.

Wat Suthat, however, is perhaps best known for the structure standing in front of it: the large, red **Giant Swing**. Standing at over 30 m high, the swing was once used as part of a special Brahmanic ritual in honor of Shiva. Teams would swing back and forth, attempting to grab a bag of gold at the top with their teeth. As one might expect, the ritual resulted in a number of deaths, and the tradition was scrapped in 1935. The swing standing there now is actually a replacement constructed in 2007.

Speaking of ancient Hindu traditions, nearby you can also find

▲ *An amulet shop*

▲ *Wat Suthat*

the little-known **Devasathan Brahmin Temple**. The Rattanakosin Kingdom adopted many court rituals from the Ayutthaya Kingdom, which itself was greatly influenced by the Khmer Empire. Despite being a Buddhist nation, a small community of Brahmin priests is still called upon by the Thai monarchy for special royal rituals. To this day, Wat Devasathan functions as the de facto Brahmin headquarters of Thailand.

Another popular landmark is the **Golden Mount**, an artificial hill topped with a large golden *chedi*. It represents Mt. Meru, the abode of the gods, and stands at 76 m high. The hill is a popular tourist destination for those hoping to get panoramic views of the city. The mount is part of the larger temple complex of **Wat Saket**, yet another temple established by King Rama I.

More Around Bangkok

Outside of the historical districts of Rattanakosin and Thonburi, there's still plenty more to experience in this sprawling city of over 15 million. As Bangkok is so spread out, be sure to take logistics from your hotel into consideration when planning your trip.

Jim Thompson House

- 6 Soi Kasemsan 2 Rama I Rd.
- 9:00 - 17:00
- Daily
- ฿ 150

One of Bangkok's best examples of a traditional Thai home happens to be the former residence of an American silk trader. Jim Thompson assembled his house with parts from several other old teak homes from Bangkok and Ayutthaya. Thompson was also a connoisseur of the Thai fine arts, and his home is full of rare Buddha images, wood carvings and old paintings. Sadly, Jim Thompson mysteriously disappeared in 1967 while traveling in Malaysia, and was never heard from again.

His well-preserved house must be visited as part of a group tour, which visitors are assigned to after purchasing a ticket.

The Erawan Museum

- 1 99/9 Bangmuangmai Muang Samut Prakan
- 9:00 - 19:00
- Daily
- ฿ 400

The unassuming suburb of Samut Prakan is home to one of the region's most unique and awe-inspiring attractions. A huge 29 m-high three-headed elephant contains a full three-story museum. Inside, you'll encounter a stained glass ceiling, intricate wood carvings and even a Buddhist temple.

The mastermind behind the project was Lek Viriyaphant, a millionaire with a passion for architecture, historical artifacts and world religions. He spent much of his wealth on projects like the Erawan Museum, Bangkok's Ancient City complex and Pattaya's Sanctuary of Truth.

The museum is nearby BTS Chang Erawan Station.

Chinatown

Chinatown's **Yaowarat Rd** is the place to grab some street food or shop at outdoor markets. The district is also home to numerous Chinese-style temples, such as **Wat Mangkon Kamalawat**. You can also find some notable Thai Buddhist temples as well. Nearby Hua Lamphong Station, don't miss **Wat Traimit**, home to a massive solid gold Buddha from Ayutthaya whose story is described on p33. And near Chakkrawat Rd is the elaborate **Wat Chakrawatrachat**, a former home of the Phra Bang. Meanwhile, close to Saphan Taksin station is the Ayutthaya-era **Wat Yannawa**, with a *viharn* shaped like a Chinese junk.

Playful street art can be found all over Chinatown

‹ 5.5 tonnes of solid gold!

Bangkok Contemporary Art

Bangkok is emerging as a mecca for street art. Among the best places to find murals are the *sois* of **Charoen Krung** (an area with plenty of art galleries), Chinatown's **Soi Wanit 2** and **Song Wat Rd**. Near the Jim Thompson House, the graffiti-covered **Saen Saep Canal** leads to **Chalerma Park**, nicknamed 'Graffiti Park' for good reason.

Art lovers shouldn't miss the **Bangkok Art & Culture Center**, a multistory complex with exhibition spaces, shops, and cafes.

Bangkok Shopping & Nightlife

Both shopping and nightlife are abound along **Sukhumvit Rd** and its various *sois*, or side streets. On the main road, you'll find large shopping malls like **Emporium, Siam Paragon, Terminal 21** and a plethora of international restaurants.

Mainly from **Sukhumvit Sois 2-33**, everything from fancy rooftop bars to Western-style sports bars are teeming with activity after dark. The general area is also home to a few of the country's most infamous redlight districts. Meanwhile, electronic music lovers have a number of options, such as **Glow** on Soi 23 or **Beam** on Soi 55.

Elsewhere, other underground music venues include **Safe Room** on Si Lom Soi 8, **De Commune** on Liberty Plaza's 1st floor, and **Culture Cafe** on Charoen Krung Rd.

People of all budgets and tastes will enjoy **Chatuchak Market**, which consists of over 15,000 booths. In addition to street food, you can find all sorts of clothes and antiques for sale. See p138 for more on **floating markets**.

Muay Thai

Bangkok is home to Muay Thai's most competitive fights. The two most prestigious stadiums are **Lumpinee** and **Rajadamnern**. Lumpinee recently relocated up north near DMK airport, while Rajadamnern, in Dusit, is much more accessible. Tickets usually cost a couple thousand baht at either, but check online for prices and start times.

The capital also has an abundance of gyms to train at. Unless you have a specific pro you'd like to train with, though, you're best off looking for the most accessible gym from your accommodation.

From India to Angkor

This chapter takes us all the way back to the very beginning. After delving into the Emerald Buddha's shadowy origin myth, we'll cover the statue's movements over the following millennium, up until its arrival in the heart of the Khmer Empire.

To get the full picture of the Emerald Buddha's early years, we'll need to cover a myriad of fascinating topics, including the ancient Indian capital of Pataliputra, the creation of the world's first Buddha images and Sri Lanka's role in Buddhism's spread and development. We'll also cover Burma's major involvement in our story and in Asian history as a whole. Note that the 'Origins' section lacks any accompanying travel guide for India, Sri Lanka or Myanmar.

Our travel guide will resume with the South Thailand province of Nakhon Si Thammarat, followed by a guide to the marvelous ruins of Angkor, including all the essential sites that one shouldn't miss. Finally, we'll briefly cover Thailand's often overlooked Isaan region.

THE EMERALD BUDDHA: ORIGINS	163
THE EMERALD BUDDHA IN INDIA	166
THE EMERALD BUDDHA IN SRI LANKA	170
ANAWRAHTA & THE KINGDOM OF PAGAN	173
NAKHON SI THAMMARAT	179
THE JOURNEYS OF THE PHRA SIHING	190
EXPLORING SOUTH THAILAND	196
ANGKOR	199
BANTEAY CHHMAR	220
ISAAN	223
SAKHON NAKHON	224
PHIMAI	226

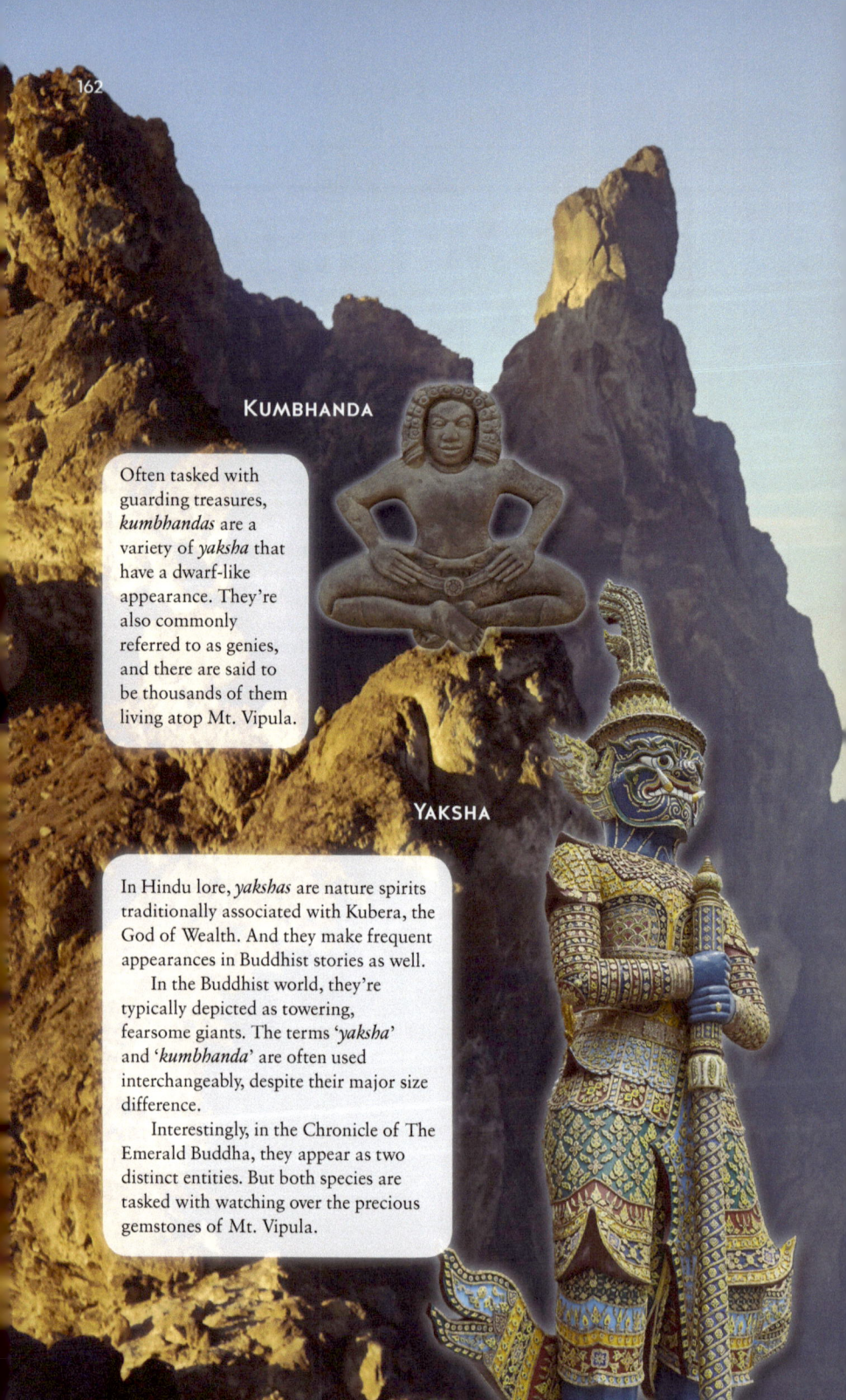

Kumbhanda

Often tasked with guarding treasures, *kumbhandas* are a variety of *yaksha* that have a dwarf-like appearance. They're also commonly referred to as genies, and there are said to be thousands of them living atop Mt. Vipula.

Yaksha

In Hindu lore, *yakshas* are nature spirits traditionally associated with Kubera, the God of Wealth. And they make frequent appearances in Buddhist stories as well.

In the Buddhist world, they're typically depicted as towering, fearsome giants. The terms '*yaksha*' and '*kumbhanda*' are often used interchangeably, despite their major size difference.

Interestingly, in the Chronicle of The Emerald Buddha, they appear as two distinct entities. But both species are tasked with watching over the precious gemstones of Mt. Vipula.

The Emerald Buddha: Origins

The Emerald Buddha's origin story takes place in the area of Bihar, India, several hundred years after the Buddha's death. According to the Chronicle, various divinities played a role in the statue's creation. But a Buddhist monk named Nagasena was the one who took the initiative to create such an image in the first place.

The scenes involving Nagasena take place in the ancient city of Pataliputra, a former capital of many Indian kingdoms like the Maurya Empire. Meanwhile, Indra and Vishwakarman take a trip to Mt. Vipula, one of several mountains surrounding the city of Rajagriha (current Rajgir).

In Buddhist lore, Vipula is inhabited by thousands of *yakshas*. And it also happens to be nearby Vulture's Peak, a favorite meditation spot of the Buddha himself.

Vishwakarman

Known as the divine craftsman and architect, Vishwakarman designed Swarga Loka, the heavenly realm over which Indra presides. And he's also behind a number of magnificent cities and structures on earth.

Indra

One of the most important Vedic gods, Indra administers the heavens in which all other demigods reside. He's also closely associated with lightning and rain and plays a major role in both Hindu and Buddhist mythology.

Nagasena

A historical monk who lived in northern India around 150 BC, Nagasena is credited with conceiving of the Emerald Buddha. He's also known for his conversations with the Indo-Greek king Menander I. In Mahayana Buddhism, he's considered one of the original 'Eighteen Arhats.'

The Creation of the Holy Emerald Jewel

Several centuries after the passing of the Buddha lived a monk named Nagasena in the grand city of Pataliputra. The learned monk was a disciple of the great master Dhammarakkhita at the monastery of King Ashoka. And Nagasena was so well-versed in the sacred scriptures that he could easily answer any riddles or questions proposed to him. In fact, he even quelled the spiritual misgivings of the clever king of the Indo-Greeks, Menander. Yet despite all this, Nagasena found himself distraught.

Though he'd worked hard to spread the Buddha's teachings, he feared that the sacred knowledge would someday be forgotten after his passing. And so he came up with an idea. Nagasena decided to create a beautiful image in the likeness of the Buddha so that all who saw it would remember the Four Noble Truths. And such an image ought to last for five thousand years - the length of time that the Buddha commanded his teachings to persist.

But with what material should such an image be crafted? Gold or silver would not do, as they might evoke feelings of greed in the hearts of wicked men. Given how the Buddha, the dharma and the sangha represent the Three Jewels of Buddhism, only a precious jewel of miraculous powers would be worthy of the task. But where could one find such a gem? Nagasena deeply pondered this question until he received some special visitors.

Sensing Nagasena's plight, the king of the gods, Indra, and the celestial architect, Vishwakarman, descended from the heavens to speak with him. 'Is it true that you intend to craft an image of the Buddha? And that you're looking for a special gem of wondrous powers?' Indra asked. 'It is true, my lord,' the monk responded. Luckily, Indra knew of such a gem.

Indra then commanded Vishwakarman to go and fetch the gem from Mt. Vipula. Vishwakarman, however, knew that at Vipula there would be 1,000 kumbhanda genies standing guard. And so Indra agreed to accompany him. 'I have come to fetch the resplendent Manjoti jewel,' Indra told the kumbhandas.

But their chieftain responded: 'I'm afraid I cannot give it to you, for in the future we must present it to the Chakravarti, the righteous and universal king that will someday come to rule. But also atop this mountain is a magnificent green gem that's under the careful watch of a thousand yaksha giants,' the chieftain explained. 'Please go ahead and take it and present it to the eminent monk.'

Indra did so and brought it to Nagasena. The monk, though overjoyed, was unsure of how to carve the image he envisioned. Vishwakarman then arrived disguised as a master sculptor, volunteering for the job. He took the stone back up to the heavens and began his work.

Over the course of seven days and seven nights, Vishwakarman, in cooperation with the other devas in heaven, crafted a marvelous Buddha image of about one cubit in height. Indra and Vishwakarman went to present it to Nagasena, who was delighted beyond words. Then, for the consecration of the image, the devas, Nagasena, the king and residents of Pataliputra gathered together with monks from around the land at Ashoka's monastery.

Celestial music filled the air as Indra, using his supernatural powers, created a splendid golden throne for the precious statue. For the next seven days and nights, people gathered around the image and brought it innumerable offerings. And finally, under the rays of a bright full moon, Nagasena consecrated and awakened the image. And he declared that it shall be called 'The Unique Emerald Buddha.'

On the same night, Nagasena placed a golden vessel containing seven holy relics of Lord Buddha in front of the statue. 'If this image is to last for 5,000 years,' he said, 'let these relics enter inside of it.' And miraculously, they did just that, with one going in the head, two each in the arms and legs, and one in the heart.

And then Nagasena made a prophecy: 'This splendid image will not remain here for long in Pataliputra. It will travel to various distant lands where it will help spread the sacred teachings of the Buddha,' he declared.

Eventually, Nagasena attained nirvana, and the king of Pataliputra entered heaven upon his death. And his successors, who ruled in an unbroken lineage, continued to care for the Emerald Buddha for about three hundred years. During that time, the Jewel Image performed many miracles and granted many wishes. But due to great conflict and turmoil in the region, the reigning king of Pataliputra decided that the image should be taken somewhere else for safekeeping.

'The king of Sri Lanka is my beloved friend,' he thought. 'Surely he will hold onto it for me until I'm ready to take it back.' And so the Emerald Buddha was sent on a junk to the island of Lanka. It was taken to Meghagiri Temple in Anuradhapura, Lanka's capital. And there the image was placed in a golden pavilion, where it was received by local residents with much celebration and reverence.

Next
p172

The Emerald Buddha In India

As the beginning of the Chronicle describes, the Emerald Buddha was created thousands of years ago in Pataliputra. Let's look at the region's history, Nagasena's interactions with a famous king, and what factors may have led to the creation of the world's first Buddha images.

Pataliputra

According to the legend, the Emerald Buddha was carved in the city of Pataliputra, India. Pataliputra, nearby modern-day Patna, Bihar Province, was one of the most prosperous and culturally significant cities of ancient India. It was established around 490 BC as the capital of the legendary Magadha Kingdom. It was also the capital of the mighty Maurya Empire and a number of later empires which succeeded it.

The Maurya Empire plays an important role in the development of Buddhism, largely thanks to King Ashoka. Ashoka, who reigned from around 268–232 BC, was one of India's most dominant kings. And he was also a Buddhist convert who worked hard to spread the religion throughout his vast empire. With Pataliputra as his capital, Ashoka ruled over most of what makes up modern-day India, along with large parts of Pakistan and Afghanistan. Though Pataliputra would continue to remain important for centuries to come, Buddhism in India would never quite be the same after the fall of the Mauryas.

In the Chronicle, the main (human, at least) character of the Emerald Buddha's origin story is Nagasena. Nagasena is an actual historical figure who was born in Kashmir, but who also spent a long time in Pataliputra. Though the original Chronicle says that the Emerald Buddha was created in 44 BC, Nagasena is believed to have lived around 150 BC. But let's overlook that error for now. It was Nagasena's interactions with the Indo-Greek king Menander I that may have given rise, directly or indirectly, to some of the world's first Buddha images.

A yaksha statue from the Shunga period (185-73 BC). The Shungas ruled Pataliputra during Nagasena's lifetime.

Who Were the Indo-Greeks?

Alexander the Great conquered much of the Persian Empire from around 323 BC. Taking over vast territories from North Africa to West and Central Asia, Alexander and his men brought their Hellenistic culture with them wherever they went. But rather than one culture completely dominating the others, what resulted were new syncretic fusions of Hellenistic ideas with local religious beliefs.

Even after Alexander's passing, the Greeks continued heading eastward. Eventually, Greek territory in Central Asia split into three separate kingdoms. The easternmost one was the Greco-Bactrian Kingdom, which formed around 256 BC. Occupying much of what makes up modern-day Afghanistan and Pakistan, Greco-Bactria was considered highly prosperous, urbanized and cosmopolitan for its time.

Notably, this eastward expansion coincided with the Maurya Empire's apex of power and influence. While some regions of Central Asia saw a melding of the Greek and Hindu pantheons, numerous Greek rulers also converted to Buddhism. This was largely thanks to Ashoka's evangelical efforts, and Buddhism continued to prosper in Greco-Bactria well after his passing.

From around 180 BC, a new kingdom called the Indo-Greek Kingdom was formed. And as their territory stretched further into what's now India, Buddhism started to spread from west to east rather than the other way around.

During Nagasena's lifetime, around 150 BC, the ruler of the Indo-Greeks was King Menander I. But he had yet to convert to Buddhism himself.

Menander's Many Questions

King Menander wasn't only a dominant king, but an avid philosophy and theology enthusiast. Menander, however, was not a follower of any particular faith. He was able to stump just about any religious leader he met in a philosophical debate. But this only made Menander feel skeptical and spiritually unsatisfied. That is, at least, until he met Nagasena.

The two had a lengthy conversation that left Menander stunned. The humble monk was able to answer every single one of his questions about topics such as the self, the soul, suffering and the nature of reality. As a result of the meeting, Menander converted to Buddhism and left his kingly duties to his son. According to legend, he eventually became an *arhat*, or one who attained enlightenment.

The conversation between Menander and Nagasena was written down, becoming an important Buddhist text called the Milinda Pañha, or 'The Questions of Menander.' Interestingly enough, this conversation took place in Pataliputra.

By this point, the Hindu Shunga dynasty had overthrown the Maurya

An illustration of the famous conversation from 'Hutchinson's Story of the Nations'

Empire and continued ruling out of Pataliputra. According to some accounts, the Shungas worked to persecute Buddhism during Nagasena's lifetime, though it's unclear to what extent this is actually true. What we do know, however, is that the Shungas favored Hinduism and fought wars against the Buddhist Indo-Greeks.

It also remains unclear whether Pataliputra ever became part of Indo-Greek territory. While it may have happened, it's also possible that Menander simply traveled there on a peaceful mission to meet with Nagasena.

The World's First Buddha Images

For the first several hundred years of the religion's existence, the Buddha's likeness was not depicted in art. He was typically represented in abstract form, such as by a pair of footprints or a Bodhi tree. Or, oftentimes, he wasn't even depicted at all. For example, in artistic renditions of stories from the Buddha's life, he was sometimes represented by an empty chair. The others around him, in contrast, would be shown in full detail. It seems as if the earliest Buddhists took an approach similar to how Muslims avoid painting the Prophet Muhammad to this day.

But walking through the streets of Sri Lanka or Indochina today, Buddha images can be found just about everywhere. How exactly did that come about? We likely have the Indo-Greeks to thank.

The Greeks were no strangers to sculpting lifelike statues of their gods, kings and philosophers. After converting to Buddhism, the Indo-Greeks carried on the tradition by immortalizing the Buddha in stone as well. And at some point, the once-taboo practice was destigmatized among the general population.

Scholars believe that the earliest Buddha statues were created between the 2nd-1st centuries BC, right around Nagasena's time. But many old images are impossible to date. The earliest images with agreed upon-dates, then, are those that were sculpted from the 1st-3rd centuries AD in the Gandhara region.

Gandhara was a large area which encompassed much of present-day Afghanistan and Pakistan. Conquered by the Persians, it was then taken over by Alexander the Great, and later the Maurya Empire. It was then controlled by the Greco-Bactrians and after that, the Indo-Greeks under the rule of King Menander.

Even later, Gandhara was taken over by the Kushan Empire, which persisted from around the 1st-3rd centuries (and even expanded as far east as Pataliputra). Fascinatingly, the Kushans fused Buddhist, Zoroastrian and Hellenistic ideas. Buddhist art and sculpture, with noticeable Greek influence, thrived around this time, especially under the patronage of Kanishka the Great.

But it's not farfetched to think that Buddha images could've been produced even earlier in Pataliputra. Nagasena's teacher, Dhammarakkhita, in fact, was a Buddhist of Greek descent. The Emerald Buddha is not Hellenistic in appearance,

A 3rd-century AD Gandhara image

but the idea to carve an image in the first place may have come from Nagasena's Greek associates.

As for the light green jade used to create the Emerald Buddha, it's not exactly clear where it would've come from. It may have been sourced from Kashmir, Nagasena's hometown. But as mentioned on p39, Thailand's King Rama IV postulated in the 19th century that the jade came from China. And this could very well be true. Thanks to the Silk Road, trade between the Indo-Greeks and China's Han dynasty was flourishing in Nagasena's time. And many Chinese goods ended up in North India via Gandhara.

But who could've carved such a beautiful statue? As religious images are typically created without signatures, we'll never know for sure. Let's take a moment, then, to look at the Emerald Buddha's mythological creator, Vishwakarman.

Vishwakarman

As mentioned on p163, Vishwakarman is a Hindu deity considered to be the celestial architect. In India to this day, he's revered by creators, designers, craftsmen and architects.

Aside from heaven itself, other mythological achievements of Vishwakarman include the golden city of Lanka (current Sri Lanka), as mentioned in the Ramayana *(see p153)*. And in the Mahabharata epic *(p217)*, Vishwakarman is credited with creating Krishna's abode of Dwarka and the splendid city of Indraprastha (modern-day Delhi).

More recently, as mentioned on p142, Bangkok's incredibly long official name even refers to the city and its Grand Palace as having been created by Vishwakarman himself!

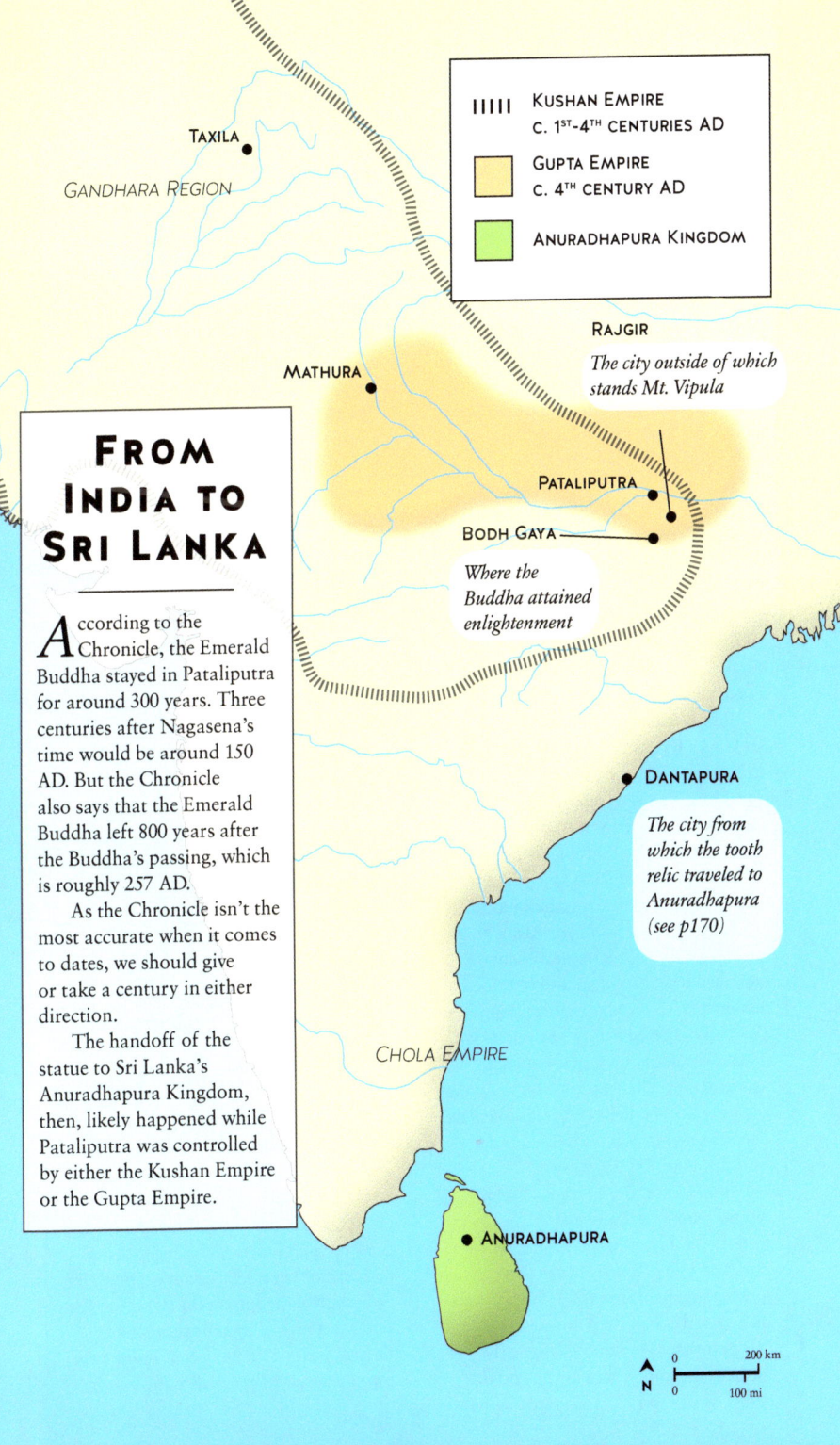

FROM INDIA TO SRI LANKA

According to the Chronicle, the Emerald Buddha stayed in Pataliputra for around 300 years. Three centuries after Nagasena's time would be around 150 AD. But the Chronicle also says that the Emerald Buddha left 800 years after the Buddha's passing, which is roughly 257 AD.

As the Chronicle isn't the most accurate when it comes to dates, we should give or take a century in either direction.

The handoff of the statue to Sri Lanka's Anuradhapura Kingdom, then, likely happened while Pataliputra was controlled by either the Kushan Empire or the Gupta Empire.

The Emerald Buddha In Sri Lanka

Arrival on the Island

According to the Chronicle, the king reigning over Pataliputra in the 3rd century AD feared for the Emerald Buddha's safety. A civil war had broken out, and the king decided that his good friend, the king of Lanka, could hold onto it until things quieted down at home.

Intending to eventually retrieve it, he placed the Emerald Buddha on a junk with some of his men. Upon arrival in Sri Lanka, says the Chronicle, it was placed in Meghagiri Temple in the capital of Anuradhapura. That temple is now known as Isurumuniya and is famous for its rock carvings.

Buddhism was first introduced to Sri Lanka by King Ashoka's children, and the link between Pataliputra and Anuradhapura remained strong. Pataliputra was also nearby Bodh Gaya, the site where the Buddha attained enlightenment, which was a popular pilgrimage spot for Sri Lankan monks.

In the early 4th century AD, a king named Kitti Sri Meghavanna sent an emissary to Pataliputra and obtained permission to build an official Sinhalese (Sri Lankan) monastery at Bodh Gaya. This is the same king who obtained the sacred tooth relic (more below). Though the timeline is a little off, might he have been the one to receive the Emerald Buddha as well?

In any case, the Emerald Buddha would remain in Lanka for a very long time - possibly even seven or eight hundred years! But would it have stayed at Meghagiri all that time? As we'll go over shortly, definitely not.

Before moving on, let's quickly address the addendum at the end of Camille Notton's translation of the Chronicle, which details a much more convoluted series of events. According to the Chiang Mai version of the manuscript, the Emerald Buddha first traveled from Pataliputra to Taxila, Gandhara (current Pakistan) and from there it was taken to Sri Lanka. It then went back again to Pataliputra, and from there back to Sri Lanka a second time! Most versions, however, simply state that the sacred image traveled directly from Pataliputra to Sri Lanka.

The Tooth Relic

Throughout Sri Lanka's history, the most important and celebrated Buddhist relic on the island has long been a tooth belonging to the Buddha himself, now enshrined in the city of Kandy. And while the Buddha's tooth is not mentioned anywhere in the Chronicle of the Emerald Buddha, one can't help but notice some striking similarities between the two stories.

The Temple of the Tooth, Kandy

According to the tooth relic legend, the Buddha's left canine tooth was taken right from his cremation pyre. It eventually ended up in the hands of King Guhasiva of Kalinga, or present-day Orissa, India. Learning that many other kings wanted to get their hands on it,

The Emerald Buddha: Origins

Guhasiva decided to hide it, and so he gave it to his daughter Princess Hemmali.

Around the year 317 AD, Princess Hemmali and her husband Prince Danta set sail from the city of Dantapura to Sri Lanka to hide the sacred tooth *(see map on p169)*. The princess had put the tooth in a jewel-encrusted case which she kept in her hair. That way, it appeared to observers as nothing more than a piece of jewelry. Furthermore, the couple disguised themselves as Brahmin priests, concealing the fact that they were royalty.

After a long journey, they ended up on the eastern coast of Sri Lanka. Wandering through the country on foot, they eventually arrived at Meghagiri Temple in Anuradhapura, where the relic was received with much celebration.

The tooth relic wouldn't stay at Meghagiri for long, though. Over time, Sri Lanka experienced its own share of internal strife and shifting of capitals. And the tooth relic would travel around the country with each major political change. On top of that, replicas of the tooth were frequently made to trick invading armies.

Learning this, one can't help but wonder: Did the authors of the Chronicle of the Emerald Buddha merely paraphrase parts of the tooth relic legend? Or did these two relics really join each other at Meghagiri temple? And if so, would they later accompany one another on travels around the island?

The Abhayagiri Monastery

In the 5th century, a Chinese monk named Faxian traveled to Sri Lanka, and his old travel writings may provide us with some answers to these questions. At the time, the tooth relic was being kept at a temple called Abhayagiri, also in Anuradhapura, and about 6 km away from Meghagiri.

What's especially noteworthy is Faxian's description of Abhayagiri's main hall. He writes:

'There is in it a hall of Buddha, adorned with carved and inlaid works of gold and silver, and rich in the seven precious substances, in which there is an image (of Buddha) in green jade, more than twenty cubits in height, glittering all over with those substances, and having an appearance of solemn dignity which words cannot express.' (Legge, 1886)

Now we have a clear reference to a green jade Buddha image being kept at the same temple as the tooth relic! But 'twenty cubits in height'? That's about 9 meters high. Not only is the Emerald Buddha nowhere near that large, but there is no jade Buddha image in the world that big. The largest we know of, in Anshan, China, stands at 7.95 m high. The tallest Buddha in Sri Lanka, the Aukuna Buddha, is 11.4 m high, but was carved from a boulder. And in Sri Lanka today, there don't seem to be any other jade images dating back to that era, period.

A 6th-century Sri Lankan image

Perhaps Faxian was simply describing the height of the image on its platform. Today in Wat Phra Kaew, the Emerald Buddha sits on a platform that also happens to be around 9 meters, or 20 cubits high *(see p149)*. If Faxian was describing a similar pedestal, we can conclude that the Emerald Buddha was indeed at Abhayagiri together with the tooth relic. And it's also likely that the two relics were transported around the island together until the jade statue's eventual departure.

Lanka's Precious Gift

Centuries later, in the land of Burma, a powerful king was born who possessed the ability to fly through the air. His name was Anawrahta and he ruled the mighty Kingdom of Pagan. He was a devout Buddhist who worked hard to propagate the Three Jewels throughout his vast territory. But one day, his head priest, Shin Arahan, sensed that something was amiss.

Shin Arahan had been a monk for fifty years and knew the entirety of the Tripitaka scriptures by heart. And at the temples of Pagan, he noticed the improper use of words in some of the sacred rites. 'Can you confirm whether the copy of the Tripitaka we have in our kingdom is truly authentic?' Shin Arahan asked the local temple chiefs. 'We cannot,' they told him. 'We are only following the traditions of our elders. But surely, the island of Lanka must have a version that is free from error.'

Learning of this, King Anawrahta decided to make a visit. He sent two boats filled with valuable gifts, together with a group of eight monks led by Shin Arahan. Anawrahta himself then flew over to Lanka on his flying horse.

After presenting the king of Lanka with the precious gifts, Anawrahta requested copies of the Tripitaka scriptures. Additionally, Shin Arahan asked that he and his monks be ordained again into the holy order according to the proper rituals.

The king of Lanka had hoped to spread the teachings of the Buddha to other lands, and he happily agreed. He even allowed Anawrahta to make copies of the Tripitaka and additional Buddhist commentaries himself. And the Lankan monarch also presented Anawrahta with another spectacular gift: the sacred Emerald Buddha.

Once the scriptures were copied, they were divided up among the two boats. On one boat rode Shin Arahan and the monks, while the Jewel Image was placed on the other. Anawrahta, of course, returned to Pagan on his horse. The mission had been a great success. However, not all would end according to plan.

While the boat with the monks and half of the scriptures successfully made it to Pagan, the other boat got blown off course midway through the journey. It arrived not within Anawrahta's territory, but in the Khmer Empire. Hearing the news, King Anawrahta hastily took off again on his magical steed.

Previous
p164

Next
p180

Anawrahta & The Kingdom of Pagan

Though the Burmese would never get ahold of the Emerald Buddha, their role in the story cannot be understated. It was the Burmese king Anawrahta, in fact, that helped set the statue's journeys throughout Indochina in motion.

Anawrahta of Pagan

King Anawrahta, or 'Anuruddha' as he's sometimes called, is one of Southeast Asia's most legendary kings. Even in Myanmar today, he's widely revered as the father of the Burmese nation. Remarkably, the borders of Anawrahta's Pagan Kingdom a thousand years ago are very similar to those of modern-day Myanmar.

Anawrahta, who took the throne in 1044, saw his life change dramatically after encountering the mysterious monk Shin Arahan (or 'Silakhanda' in the original Chronicle). Shin Arahan hailed from Thaton, a Mon kingdom in the Lower Burma region where Theravada Buddhism had long flourished. Dissatisfied with the growing influence of Hinduism, however, he left for Pagan. It was good timing, as King Anawrahta himself was frustrated with the depraved behavior of the local Pagan monks. Upon meeting Shin Arahan, he was more than happy to convert to the more austere Theravada tradition.

Following his conversion, Anawrahta vowed to make Theravada Buddhism the dominant religion of his kingdom. He lacked copies of the important Buddhist scriptures, however, not to mention clergymen. Following Shin Arahan's suggestion, he made his way to Thaton and lavished the local king with expensive gifts *(see map on p177-78)*.

But when the king refused to give up his scriptures, Anawrahta followed through with an all-out invasion in the year 1057. While the takeover of Thaton is not mentioned in Chronicle, the event is widely agreed upon by historians.

Anawrahta not only brought back scriptures but also monks and craftsmen who helped build Pagan's innumerable pagodas. The motivation for invading Thaton, though, may have been twofold. In addition to obtaining the texts, it also allowed Pagan to establish a base in the upper Malay Peninsula. This would've been vital for stopping further encroachments by the Khmer Empire.

Shwezigon Pagoda in Bagan (formerly Pagan)

As mentioned in the Chronicle, the accuracy of the scriptures obtained from Thaton would later come into question. And these doubts caused Pagan to forge a close relationship with the Theravada Buddhist stronghold of Sri Lanka. It was there, of course, that the Tripitaka scriptures were first transcribed centuries prior *(see p13)*.

Other than the Chronicle of the Emerald Buddha, there are no mentions of Anawrahta requesting the Tripitaka from Sri Lanka in other ancient manuscripts. But it's widely accepted that the two kingdoms became friendly during

Anawrahta's reign.

Interestingly, a famous Burmese text called the Glass Palace Chronicle does mention a similar visit. But instead of the scriptures, Anawrahta requests the sacred tooth relic *(see p170)*! Despite pampering the Lankan monarch with numerous gifts, all he ends up getting is a replica, now enshrined at Bagan's Shwezigon Pagoda. Meanwhile, replicas of the replica (!) are enshrined at a few other temples around town.

Could the Glass Palace and the Emerald Buddha chronicles be describing the same visit? Perhaps Sri Lanka sent the scriptures, the Emerald Buddha and the tooth replica divided among two boats. But only one of them would successfully reach Burma.

The Chola Dynasty

While not mentioned in the Chronicle of the Emerald Buddha, in the 11th century, the Pagan Kingdom and Sri Lanka also shared a common enemy: the Chola Empire. Based in southern India's Tamil Nadu region, the Cholas are considered one of the longest-reigning dynasties in all of world history. They lasted from the 3rd century BC all the way up until the 13th century AD. But the Cholas were at the very peak of their power around the time our story takes place.

In 993, the Cholas invaded Sri Lanka, taking over the capital of Anuradhapura. The Sri Lankan elite then had to retreat to the southern area of Ruhuna. The Buddhist monkhood was also under threat, as the Hindu Cholas were not especially favorable toward Buddhism. Therefore, we can surmise that the Emerald Buddha was likely brought to Ruhuna in the late 10th century. This is also where Anawrahta's meeting with the king would've taken place.

The 'king of Lanka' mentioned in the Chronicle would've been Vijayabahu I (r.1055-1110). He was the one to finally liberate Sri Lanka from Chola rule in 1070, but not without Burmese support. Scholars generally agree that Anawrahta assisted Vijayabahu during his liberational struggle, probably in the form of goods or military equipment. This may have been a 'thank you' for the earlier gift of scriptures and relics.

Taking the tumultuous times into account, it's easy to see why Vijayabahu would've been so generous to Anawrahta. On the one hand, he may have really envisioned spreading Theravada Buddhism around the world. But he also likely had the long-term survival of Sri Lanka's own Buddhist community in mind. Just as numerous relics and scriptures were brought to Sri Lanka from India for safekeeping centuries prior, Vijayabahu probably saw Burma as the safest haven for Buddhism at that time.

In fact, after the Cholas were driven out, Sri Lanka made a special request for Burma to bring back copies of the scriptures along with Sri Lankan monks who'd been staying there. This event is widely agreed upon by historians, and it likely occurred in the year 1071.

Numerous scholars, however, imply that these scriptures were the ones which Burma had obtained from Thaton in 1057. But as Sri Lanka was (and often still is) considered the home of Theravada Buddhism in its 'purest' form, would they really have been satisfied with these third-party scriptures?

Though the event is absent from historical documents, it's probable that the scene described in the Chronicle is at least partly true. Sri Lanka likely gifted Anawrahta with the Tripitaka scriptures and the Emerald Buddha with every intention of asking for them back once the war was over. But the jade statue, of course, is the one thing they would never get back.

BURMA'S MAJOR ROLE

As mentioned, the Emerald Buddha would never end up in Burma, but the country still plays a huge part in our story. On multiple occasions, various Burmese dynasties would directly or indirectly influence the statue's path of travel.

Strangely, though, after the scenes involving Anawrahta, Burma doesn't get mentioned directly again in the Chronicle. This is likely because numerous versions of the manuscript were written down in Lanna while it was a Burmese vassal. Rather than upset their overlords, perhaps the authors felt it best to leave out mentions of Burma altogether.

Nevertheless, historical records reveal what a major role the country played in both the Emerald Buddha's story and in Indochina's history as a whole.

Below is a list of all the times that various dynasties of Burma altered the course of the Emerald Buddha's travels:

- According to the Chronicle, in the 11th century, King Anawrahta of Pagan received the Emerald Buddha as a gift from Sri Lanka, but the ship got blown off course. *(p172)*

- In the 1550s, King Setthathirath of Lan Chang intended to retake the Lanna Kingdom, but the invading Burmese Toungoo dynasty kept him out. The threat of King Bayinnaung was so great that Setthathirath even moved his capital south to Vientiane, taking the Emerald Buddha with him. *(p109)*

- Shortly after Setthathirath's death, the Toungoo dynasty occupied Vientiane for around 18 years. For whatever reason, though, they did not take the Emerald Buddha.

- In 1767, the Burmese Konbaung dynasty sacked Ayutthaya, but Siam was quickly reunited by Taksin. Siam then invaded the Kingdom of Vientiane in 1778 due to their allegiance with Burma, taking the Emerald Buddha in the process. *(p126)*

- The threat of another potential Burmese invasion is one reason why King Rama I moved the capital from Thonburi to the other side of the Chao Phraya River. There, he built the Grand Palace and the brand new city of Bangkok. *(p142)*

South & Southeast Asia: c. 1060s

When the Emerald Buddha arrived in Indochina around 1,000 years ago, kingdoms like Lanna, Sukhothai and Lan Chang did not yet exist. The two main powers were the Khmer Empire and the Kingdom of Pagan, both of which were rapidly expanding.

During the reign of Suryavarman I (1002-1050), the Khmer Empire absorbed the Mon kingdom of Lavo into its territory, and then made encroachments much further south (the Haripunchai Kingdom, notably, was able to maintain independence).

The Khmer takeover of both Lavo and the Malay Peninsula opened up new trading routes which utilized the Chao Phraya River. While the Chronicle merely states that the Emerald Buddha left Sri Lanka and ended up in Cambodia, the route shown here is likely the one which the statue took.

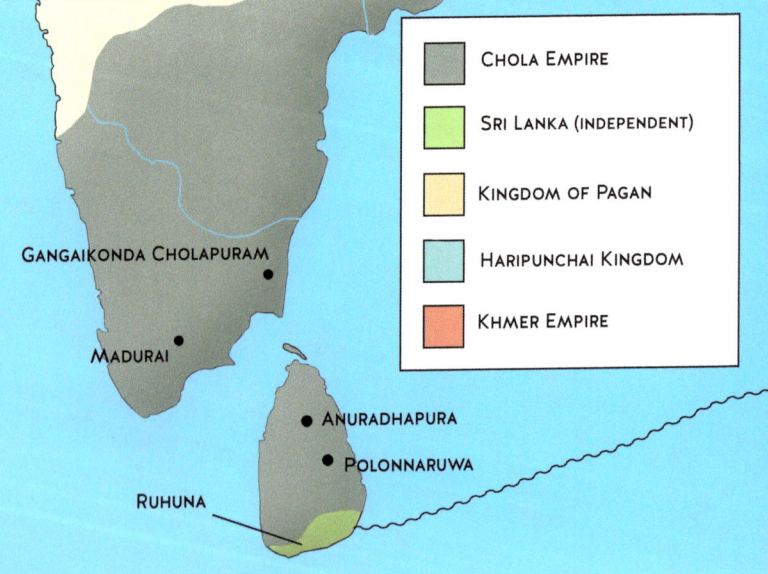

1050
Suryavarman I dies. Udayadityavarman II, the likely builder of the Baphuon temple, takes the throne at Angkor.

1060s (?)
King Anawrahta receives monks, scriptures and the Emerald Buddha from Sri Lanka. But one boat gets blown off course.

1050s

1060s

1057
King Anawrahta of Pagan takes over Thaton, followed by Mergui.

1066
Harshavarman III takes the throne at Angkor.

From this point on, the Emerald Buddha would remain in Khmer territory for hundreds of years.

1070-1
Vijayabahu I liberates Sri Lanka from the Cholas, making Polonnaruwa his capital. He then asks King Anawrahta for copies of the scriptures and for the return of Sinhalese monks.

| 1070s | 1080s |

1080
Jayavarman VI becomes Khmer king, ruling out of Phimai instead of Angkor

Nakhon Si Thammarat

11th Century

The Merit of the King

Coming down from the sky, King Anawrahta arrived in the Khmer precinct where the Emerald Buddha and the scriptures had arrived by mistake. He rode up to a monastery and dismounted from his horse.

But before going about his business, he stopped to pass urine on a nearby rock. Amazingly, Anawrahta's powerful stream split the rock in two, and a nearby monk could tell that this was no ordinary man. 'Who are you?' asked the monk, mystified.

'I am a servant of King Anawrahta,' he replied, concealing his true identity. 'I have come to retrieve the scriptures and the Jewel Image which belong to the Kingdom of Pagan.' The monk went to inform the temple chief who then told the king. But the local king said, 'These treasures have come to my land thanks to my good merit, and are therefore rightfully mine. Anawrahta gets nothing.'

Enraged, but careful not to commit such a grave sin as murder, Anawrahta picked up a long piece of wood. He then applied a chalky powder to its tip and mounted his horse. Speedily riding around the city walls three times in the manner of pradakshina, he waved the stick in the air so quickly that it appeared as nothing but a blur.

'Feel your necks,' Anawrahta told the townsfolk and the king. They did, and noticed the powder on their fingers. 'I easily could have killed you all,' said Anawrahta. 'I demand that you bring me what rightfully belongs to Pagan, or suffer the consequences.'

With everyone fearing for their lives, the local king trembled as he assured the mysterious visitor of his cooperation. Anawrahta received the scriptures before quickly heading back to Pagan. But in his haste, he did not notice that the Emerald Buddha was absent, as his mind had been so focused on the sacred texts.

'It must have been meant to be this way,' he told himself. And from then on, the Emerald Buddha remained in the Khmer Empire for a very long time.

Previous p172

Next p218

The Emerald Buddha in Nakhon Si Thammarat?

The Chronicle's Missing Link

According to the story, the ship with the statue that was destined for Burma got blown off course and ended up in the Khmer Empire, based out of Angkor in present-day Cambodia. But how could the statue have arrived in Cambodia? A quick look at a map reveals the extreme unlikelihood of such a journey happening by accident.

As we know that the boat with the Emerald Buddha did not arrive somewhere within King Anawrahta's territory, it most likely ended up south of Mergui on the west coast of the Malay Peninsula. (King Anawrahta took over Mergui following his conquest of Thaton.)

At the time, the Kingdom of Ligor, based out of present-day Nakhon Si Thammarat, controlled much of the peninsula. The kingdom, also referred to as Tambralinga in ancient texts, rose to prominence from the 7th century, or possibly even earlier.

Ligor also controlled vital trade routes connecting South Asia with Indochina. In those days, the peninsula's coasts were connected by an extensive canal system. Ships coming from India or Sri Lanka would've arrived at the Isthmus of Kra or numerous west coast ports further south, such as Takua Pa in current Phang Nga Province. And from there, many ships would sail to the capital of Nakhon Si Thammarat near the east coast. (In the case of our story, of course, the boat arrived by accident, but it likely followed a similar path.)

Due to Ligor's strategic and economic importance, it was often a vassal of larger, more powerful empires throughout its history. For centuries, Ligor was under the control of the Srivijaya Empire, a Mahayana Buddhist kingdom based on the island of Sumatra. To this day, old Srivijaya-style *chedis* can still be found at numerous Nakhon Si Thammarat temples.

But how long were the Srivijaya in control? There are no definitive historical records on the matter. But we do know that throughout the 11th century, the Srivijaya were embroiled in conflicts with the Sailendra dynasty of Java, and also the Chola dynasty of southern India *(see p174)*. Numerous attacks were launched on the peninsula which likely caused the Srivijaya to retreat further south. An independent Ligor may have emerged as a result, with the Khmers coming in shortly after.

Scholars generally agree that the Khmers controlled the Malay Peninsula throughout the 12th and 13th centuries. But they may have already been there by the time the Emerald Buddha left Sri Lanka. While they may or may not have not absorbed Ligor into their territory outright, the Khmers likely did at least establish close relations with the local king to take advantage of lucrative trade routes.

And if so, that would explain a major gap in our story. Nakhon Si Thammarat, while not named in the Chronicle, may be an important piece of the puzzle that would explain how the statue eventually got to Angkor.

A Khmer-style Vishnu statue found in Ligor, possibly as old as the 11th century

Expansion Under Suryavarman I

While we'll take a much deeper look at the history and culture of the Khmer Empire in the following section on Angkor *(p200)*, for now, let's turn our attention to an Angkorian king named Suryavarman I. He ruled from 1002-1050 and is credited with greatly expanding the empire. To the west he took over places like Phimai and Lopburi (both now in Thailand), eventually gaining control over the Chao Phraya River valley. And to the south, he made incursions into the Isthmus of Kra on the Malay Peninsula. And it's quite likely that he even went as far as Ligor, or Nakhon Si Thammarat.

This idea is proposed by Kenneth R. Hall in his book *A History of Early Southeast Asia*. Suryavarman's territorial expansion would've opened up new and important trade routes throughout the Khmer Empire. Goods coming from the west, from places like the Middle East or the Indian subcontinent, would've first sailed through the Malay Peninsula and then up toward the Chao Phraya River, past the site of modern Bangkok.

From there, the goods would sail up the river to Lopburi, before being taken overland eastward toward Sisophon and Battambang. And finally, further east to the capital of Angkor. When taking the region's mountainous terrain into account, this would've been the quickest and most direct route.

Modern roads connecting Cambodia with Thailand, in fact, largely follow parts of this same ancient trading route. And this was likely the path which the Emerald Buddha took to get to Angkor *(see 'Boat 2' route on p177)*.

Interestingly, Suryavarman also had a personal connection with the Malay Peninsula. Early on in his reign, he waged a brutal civil war against another claimant to the Khmer throne, Jayaviravarman. That king, who was only in power for several years, is widely believed to be a usurper who came all the way from Nakhon Si Thammarat! In fact, he'd once been a prince of the Kingdom of Ligor.

In addition to establishing new trade routes, Suryavarman may have conquered Ligor to ensure that Jayaviravarman's family could never avenge his death.

Burmese Presence

Now, considering that the Malay Peninsula was likely under Khmer control by the time our story takes place, we can picture the scene with Anawrahta and the wooden sword as having happened at the Malay Peninsula and not at Angkor. After all, it's highly unlikely that Anawrahta ever visited the Khmer capital (unless he really did have a flying horse!)

And the king in the story was probably the local ruler of Nakhon Si Thammarat rather than the Khmer emperor. But what do historical records tell us about Burmese presence in the Malay Peninsula around that time?

From 1057, the Burmese Kingdom of Pagan controlled both Thaton and Mergui in the upper part of the peninsula. But they may have even made further incursions south shortly afterward. Hall brings up a Chola raid on the west coast town of Takua Pa in 1067. Supposedly, it was in response to an attack by *another* power that forced the local ruler to flee. Was

A mysterious sculpture from peninsular Thailand, which scholars believe is a blend of Khmer and Srivijaya art styles. It seems to depict a local ruler, but who?

it perhaps the Burmese?

While we don't know for sure, Hall also suggests that the Burmese may have even occupied Takua Pa for a time. And though he died in 1050, Suryavarman I had forged an alliance with the Cholas decades earlier.

The year 1067 also fits in very neatly with our timeline. As mentioned on p174, Anawrahta grew closer with Sri Lanka (then under Chola occupation) at some point between 1057 and 1070.

Perhaps this Burmese invasion of the lower regions of the Malay Peninsula, then, is the same episode described in the Chronicle. After learning that the sacred texts and Emerald Buddha ended up in Ligor, maybe the Burmese went to intimidate the local population. But after learning that the Cholas were on their way, they hastily returned home with the scriptures.

As we can see, the situation in the Malay Peninsula was quite complex, to say the least. The Cholas, Burmese, Khmers and Srivijaya were all involved, with the semi-autonomous Kingdom of Ligor getting attacked from all sides!

But this mix of cultures is one of the reasons Nakhon Si Thammarat so fascinating to study, and also to visit.

Related Legends

Setting the convoluted history of the region aside for a moment, there are a couple of interesting legends involving Nakhon Si Thammarat that bear a striking resemblance to that of the Chronicle.

As we know, the Chronicle of the Emerald Buddha does not mention Nakhon Si Thammarat directly. But there are no less than two other stories which involve Buddhist relics, Sri Lanka, Nakhon Si Thammarat and shipwrecks.

One of them is the story of the Phra Sihing Buddha statue, whose history is deeply intertwined with that of the Emerald Buddha. As we'll discuss in more detail on p190, the Phra Sihing set sail on a boat from Sri Lanka in the 13th century. And although Nakhon Si Thammarat was its intended destination all along, the statue endured a shipwreck along the way. While the entire crew ended up perishing, somehow, the statue floated all the way to Nakhon Si Thammarat unscathed.

The other story involving a shipwreck is a local, alternate version of the Sri Lankan tooth relic story that we covered on p170. As we'll go over on p188, locals believe that a shipwreck brought the original tooth relic from India to Nakhon Si Thammarat instead of Sri Lanka!

In conclusion, considering the likelihood of a Khmer presence in the 11th century, Burmese attacks on the peninsula, and the two similar legends involving relics and shipwrecks, it's highly probable that the Emerald Buddha did indeed pass through Nakhon Si Thammarat.

But where was it kept and for how long? While we don't know for sure, if it stuck around for any significant length of time, it would've likely been on display at Wat Phra Mahathat, the oldest and most important temple in all of South Thailand.

Despite Nakhon Si Thammarat being relatively unknown to tourists, the city is widely regarded as South Thailand's historical center. And the inland destination makes for a surprisingly easy stopover during your travels around the region *(see pp196-7)*.

What's more is that the city also has a historical connection with another major character from our story: King Taksin! *(see p127)* As you'll see, shrines for the Thonburi king are abundant throughout town *(more on p189)*.

NAKHON SI THAMMARAT TRAVEL TIPS

Nakhon Si Thammarat doesn't appear on most people's itineraries – even those doing extended stays in South Thailand. And that's a shame, as it's one of Thailand's most historically significant cities, and also one of its oldest. It's also within easy reach of tourism hotspots like Krabi and Surat Thani.

With so much to see, visiting all the sites detailed in this section requires at least two days. But if you only have a day to explore the city, don't miss Wat Phra Mahathat, the Isuan (Shiva) and Narai (Vishnu) shrines, Phra Phuttha Sihing Hall and the Shadow Puppet Museum.

Visit the Thailand Tourism Authority office if you need any English assistance

GETTING THERE

A few budget airlines operate direct **flights** between Nakhon Si Thammarat and Bangkok, such as Thai Lion Air and Nok Air.

There are also a few **trains** a day connecting Nakhon Si Thammarat with Bangkok's Hua Lamphong Station. Rides last around 12 hours, while **long-distance buses** also take around the same amount of time.

Both regular **buses and minibuses** can take you to Nakhon Si Thammarat from other parts of South Thailand. Direct rides between places like Krabi, Surat Thani or Hat Yai last just a few hours each.

You can easily fit Nakhon Si Thammarat into your broader South Thailand itinerary. Learn more on pp196-97.

GETTING AROUND

Nearly all of the noteworthy sites in Nakhon Si Thammarat are situated north-south along a single road: Ratchadamnoen Rd. This is because long ago, the city was actually situated along the coast. But due to years of siltation, it's currently about 12 km from the ocean.

While many locations are walkable from one another, Ratchadamnoen is a pretty long road. Fortunately, numerous **blue songthaews** go up and down the road for just 10 baht per ride. Flag one down, hop in, and get off wherever you like.

Away from Ratchadamnoen Rd, there are hardly any songthaews or tuk tuks riding around, so it's best to book your accommodation as close to the main road as possible.

For day trips out of town, visit the **songthaew** 'station' situated in Talat Yao Market across from Wat Chedi Yak. From here you can ride to nearby waterfalls, beaches or the Ban Khiri Wong ecovillage.

You can also get around the city via **ridesharing** apps. This is the best way to get back and forth between your hotel and the bus terminal, train station or airport. There are also some **motorbike taxis** waiting outside the main bus terminal.

A roundabout on Ratchadamnoen Rd

WHERE TO STAY

When choosing accommodation in Nakhon Si Thammarat, don't worry so much about how close you are to a particular landmark. Instead, find somewhere as close as possible to Ratchadamnoen Rd, such as Thai Hotel. As mentioned, numerous blue songthaews ride up and down this road throughout the day. Away from the main road, in contrast, public transport is nearly non-existent.

Given the city's relative obscurity, finding accommodation can be a bit tricky, but you should find several options on the usual international hotel booking sites. Don't be surprised, however, if your hotel staff lacks English ability. Translation apps will certainly come in handy!

 ## SHOPPING

You can find local crafts, such as Yan Lipao traditional basketry, at places along Ratchadamnoen Rd and Tha Chang Rd.

One of the city center's only shopping malls is the Big C Supercenter on Pak Nakhon Rd, north of Wat Wang Tawan Ok.

 ## FOOD

Local South Thailand delicacies include Gaeng Som (a type of sour and spicy curry), fried liang leaves with egg and Pad Sataw Goong (stir-fried prawns with bitter beans).

Kopi, situated on an alley around 450 m east of Wat Chedi Yak, has been a local mainstay since the 1940s. Meanwhile, diners at the Krua Nai Nang restaurant can enjoy traditional southern food while watching a shadow puppet show.

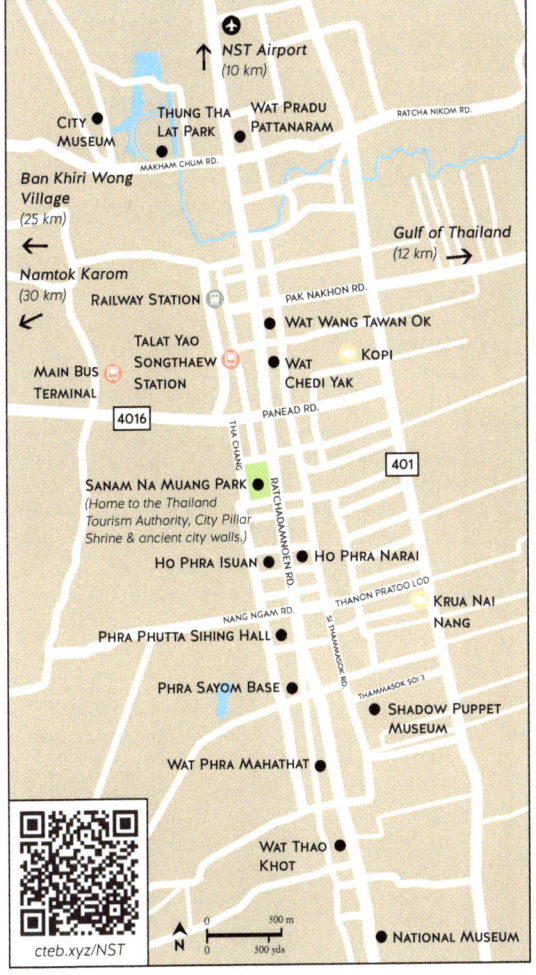

Wat Phra Mahathat • วัดพระมหาธาตุวรมหาวิหาร

Built in the 13th century, Wat Phra Mahathat is South Thailand's oldest and most important Buddhist temple. Its mostly known for its massive *chedi* which is visible from blocks away.

- Ratchadamnoen Rd.
- Daily
- ฿ 20 (for museum)

According to legend, an earlier version of the temple was built in the 4th century. At that time, the temple would've been situated right along the coast. But it's not anywhere near the water now due to centuries of siltation.

A nun strolls through the courtyard

Viharn Luang

The elaborate *viharn* contains a large standing Buddha image, while its ceiling was painted in the 18th century. Note that the structure is normally locked except for special ceremonies.

Small Viharns

Exploring the outer courtyard area, you'll encounter a shrine for King Taksin *(see p127)* and a few small *viharns*, one of which is the Viharn Phra Maha Kaccayana. This is where locals come to pray for backache relief!

‹ Viharn Phra Ma

One of the most impressive rooms of the temple, this *viharn* is at the base of a staircase which leads to the main *chedi*. Inside you'll find intricate carvings of mythological scenes along with statues of *chinthes*, *yakshas* and *garudas* (see p22).

Phra That Borommathat Chedi & Gallery

The highlight of the temple is its principle *chedi*, known as Phra That Borommathat. This massive *chedi*, which stands at 78 m high, is believed to contain a tiny tooth relic of the Buddha himself.

Though its current incarnation dates back to the 13th century, an older Srivijaya-style *chedi* may have once stood here in the far distant past.

The central spire is surrounded by no less than 173 smaller ones. Many of them have recently received a fresh coat of paint, concealing their true age.

Surrounding the *chedi* is a large gallery area with Buddha statues of all shapes and sizes. If ancient, rustic temples are your thing, you can do no better than Wat Phra Mahathat.

The gallery will also lead you to a sizeable **museum** containing all sorts of relics from Nakhon Si Thammmarat's long and storied past.

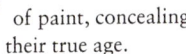
Bhumi, the Earth goddess

A familiar image ⌄

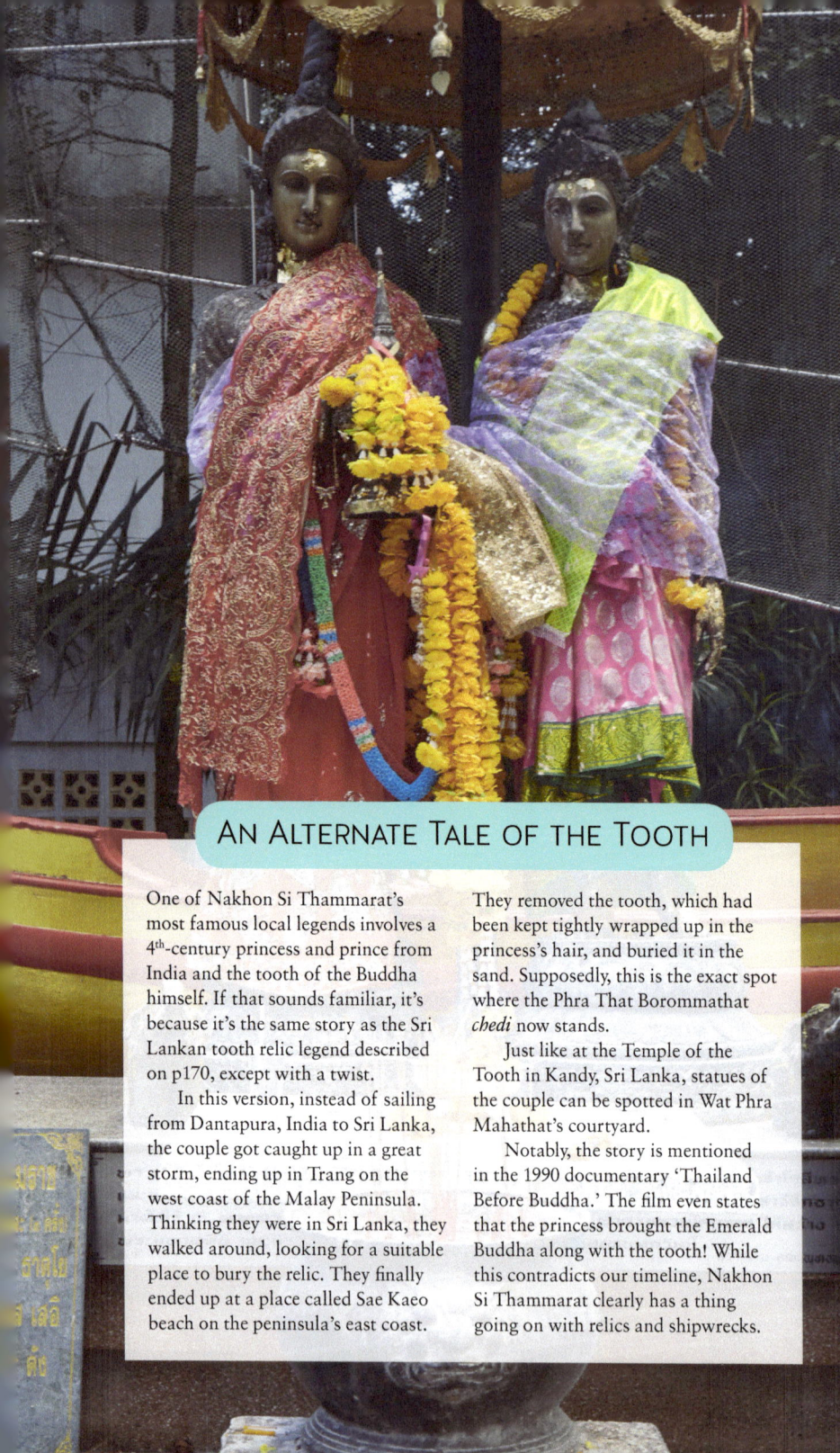

An Alternate Tale of the Tooth

One of Nakhon Si Thammarat's most famous local legends involves a 4th-century princess and prince from India and the tooth of the Buddha himself. If that sounds familiar, it's because it's the same story as the Sri Lankan tooth relic legend described on p170, except with a twist.

In this version, instead of sailing from Dantapura, India to Sri Lanka, the couple got caught up in a great storm, ending up in Trang on the west coast of the Malay Peninsula. Thinking they were in Sri Lanka, they walked around, looking for a suitable place to bury the relic. They finally ended up at a place called Sae Kaeo beach on the peninsula's east coast.

They removed the tooth, which had been kept tightly wrapped up in the princess's hair, and buried it in the sand. Supposedly, this is the exact spot where the Phra That Borommathat *chedi* now stands.

Just like at the Temple of the Tooth in Kandy, Sri Lanka, statues of the couple can be spotted in Wat Phra Mahathat's courtyard.

Notably, the story is mentioned in the 1990 documentary 'Thailand Before Buddha.' The film even states that the princess brought the Emerald Buddha along with the tooth! While this contradicts our timeline, Nakhon Si Thammarat clearly has a thing going on with relics and shipwrecks.

Wat Pradu Pattanaram • วัดประดู่พัฒนาราม

Ratchadamnoen Rd. (N of Ratchanikhom)
8:00 - 16:30
Daily
Free

After the Khmer Empire, Nakhon Si Thammarat was overtaken by the Sukhothai Kingdom in the 13th century, followed by Ayutthaya. And in the 18th century, King Taksin took the territory for Thonburi. In fact, some say he was never really executed in Thonburi but came down south to live out the rest of his days *(see p143)*.

If true, Taksin's ashes are not at Wat Intharam *(p137)* but here at Wat Pradu Pattanaram on Ratchadamnoen Rd.

Fittingly, the temple compound features Chinese-style structures in honor of Taksin's Chinese heritage. And the ashes of 19th-century governor Phraya Nakhon (rumored to be Taksin's son) are enshrined here as well.

Phra Phuttha Sihing Hall • พระพุทธสิหิงค์

Ratchadamnoen Rd.
8:00 - 17:00
Daily
Free

The Phra Phuttha Sihing Hall is home to the Phra Sihing Buddha image. Well, at least one of them! The other two, as mentioned previously, are in Chiang Mai and Bangkok. According to legend, the statue first arrived here in Nakhon Si Thammarat from Sri Lanka before being taken all over Thailand.

The modest structure housing the image is located just next to City Hall. As with its counterparts in Bangkok and Chiang Mai, the Phra Sihing of Nakhon Si Thammarat is paraded around the city each year in April during the Songkran festivities.

The hall is free to enter, but it might be locked around lunchtime. For a full summary of the Phra Sihing's journeys, check out the next page.

The Journeys of the Phra Sihing

The Phra Sihing is Thailand's second most significant Buddha image after the Emerald Buddha. Oddly enough, however, there's still some uncertainty over which statue is the *real* Phra Sihing. The creation of so many replicas in various towns the statue visited has resulted in multiple claimants, which we'll cover on p193.

The statue's history was written down on dried palm leaves in the 15th century. The manuscript, now commonly referred to as the 'Chronicle of the Phra Sihing,' was also translated to English by Camille Notton

The Phra Sihing's Creation

The story begins in Sri Lanka in the 2nd century AD, when three different kings gathered together and called for a meeting with the local holy men.

'Has anyone here seen our Lord Buddha when he was still alive?' one of the kings asked. But the holy men replied that they had not.

A chief of the *naga* serpents, however, spoke up. He said that he'd once met the Buddha, and he would be happy to show everyone what the 'Omniscient One' looked like. And so, at Anuradhapura's Jetavana Monastery, in front of a large audience, the *naga* shapeshifted into the exact likeness of Lord Buddha. He sat in the *dhyana mudra*, or meditation posture, and remained that way for seven days.

in the 1930s *(see p6)*. And we'll go over the Phra Sihing's entire journeys over the next several pages.

As will be covered again in later sections, the Chronicle of the Phra Sihing also provides us with vital information on the Emerald Buddha's 14th and 15th-century whereabouts.

Note: *Over the next few pages, the term 'Chronicle' will refer to that of the Phra Sihing and not the Chronicle of the Emerald Buddha, as is normally the case throughout this book.*

Lest anyone forget the miraculous sight, the kings decided to cast a metal image of the Buddha's likeness. Priests, sages and all sorts of celestial beings gathered to contribute metals such as gold, silver, tin and copper.

At one point during the laborious casting process, one of the workers was having a difficult time following orders. His boss struck him with a stick to keep him in line, but the blow only landed on a single finger. Curiously, once the Phra Sihing image was finished, one of its fingers happened to turn out defective.

Rather than fix it, the holy men prophesied that 'the finger will be fixed in the future by a devout king who comes into possession of the statue. And in the year 1457, a righteous king from Sri Lanka will visit that land to retrieve it.' After a weeklong celebration, the Phra Sihing image was then placed together with Sri Lanka's sacred tooth relic (see p170).

‹ *Crafting the image (murals of Wat Phra Singh, Chiang Rai)*

From Sri Lanka to Nakhon Si Thammarat & Sukhothai

The story fast-forwards over a thousand years to the reign of King Ram Khamhaeng who ruled over Sukhothai from around

1279–98. Ram Khamhaeng had greatly expanded the kingdom's territory, taking over parts of modern-day Laos, as well as most of the Malay Peninsula, including Nakhon Si Thammarat *(see p230)*.

And Ram Khamhaeng maintained close relations with Nakhon Si Thammarat, even bringing some of its monks to live and teach in Sukhothai. One day, when visiting the city, Ram Khamhaeng was conversing with the local king when he learned of the golden Buddha image across the sea in Sri Lanka. As the local king was close with Sri Lankan royalty, Ram Khamhaeng requested for him to retrieve the statue during his next visit there.

And so the king of Nakhon Si Thammarat did as he was told. Using flattery and gifts, he was able to convince the King of Lanka to part with the Phra Sihing. The holy men of Lanka were unconcerned, as they knew of the prophecy of the damaged finger, and that the Phra Sihing was destined to travel to other lands.

The king of Nakhon Si Thammarat went back home on his own, and the king of Sri Lanka later sent the Phra Sihing on a boat after a week of festivities in the image's honor. But on the ride over, stormy weather caused the boat to sink, with all the men on board perishing.

Miraculously, the Phra Sihing image did not sink but continued floating on top of the water. As if knowing exactly where to go, it floated all the way to the peninsula's west coast! It was not through the power of angels, the Chronicle states, but through the will of the statue itself (saving the men on board, however, was beyond its abilities).

Learning that the statue was steadily approaching, the king sent out boats to retrieve it. The people living near the port celebrated its arrival and brought the Phra Sihing all sorts of offerings. The statue was then brought to the capital where it was kept in a pavilion within the royal plaza.

After seven days and nights of festivities, the Phra Sihing floated in the air, emitting brilliant rays of light, the Chronicle states. Not long afterward, King Ram Khamhaeng came down to Nakhon Si Thammarat to retrieve the statue, bringing it to the Siamese capital of Sukhothai.

From Sukhothai to Ayutthaya

While the image was still in Sukhothai *(see p266)*, the rival kingdom of Ayutthaya formed in the year 1351. U Thong, the first king of Ayutthaya, pursued dominance over Sukhothai, forcing the kingdom to pay an annual tribute early on in his reign. But later, he sought outright control. He knew that Sukhothai's reigning king, Lithai, was a devout Buddhist and learned philosopher who had little interest in fighting. And around the year 1368, U Thong easily made Sukhothai an Ayutthaya vassal.

According to one version of the story, Lithai was then sent to rule in the satellite city of Phitsanulok and was permitted to take the Phra Sihing with him. Another version states that the statue was taken to the central province of Chainat. In either case, upon Lithai's death, it was finally taken to Ayutthaya and likely installed at Wat Phra Si Sanphet *(see p238)*.

The transition occurred around 1378, when King Borommaracha I, U Thong's brother-in-law, ruled over Ayutthaya. Around this time, Ayutthaya was embroiled in conflicts with Lanna, with both kingdoms vying for control over Sukhothai's former territory. But more on Lanna later.

A completed replica ▸

From Ayutthaya to Kamphaeng Phet

The story goes on to describe a king of the city of Kamphaeng Phet, situated near Sukhothai. Kamphaeng Phet was originally part of the Sukhothai Kingdom and would eventually become a vassal of Ayutthaya. But at the time the story takes place, it was probably somewhat autonomous. Kamphaeng Phet's king then was named Nanatissa, and he desired the Phra Sihing for himself at all costs.

He came up with a scheme that involved his own mother, who was still a strikingly beautiful woman. She traveled to Ayutthaya and easily made King Borommaracha fall in love with her.

One day, the woman asked the king for an alloyed Buddha image to send back to her hometown. The king agreed, telling her to choose one from the royal temple's main pavilion. He never imagined that she'd be able to single out the Phra Sihing from all the other statues in the temple - let alone have the nerve to take such a valued relic!

And it was true that she couldn't identify it. But all she had to do was bribe a temple guard with copious amounts of gold to point it out for her.

She then sent the image up to Kamphaeng Phet on a boat, to the great delight of her son. But after a few days, Borommaracha caught on and called in his concubine for questioning. She feigned innocence, claiming that it was a complete coincidence that the statue she chose was the Phra Sihing. And her son Nanatissa, unfortunately, would not easily part with it. But he would at least create a replica which he would later send down to Ayutthaya.

From Kamphaeng Phet to Chiang Rai

In the Lanna kingdom, a prince who ruled over Chiang Rai named Maha Proma heard that a beautiful Buddha image had arrived in Kamphaeng Phet. He wanted it and hoped that Nanatissa would voluntarily hand it over. But just in case, he marched over to Kamphaeng Phet with a huge army of 80,000 men! Maha Proma was the younger brother of King Kue Na of Lanna, who generously lent him the men and elephants required for the task.

At first, Maha Proma and Nanatissa communicated through an intermediary. Nanatissa, relieved to learn that Maha Proma had simply come for the statue, agreed to hand it over. The two men then met in person and exchanged gifts. But Nanatissa told Maha Proma to wait several days, as he would make the handoff not right then and there, but in Tak Province.

Meanwhile, Borommaracha of Ayutthaya was already on his way to Kamphaeng Phet with a group of men. In one version of the story, Nanatissa had contacted Ayutthaya for help after learning of Maha Proma's approach. But in order to avoid further complications and violence, he wanted Borommaracha to think that he'd managed to send Maha Proma back on his own. In another version, though, it was Nanatissa who Borommaracha was coming after, as he wanted the Sihing image back.

In either case, Maha Proma finally received the statue, taking it first to his older brother in Chiang Mai, King Kue Na. And while Kue Na was busy creating a niche in a large chedi suitable to house the image, Maha Proma took it to his city of Chiang Rai, where it would remain for a number of years. Not only did Maha Proma create another golden replica, but he was also the one to finally repair the original's defective finger!

From Chiang Rai to Chiang Mai

Upon Kue Na's death in 1385, his son Saen Muang Ma ascended the throne at the young age of fourteen. But the greedy Maha Proma decided to plan a covert attack on his inexperienced nephew to take control over Lanna for himself. He sent a message to Saen Muang Ma, telling him that he was coming to pay respects to his late older brother. But Saen Muang Ma suspected an ulterior motive, and he fortified the city.

Maha Proma's attack was repelled and he fled to Wiang Kum Kam. Saen Muang Ma's minister, Saenphanong, then followed after him. In an act of treachery, Maha Proma even called upon Lanna's archnemesis, the Ayutthaya Kingdom, to come and help him. The Lanna army then had to repel Ayutthaya forces at Lampang.

Amidst all the violence and confusion, Saen Muang Ma was able to gain possession of the Phra Sihing, and it was installed in Chiang Mai's Wat Phra Singh.

Interestingly, the Chronicle, written in 1417, ends by reminding the reader of the Sri Lankan monarch prophesied to come for the statue in 1457. But ultimately, this prophecy would not come true, and the statue never returned to Sri Lanka.

The Journey to Bangkok

In 1468, King Tilokarat brought the Emerald Buddha to Chiang Mai from Lampang. Both the Phra Sihing and Emerald Buddha were then taken to Luang Prabang together in 1551 by Setthathirath, where they joined the Phra Bang. But upon the request of King Mekuti, the Phra Sihing was returned to Chiang Mai after several years. It remained there until 1662 when it was captured by Ayutthaya yet again.

The Burmese sacked Ayutthaya in 1767, and they decided to bring the Phra Sihing back to Chiang Mai, which they then controlled. Following the defeat of Burma and the absorption of Lanna into Siam, however, King Rama I brought it to Bangkok, where it resides to this day.

The 'Real' Phra Sihing?

Today, three different statues could potentially be the real Phra Sihing, but the one at Bangkok's National Museum is generally recognized as the original. This is mainly because its meditation posture is typical of Sri Lankan images. The decoration of its platform, however, links it with images of Lanna origin.

All three images get paraded around their respective towns during the Songkran festivities each April, where they're splashed with water as part of a ritual cleansing. This is fitting, as symbolically speaking, the Phra Sihing is associated with water, *naga* serpents and the underworld. The Emerald Buddha, meanwhile, is generally associated with the sky and the heavens.

The name Phra Sihing, or Sihala Image, translates to 'Lion Image.' This is a reference to Sri Lanka, also nicknamed 'The Abode of Lions.'

Posture: Dhyana mudra
Location: Buddhaisawan Chapel of the Bangkok National Museum (p157)

Posture: Bhumisparsa
Location: Wat Phra Singh, Chiang Mai (p74)

Posture: Bhumisparsa
Location: Phra Putta Sihing Hall, Nakhon Si Thammarat (p189)

Namtok Karom • น้ำตกกะโรม

Situated about 30 km from the city in Khao Luang National Park, Namtok Karom is one of the area's most beautiful waterfalls. It makes for an easy and worthwhile half-day trip.

📍 Off of Highway 4015
🕒 8:00 - 16:00
📅 Daily
฿ 200

In total, there are 19 levels to the waterfall, though visitors only have access to the first seven. About halfway up is a place where you can take a dip in the water, while the highest level provides the most beautiful views. Looking closely, you can even see initials carved in the rock by both kings Rama V and VI, who visited the waterfall during their reigns.

GETTING THERE:
Take a songthaew from Talat Yao Market across from Wat Chedi Yak (see p185). You'll be dropped off at the base of a hill, from where it's a 10-minute walk to the entrance.

All along Ratchadamnoen Rd, between the National Museum and Wat Pradu, are numerous cultural landmarks. As mentioned below, the city also features large parks and a puppet museum.

AROUND TOWN

ANCIENT HINDU SHRINES

Across the street from one another on Ratchadamnoen Rd are two Hindu shrines which date back to the Ayutthaya period. **Ho Phra Isuan**, a small Shiva shrine, contains a *linga* and a dancing Shiva statue in the style of the Chola dynasty (the National Museum houses the original).

And outside is a tall red swing, much like the one in Bangkok *(see p157)*.

Ho Phra Narai, meanwhile, is a similar shrine dedicated to Vishnu. A statue was found here believed to be as old as the 5th century. And on a side street near the fruit market is the mysterious **Phra Sayom Base**, a Shiva shrine of unknown age.

WAT THAO KHOT

Wat Thao Khot is made up of five former temples that were all built nearby one another. But the *wat's* most notable feature is its large brick *chedi* built during the Srivijaya era. The *ubosot*, meanwhile, was built while Ayutthaya controlled the region. You can find it north of the National Museum on Ratchadamnoen Rd.

NANG TALUNG SHADOW PUPPET MUSEUM

- 📍 Si Thammasok Soi 3
- 🕘 9:00 - 16:30
- 📅 Daily
- 📞 (075) 346 394

Shadow puppetry has long been a popular means of storytelling in Southeast Asia, and this local museum is one of the best places to learn about it.

In addition to local puppets, you'll find some from Cambodia, Isaan, and central Thailand. The friendly family who runs it will even give you a brief explanation in English on how the leather puppets are made. Performances sometimes take place here, though you may need to call in advance.

THUNG THA LAT PARK

Located a few blocks west of Wat Pradu *(p189)*, this massive park may be one of the city's best-kept secrets. Thung Tha Lat even contains a zoo, along with a museum that's every bit as good as the National Museum at the opposite end of the city. Also around the park, you can find replicas of famous *chedis* from all throughout Asia.

Exploring
South Thailand

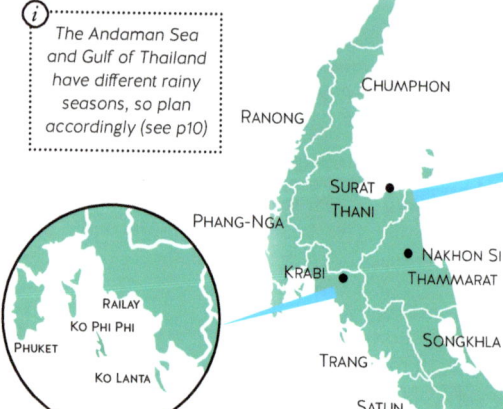

> The Andaman Sea and Gulf of Thailand have different rainy seasons, so plan accordingly (see p10)

South Thailand, home to the country's most pristine beaches, is a big hit with tourists. There's plenty to explore in the region overall, but the most visited provinces are Krabi, Phuket and Surat Thani.

Krabi Province

Railay Beach, while technically on the mainland, can only be accessed by boat, giving it an island feel. It's home to some of Krabi's most beautiful beaches and it also has some limestone caves to explore. Its cliffs, meanwhile, are a favorite among rock climbers.

Ko Lanta, home to some pristine beaches and a national park, has long been touted as the region's best-kept secret. While still beautiful, the secret is out, and the island is currently undergoing a major construction boom.

▲ Fastboats are the most comfortable way to go island hopping, but longboats are fine for shorter rides

Ko Phi Phi is comprised of two main islands. Phi Phi Leh is a protected national park, while Phi Phi Don is where people stay and party. Many complain that the gorgeous islands have become too popular for their own good, but nature lovers may still want to consider a day trip.

Krabi Town, the area's main transport hub, is home to the Tiger Cave Temple. Its stunning views are worth the 1,200 step climb! Also in town are the Khao Kanab Nam limestone caves, as well as a lively night market.

Elsewhere on the mainland, Ao Nang is a popular tourist hub. It has several beaches of its own, but offers easy boat access to nearby islands like the secluded Ko Poda.

Surat Thani Province

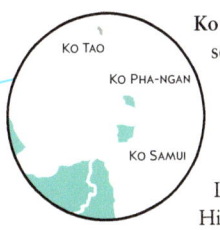

Ko Samui, Thailand's second-largest island, is home to stunning viewpoints like Loh Wua Tu Lub and Lat Koh. Hin Ta Hin Yai, meanwhile, is known for its peculiar rock formations which closely resemble male and female organs. Chaweng Beach is the island's most popular, but also the most commercialized. Nearby Mae Koh island features an emerald green lagoon, while the 'Big Buddha' temple can be found on Fan Island.

Ko Pha-ngan these days is most known for its full moon parties, for which tens of thousands gather every month. But the island is also home to some beautiful beaches, waterfalls and hiking spots. If you're going to party, be sure to book accommodation well in advance. If you're not, avoid the full moon period altogether.

Snorkeling and diving opportunities are easy to find

Ko Tao is considered one of Thailand's top places for diving. It's popular with both experts and beginners who are looking for an affordable diving school.

Also within Surat Thani Province is **Khao Sok National Park**, much of which surrounds the gorgeous Chiow Lan Lake. The turquoise lake features numerous limestone cliffs, while the surrounding jungle is home to everything from wild elephants to the Rafflesia flower.

The world's largest flower ›

TRANSPORT:

Krabi airport is well connected to the rest of the country, and you can even fly directly from places like Chiang Mai and Chiang Rai. Furthermore, it's connected to international airports like Kuala Lumpur, Malaysia.

Shared or private minivans from the airport can take you to places like Ko Lanta and Ao Nang. Ko Phi Phi, however, requires a high-speed ferry. From Krabi Town, you can take a bus over to Nakhon Si Thammarat (2-3 hours) which also has its own airport *(see p184)*.

Surat Thani has an airport as well. A ferry from there is the cheapest way to get to Ko Samui. While there is an airport on the island, direct flights are costly. From Surat Thani, a bus ride to Nakhon Si Thammarat takes about 2 hours.

Phuket also has a very well-connected airport, while the island is connected to the mainland by bridge.

Given South Thailand's popularity, the region is unfortunately rife with scams. Whenever possible, try to arrange transport in advance with a reputable company.

Beyond

The popular island of **Phuket** is easy to reach and has a well-developed tourism infrastructure. But some complain that it's overcrowded and a bit seedy. Between Phuket and Krabi are the stunning limestone formations of **Phang Nga Bay**. The province is also home to the Similan and Surin islands. Further south, **Ko Lipe** remains one of Thailand's most remote and scenic islands, but it's gaining popularity fast.

The Emerald Buddha In The Khmer Empire

The Emerald Buddha resided in the Khmer Empire for nearly three hundred years, during which the kingdom reached its height of power and influence. But just who were the Khmers, and where would they have kept the statue?

Arrival in The Empire

The Emerald Buddha's arrival in Khmer territory was detailed in the previous section *(p180)*. As mentioned, the statue probably first arrived in Nakhon Si Thammarat after the ship from Sri Lanka got blown off course. Nakhon Si Thammarat was likely part of, or at least allied with, the Khmer Empire by that time. And at some point, the statue was transferred to the Khmer capital of Angkor, nearby modern-day Siem Reap. *(see map on pp176-77).*

The Chronicle mentions nothing of the Emerald Buddha's time in Angkor other than what led to its eventual departure, which we'll go over on p218. And after Angkor, it stayed for an unspecified period of time in one of the empire's rural outposts.

When it comes to guessing which temple the Emerald Buddha may have stayed at, the Chronicle really doesn't give us much to work with. But the more we delve into the history of the Khmer Empire, one of world history's most fascinating civilizations, the more we're able to narrow things down.

For now, let's briefly go over the history and culture of the Khmers. We'll also consider how a jade Buddha statue would've likely been received in what was a Hindu kingdom until the late 12th century.

From p206, in our guide to the Angkor temples, we'll examine the Emerald Buddha's most probable hosts, which are also among Angkor's most impressive structures.

The Khmer Empire: A Brief Introduction

The Khmer Empire was founded in the year 802 AD, when King Jayavarman II declared independence from Java. The empire's original capital was situated on top of Mt. Kulen, some 50 km north of modern-day Siem Reap. And several decades later in 877, the capital moved to a city called Harihalaya. Not long after, around 893, a king named Yashovarman I moved the capital to Yasodharapura, which we now know as Angkor.

Aside from a brief move to Koh Ker in the 900s, Angkor remained the Khmer capital up until the 15th century. But the mighty empire's borders extended well beyond those of modern-day Cambodia.

The Khmer Empire started a massive expansion campaign from 11th century during the reign of Suryavarman I *(see p182)*. This ambitious king conquered much of what makes up modern-day Thailand and also Laos. Later in the 12th century, kings like Suryavarman II and Jayavarman VII would also look eastward, occupying parts of the Champa Kingdom in present-day Vietnam.

Khmer culture was heavily influenced by India. The ancient Indian language of Sanskrit was prevalent in Khmer society, and many stone inscriptions were written in Sanskrit using the Khmer script. Shiva was the favored god of most (but not all) kings, while a large community of Brahmin priests presided over important court rituals *(see p15)*.

The Khmers also placed a high importance on the Indian Ramayana and Mahabharata epics, using them as the subject matter for much of their intricate art and sculptures.

The Khmers, if anything, were fantastic builders. They left behind some of the world's most impressive man-made structures, such as Angkor Wat and the Bayon, which continue to mystify visitors to this day. Their temples, which resembled Hindu *mandala* patterns, also played a major role in town planning. Entire cities were often built surrounding these sacred stone monuments.

Like many other Asian societies, the Khmers also worshipped their ancestors and probably an array of local nature spirits as well. And, as we'll cover shortly, Buddhism was widely tolerated even before it became the official religion in the late 12th century.

According to tradition, kings would start their reigns by building an ancestral temple dedicated to their parents and a large pyramidal temple for their favored god. And they'd also construct a new *baray*, or massive rectangular reservoir.

The Khmers were extraordinarily efficient at altering the landscape of their empire, with much of their territory being traversable by boat thanks to an intricate canal system.

But there's still a lot we don't know about the Khmer Empire, and our current understanding could easily be challenged in the near future. As archaeologists utilize new technology like LIDAR (laser scanners), entire cities lost to time and the jungle could soon be unearthed.

Sadly, none of the Khmers' ancient palm leaf manuscripts have survived. And strangely, there's only one surviving written account of a foreigner who visited Angkor in its prime (see p202). With that in mind, it's not surprising that there are no surviving written records mentioning the Emerald Buddha's time there.

EARLY KHMER BUDDHISM

The Khmer Empire was largely Hindu up until the late 12th century. We can't help but wonder, then, how they would've reacted to the Emerald Buddha's arrival in their territory. Would it have been placed prominently at one of the main temples? Or would it have been merely kept off to the side somewhere?

While Hinduism, and in particular Shaivism (Shiva worship) remained the dominant religion for centuries, Mahayana Buddhism was largely tolerated the whole time. The two religions coexisted side by side, and some early Khmer kings even helped open Buddhist monasteries. And from as early as the 10th century onward, the Khmers produced many sculptures of Avalokiteshvara, one of Mahayana Buddhism's most important divinities (see p14).

Nevertheless, up until the reign of Jayavarman VII, Buddhist temples made of stone were incredibly rare. One exception would be a small temple called Bat Chum, built in 952 by the Buddhist architect Kavindrarimathana. He was the same man who built East Mebon, a Hindu Shiva temple, for King Rajendravarman II. Therefore, numerous other Hindu temples may have also been constructed by those who personally identified with Buddhism.

But what's more, is that some of the early Khmer kings themselves may have been Buddhist. Many scholars even think that none other than Suryavarman I was a Mahayana Buddhist. His posthumous name, after all, was *Nirvanapada*. While

An early 11th-century Khmer sculpture of Avalokiteshvara

the temples in Angkor he commissioned are thought to be Hindu, he may have been responsible for the elaborate Buddhist temple of Phimai, located in current-day Thailand. We'll be going over Phimai in more detail on p226.

Suryavarman I died shortly before the Emerald Buddha's arrival in the Khmer Empire. And as far as historians can tell, his successors were followers of Hinduism. But interestingly enough, in addition to Avalokiteshvara, the Khmers started sculpting numerous images of the Buddha himself from the 11th century, mainly during what we now call the 'Baphuon period' of Khmer art. This period lasted from 1010-1080, which overlaps with the Emerald Buddha's departure from Sri Lanka.

Therefore, it's likely that even before the reign of devout Buddhist king Jayavarman VII, a highly refined carving such as the Emerald Buddha would've been received with great esteem.

If the Emerald Buddha only stayed in the Malay Peninsula for a few years, it would've arrived in Angkor during the reign of either Udayadityavarman II or Harshavarman III *(see p176)*. And at that time, the Khmer Empire would've been centered around the Baphuon temple *(p207)*.

The Reign of Jayavarman VII

Fast-forward over 100 years later, and Jayavarman VII would completely transform Khmer society. An ardent follower of Mahayana Buddhism, Jayavarman VII was the first king to build major stone temples in Angkor for the Buddha and various *bodhisattvas*.

But the king did not do away with Hinduism or abolish the Brahmin priesthood. Priests still presided over state rituals, while the new temples featured plenty of sanctuaries for the Hindu pantheon. Jayavarman VII's temples, while predominantly Buddhist, were also highly syncretic.

Wherever the Emerald Buddha resided before Jayavarman VII's ascension to the throne in 1181, he probably would've moved it to one of his brand new constructions.

Zhou Daguan's Memoir

Despite the Khmer Empire lasting for centuries as one of Southeast Asia's most powerful kingdoms, we only have one single account written by a foreign visitor to Angkor. It comes from a man named Zhou Daguan, a Chinese diplomat who stayed for around a year in 1296. This was well after the reign of Jayavarman VII, Angkor's last great king. The Khmers had long stopped building temples by this point, but Daguan's writings reveal that Angkor was still thriving at the end of the 13th century.

The exact purpose of Zhou Daguan's trip remains unclear, but he traveled on behalf of the ruling Yuan dynasty, or the Mongol Empire which controlled China at the time. And considering how Daguan spent a year there, his work is surprisingly brief. Nevertheless, it's become an extremely important source for researchers looking to learn more about Angkor's main temples, as well as the daily life of the commoner. And the sense of awe and wonder he experienced when seeing Angkor's monuments is something still felt by tourists today.

Though the Emerald Buddha should've still been in Khmer territory in 1296, Daguan doesn't mention it. We'll cover the likely reason why on p215.

Khmer Temple Architecture

The Prasat

The *prasat*, or sanctuary, is the basis of all Khmer temple architecture. Early temples consisted of just a single *prasat*. Later, more elaborate temples would utilize many. Too small for congregations, *prasats* were just big enough for priests to conduct the necessary rituals. They typically contained an idol or a *linga (see p15)*.

Prasats were first made of brick, then laterite, and eventually sandstone.

This early 9th-century prasat *features one east-facing entrance and three 'false doors' on the other sides.*

From the late 10th century onward, a temple's primary prasat *would often have a* gopura *attached to the eastern entrance. And regular openings on the other sides would replace the false doors.*

At the top of the prasat *door is the* lintel. *These always feature intricate carvings of mythological beings. Though designs often repeat themselves, there are also many one-of-a-kind carvings throughout Angkor.*

Intricate floral patterns can often be found along the pilasters.

Above the lintels of more elaborate temples, pediments *provide space for even more detailed mythological scenes.*

On either side of most doorways are two colonettes. *They're usually octagonal and carved with vegetal motifs.*

Temple Layouts

‹ *The most popular temple layout throughout the 9th and 10th centuries was the* trimurti. *Three* prasats *lined up in a row often represented the Hindu triad (see p16).*

Most Khmer kings built an official state temple during their reign, and these were always stepped pyramids. Many of them, such as Angkor Wat, have five prasats *arranged in a quincunx layout. From above, they're meant to resemble mandalas.* ›

SIEM REAP & ANGKOR TRAVEL TIPS

Siem Reap, which means 'Siam Defeated' in Khmer, is one of Cambodia's largest cities and the gateway to the Angkor Archaeological Park. Formerly a small village, Siem Reap started to grow in the early 20th century as colonial France cleared the Angkorian ruins, opening them up for tourism. Nowadays, this city of 140,000 has just about every tourist amenity that you can think of.

GETTING THERE

Siem Reap can be reached by direct **flight** from cities like Bangkok, Hong Kong, Singapore and Kuala Lumpur. And you can also fly domestically from Phnom Penh and Sihanoukville.

While traveling **overland from Thailand** is possible, the border area is notorious for its scams. Also note that there are no true 'direct' buses from Bangkok, as you will always need to go through immigration at the border. The opposite route from Cambodia into Thailand, on the other hand, comes with much less hassle.

Siem Reap is also reachable by **bus** from many other parts of Cambodia. Given the state of Cambodian roads, however, consider minimizing your safety risk by avoiding long bus rides at night. Learn more about transport in Cambodia on p280.

THE PARK PASS

All visitors to the Angkor Archaeological Park require a park pass. These allow for unlimited visits to any of the Angkorian temples during the allotted time period. Staff will punch a hole in your pass upon each entry to the park, while additional checks take place at the major temples.

The ticket vending area is located at the intersection of Apsara Rd and Street 60. At the time of writing, a 1-day pass costs $37, a 3-day pass $62, and a 7-day pass $72. (Passes don't need to be used on consecutive days.) Three days are enough for the highlights, while at least five are recommended for true temple fanatics!

To avoid waiting in line on the first morning, visitors can purchase their passes for the following day from 17:00 in the evening. Every temple covered between pp206-17 is accessible with the pass.

GETTING AROUND

The best way to get around the Angkor Archaeological Park is to hire a **tuk tuk** for the day. Unlike the tuk tuks in Thailand, these are basically wooden carriages attached to a motorbike. The ride may be bumpy, but it's a convenient and affordable way to visit the temples independently.

The standard price is generally $15 per day, plus a bit extra for more distant excursions or sunrises.

Air-conditioned **taxis**, meanwhile, usually cost around $40 per day.

Foreigners aren't allowed to rent motorbikes in Cambodia, but you can rent a **bicycle** from your hotel. Cycling to Angkor Wat and Angkor Thom is easy, but hire a driver for the more distant temples (see pp216-17).

LODGING

With so many tourists coming to Angkor, Siem Reap features hotels and guest houses for just about every budget. In regards to location, the closer you are to the entrance of the Angkor Archaeological Park, the better.

ANGKOR

⏱ TIMING

Get started each morning as early as possible. As most Angkorian temples face east, they look their best in the early morning light. Furthermore, the major temples get flooded with tourists from around 8:30. All temples open at 7:30, with the exception of Angkor Wat, which opens at 5:00 for sunrise (it gets packed!).

Most temples close at 17:30, with the exception of Phnom Bakheng and Pre Rup, which stay open until 19:00 for sunset viewings.

It can get very hot during midday, but the temples are also relatively calm and quiet at this time.

🛏 SIEM REAP & BEYOND

This guide only focuses on the Angkor temples, but some of the main attractions in Siem Reap itself are the **Angkor National Museum**, the floating villages of **Tonle Sap Lake**, and the **Artisans Angkor** crafts workshop. **Pub Street**, meanwhile, is wildly popular after dark.

Beyond Angkor, there are many fantastic ruins to explore, such as **Sambor Prei Kuk**, **Preah Khan of Kampong Svay**, **Preah Vihear**, **Koh Ker**, **Beng Mealea** and **Banteay Chhmar** (see p220). You can find articles on each by scanning the QR code below. Most outlying temples can be seen within three days with a private driver.

In **Phnom Penh**, be sure to check out the **Royal Palace**, which was largely inspired by Bangkok's, complete with its own Emerald Buddha replica! And the **National Museum of Cambodia** is the best place to see ancient Khmer sculptures. The capital also contains many sites related to the horrors of the Khmer Rouge.

Elsewhere, **Sihanoukville** is popular with beach lovers while **Battambang** is known for its colonial architecture.

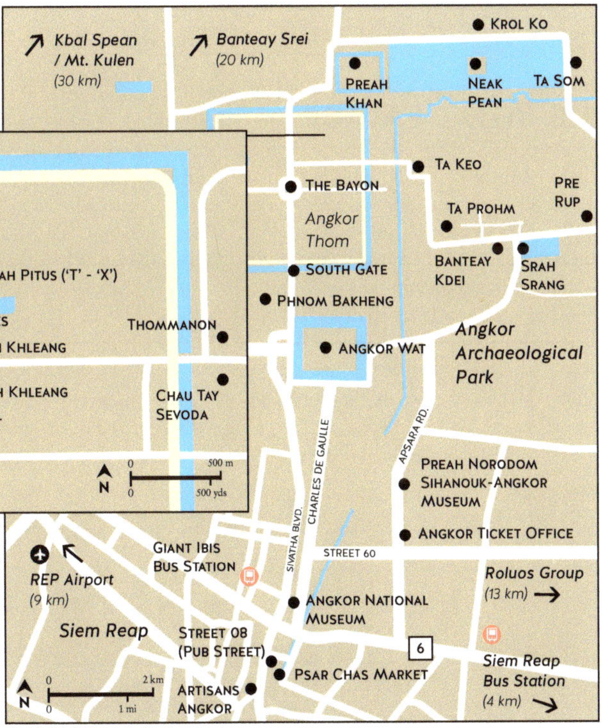

PHIMEANAKAS • ប្រាសាទភិមានអាកាស

Phimeanakas was used as a private temple for the Khmer king. It may even be one of the oldest structures at Angkor, though it was renovated by Suryavarman I in the early the 11th century. Later kings would also use it as their private temple for centuries to come. As monarchs in Asia traditionally kept their most prized relics in private royal temples, could Phimeanakas have hosted the Emerald Buddha?

The temple, built as a pyramid, is quite small (36 by 28 m) compared to other Angkorian pyramids. One reason could be that even priests were possibly barred access, with only the king allowed entry.

When restoration is taking place, Phimeanakas may not be climbable, but you can still see a lot from the ground level. Notice the small concentric gallery on top. This may be the first use of such an architectural feature in all of Angkor.

There's also a single *prasat* in the center. According to Zhou Daguan, a golden tower (a *linga* symbolic of Shiva, perhaps?) once rose out from its top. No evidence of it remains today, however.

THE KING & THE SERPENT

Zhou Daguan described how the king would visit Phimeanakas nightly. At the top, he would make love to a nine-headed *naga* spirit that would take on the form of a beautiful woman. According to local belief, if the king failed to do so, disaster would strike the kingdom. Or, if the *naga* spirit herself failed to show, it was a sign that the king's days were numbered.

THE ROYAL PALACE

King Suryavarman I also established the Royal Palace area right next to Phimeanakas. As the structures here were made entirely of wood, nothing but the entrance gate and the pond remain today. Zhou Daguan described it as having long corridors with complicated walkways and lead tiles. It was also held up by huge pillars carved with Buddha images (at least during his 1296 visit).

The stone gates that lead to this private 'city within a city' still remain, but for the rest, we'll just have to use our imagination. As mentioned above, kings would often keep prized relics within their living quarters. If not at Phimeanakas, then the Emerald Buddha might've been kept on palace grounds.

Nearby, don't miss the royal pond, a peaceful spot with steps entirely carved with bas-reliefs.

BAPHUON · ប្រាសាទបាពួន

The Baphuon was completed around the year 1060 by King Udayadityavarman II (r.1050-1066), though it was likely started by Suryavarman I. At the time, it was Angkor's most ambitious ever project. And even over 200 years later, it was the temple that Zhou Daguan was most impressed with during his time in Angkor.

The temple, originally dedicated to Shiva, features one large sanctuary on top of a massive pyramidal base. Zhou Daguan mentioned a tall bronze tower (probably a *linga*) extending out from the top, making it even taller than the Bayon *(p210)*.

When it was built, it was the largest structure the Khmers had yet attempted, and its core was actually a large earthen mound. Sadly, this is probably what led to the Baphuon's collapse by the 20th century. Archaeologists then had to rebuild it almost entirely from scratch, with the temple finally opening up to visitors in 2011.

Entering the complex, you'll walk along an elevated causeway that stretches out to 225 m, before arriving at the elaborate entrance gate *(pictured on pp198-99)*. From there, you can begin your ascent to the top.

This would've been the largest temple in Angkor upon the Emerald Buddha's arrival. You can find it within Angkor Thom (though it long predates the city walls) next to Phimeanakas.

The Baphuon is highly regarded for its art. The various carvings are mainly battle scenes from the Ramayana and Mahabharata epics. ›

The concentric gallery, which lacks the baluster windows of later temples, has a design that's unique to the Baphuon. ⌄

What's left of the top sanctuary

ANGKOR WAT · អង្គរវត្ត

THE APEX OF KHMER ARCHITECTURE

Angkor Wat is widely considered to be the finest single example of a Khmer temple. Many of its features, though, such as the quincunx layout of the *prasats*, the concentric galleries, and the long causeway at the entrance, had already been tried before.

But Angkor Wat's builders reimplemented these ideas in a more refined manner and on a much larger scale. Special care was also taken with the placement of the sandstone blocks. This is likely why it's among the best-preserved Khmer temples today.

A WEST-FACING TEMPLE

While most Hindu Khmer temples were built for Shiva, Angkor Wat was dedicated to Vishnu. This is likely why it faces west and not east. On the equinoxes, the sun can be seen rising directly above the central *prasat*.

Angkor Wat, the state temple of Suryavarman II (r.1115-1150), is the planet's largest religious monument and one of the finest engineering feats of the ancient world. The central temple is comprised of three separate levels while the entire complex takes up 2 km². For much of the 12th century, it even functioned as its own city.

But was the Emerald Buddha placed here? It's certainly possible. While the exact consecration date of Angkor Wat is unknown, the Khmers still possessed the image throughout Suryavarman II's reign. And Angkor Wat would remain the empire's central temple until the construction of the Bayon in the late 12th century. Notably, as shown on p152, a replica of Angkor Wat is now on display at Bangkok's Wat Phra Kaew!

‹ *A stunning eight-armed Vishnu statue*

The Western Gate

Passing a long causeway, you'll arrive at a massive entrance gate. The gate features its own galleries, inside of which you can find intricate lintel carvings. One of the gate's pavilions also houses the eight-armed Vishnu statue (*pictured opposite*).

The Cruciform Gallery

Just inside of the main entrance, you'll find a series of galleries in the shape of a cruciform. They're adorned with carvings, while one section contains multiple Buddha statues. Like many Angkorian temples, Angkor Wat was later converted into a Theravada Buddhist *wat*.

Angkor Wat boasts over 1800 *apsara* (celestial dancer) carvings!

The Bas-Relief Galleries

Angkor Wat was the first Khmer temple with long galleries entirely carved in bas-reliefs. Four enormous halls surround the main portion of the temple, most of which are dedicated to battle scenes. You'll find depictions of the battle at Lanka from the Ramayana epic, and the Mahabharata's grueling 18-day battle of Kurukshetra.

Other scenes represent historical battles led by Suryavarman II himself, while another shows the 'Churning of the Ocean of Milk,' a popular Hindu mythological tale.

The Upper Levels

Angkor Wat's 2nd floor is home to another series of galleries, as well as some beautiful *apsara* carvings. A total of twelve staircases lead to the third and highest level of the temple, but the only one in use today is found in the northeast corner. Be sure to have your knees and shoulders covered if you want to be allowed up.

The central *prasat* stands at 55 m high. It was here that the temple's original Vishnu statue once stood, but standing Buddhas have since taken its place.

THE BAYON · ប្រាសាទបាយ័ន

Built in the late 12th century, Jayavarman VII's state 'temple-mountain' is one of the most unique structures in all of Angkor. It sits right at the center of the walled city of Angkor Thom. In fact, the city walls themselves double as the temple's boundary walls!

The Bayon is incredibly elaborate and complex. It can be difficult to wrap your head around, even after multiple visits. But that's also what makes the temple, which once glistened with gold, such a treat to explore.

Up until the reign of Jayavarman VII, nearly every Khmer king built a brand new pyramid temple. But no subsequent king would dare try and top the Bayon.

WHO WAS JAYAVARMAN VII?

Jayavarman VII was the most powerful king in the Khmer Empire's history. Not only did he expand the empire to its largest ever size, but Jayavarman also built more structures than all the other kings combined!

As a youth, Jayavarman VII was sent to Champa (present Vietnam) to learn about their ways. Years later, in 1177, when the Champa Kingdom sacked Angkor, he raised an army and repelled the invaders - but not without the help of some useful Cham allies.

Taking the throne in 1181 (then already in his late fifties), Jayavarman implemented massive religious, political and social reforms that would change Angkor forever.

After hundreds of years of Hindu dominance, Jayavarman VII made Buddhism the kingdom's primary religion. And the Bayon was the first (and only) Buddhist pyramidal temple of Angkor.

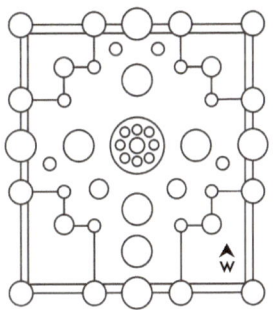

Like many Khmer temples, the Bayon was deliberately designed to be almost, yet not quite, symmetrical.

Jayavarman VII also departed from the classical quincunx tower layout. The four main surrounding prasats are located at the cardinal points instead.

A Labyrinth

Built and rebuilt in several stages, most of the Bayon's structures are jam-packed together, and hundreds of different deities were worshipped here. As you walk through the temple, you'll find yourself exploring dark corridors and dimly lit chambers, unsure of where they'll take you next. Like many temples in Angkor, the Bayon was later converted from a Mahayana temple to a Theravada one.

Bas-Reliefs

The Bayon features not one, but two layers of bas-relief galleries. One set can be found outside, encircling the temple, while further inside are more reliefs under a roof. The scenes depict Hindu and Buddhist mythological stories, while others show Jayavarman VII's military efforts against the Champa Kingdom.

In some parts, Khmer are fighting Khmer and Cham (those with helmets) are fighting other Cham! And there are also plenty of other scenes of everyday life in Angkor.

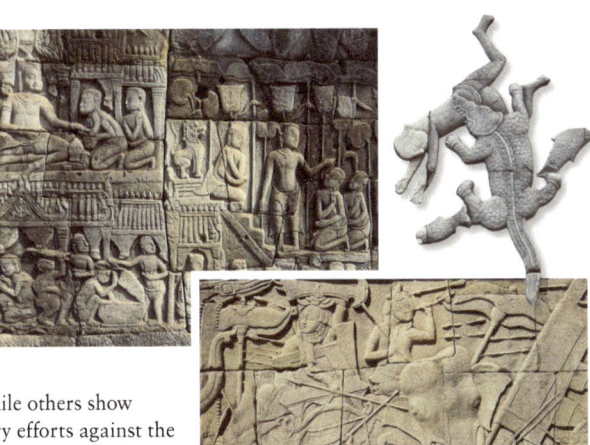

Central Sanctuary

The Bayon's central *prasat* is in a circular shape – the only one of its kind at Angkor. And the single tower actually contains nine sanctuaries within it!

A 19th-century diagram produced by France's Mekong Exploration Commission ▶

The Bayon Buddha Mystery

In 1933, broken pieces of a large Buddha statue were found deep within a pit beneath the central tower. The statue, long believed to be the Bayon's main image, is now on display at the nearby shrine of **Vihear Prampil Loveng**.

Also among the rubble, however, was a statue crafted in the U Thong art style of Ayutthaya, but sourced with local stone.

This raises the possibility that the 'Bayon Buddha' was not the Bayon's original statue, and was perhaps placed there later during a Siamese occupation. If so, which image sat at the heart of the empire during Jayavarman VII's reign?

The Face Towers

Carved into the towers are over 200 enigmatic, smiling faces. Nobody knows for sure who the faces are supposed to represent. The popular theories, though, are that they're either Avalokiteshvara, the Buddha, or even Jayavarman VII himself. It's said that the temple once consisted of 49 towers, but today only 37 of them remain standing.

Try visiting the Bayon in both early morning and late afternoon to see the towers under different lighting conditions

Arrive at 7:30 am to beat the crowds!

Ta Prohm · ប្រាសាទតាព្រហ្ម

Completed in 1186, Ta Prohm has been left largely unrestored, meaning visitors can see it how archaeologists first discovered it. Ta Prohm is most known for its large trees gripping its ancient stone structures.

The temple was dedicated to Jayavarman VII's own mother, in addition to the female *bodhisattva* Prajnaparamita. This divinity has traditionally been associated with motherhood, along with the Buddhist concept of emptiness.

All in all, no less than 260 divinities were enshrined at Ta Prohm. According to the temple's stele, over 12,000 staff members worked to maintain it all!

Hall of Dancers

A new architectural feature introduced at Jayavarman VII's temples was the 'Hall of Dancers.' Structurally, the halls were inspired by the cruciform galleries of Angkor Wat, and they were entirely decorated with dancing *apsaras*. The structures, however, are too narrow for any actual dancing.

Medallions

Jayavarman introduced 'medallions' that were carved vertically on door frames. While they mostly depicted scenes from mythology or daily life, this 'stegosaurus' near the western exit has got lots of people talking. It's probably just a rhino, however.

> ### THE TRIAD TEMPLES
>
> Ta Prohm, Preah Khan and Banteay Kdei make up Jayavarman VII's 'triad temples.' They represent Prajnaparamita, Avalokiteshvara and the Buddha. You can easily visit them all on the same day following sunrise at the **Srah Srang** reservoir. And be sure to stop at Neak Pean *(p216)*, Krol Ko and Ta Som (all by Jayavarman VII) along the way.

PREAH KHAN • ប្រាសាទព្រះខ័ន

Preah Khan, built five years after Ta Prohm, functioned as its own city, and was likely the king's base as he built up Angkor Thom. Visitors will first encounter a set of *devas* and *asuras* outside the entrance which precede those in front of Angkor Thom *(see p216)*.

The temple was primarily dedicated to Jayavarman's own father as well as Avalokiteshvara. The main statue has never been found, however. According to the stele, a whopping 430 gods were worshipped here!

Like Ta Prohm, Preah Khan also has trees overtaking some of its structures, but this is the much less crowded of the two. The temple is complicated to navigate, but come back to the Sri Lankan-style *chedi* in the very center if you lose your place.

▲ *Likely the only use of round columns at Angkor*

BANTEAY KDEI • ប្រាសាទបន្ទាយក្តី

No inscription has been found at Banteay Kdei. We can only assume, then, that in order to complete the triad, the temple was associated with the Buddha, and probably King Jayavarman himself.

Banteay Kdei follows a similar layout to the other two temples but on a smaller scale. Apparently, the temple had an association with Buddhist art, as hundreds of Buddha images were found buried within the complex *(see next page)*.

You can find the temple just southeast of Ta Prohm, and it's a great place to escape the crowds.

The 'Hindu Reaction'

When visiting Angkor's Buddhist temples, you'll notice that most images of the Buddha have been vandalized. At some point after Jayavarman VII's reign, the Hindu Shaivite sect regained control, with large-scale desecration happening at all Buddhist temples.

But why? For centuries, even before Jayavarman VII's reign, Buddhism was widely tolerated in Khmer society *(see p201)*. To this day, we're not sure of the exact reason, nor who the culprit really was.

Perhaps Jayavarman VII had gone too far when he had images carved of Hindu deities bowing down to the Buddha, or even emanating from Avalokiteshvara.

On a political level, it's also possible that the Brahmin priesthood felt their grip on Angkorian society weakening after the kingdom's Buddhist conversion. It's also worth noting that a major revival of Shaivism in India was happening at around this time, and there was likely ongoing communication between the two countries.

Whatever the case may be, Cambodia would eventually revert to Buddhism, albeit of the Theravada variety thanks to ties with Sri Lanka.

A Discovery at Banteay Kdei

In the 1990s, researchers from Sophia University made a fascinating discovery. They unearthed parts of 274 desecrated Buddha images that were buried near Banteay Kdei's entrance.

Where the statues were found

The burials were likely carried out by monks and not the vandals, as the fragments appear to have been carefully laid to rest.

As Banteay Kdei was chosen for the burial site over all the other temples at Angkor, it must've been strongly associated with Buddhist art in its day.

As mentioned, this temple likely represented the 'Buddha' aspect of Jayavarman's favored triad.

The mass desecration of Buddha images all over Angkor also implies that at some point, the Emerald Buddha would've had to be whisked away to safety, a topic we'll cover from pp218-27.

As for the recovered statues, they're now on display at the **Preah Norodom Sihanouk-Angkor Museum** in Siem Reap. Interestingly, the images represent a wide range of Angkorian art styles.

Exploring Further

The temples of Angkor are among the world's most spectacular ruins, and there's enough to explore for days. Here are some additional highlights of the Angkor Archaeological Park that you shouldn't miss. Our web site also contains plenty of free comprehensive articles on these architectural marvels.

The Roluos Group

The 'Roluos group' temples are situated in the early 9th-century capital of Harihalaya (13 km east of Siem Reap). The three temples are **Preah Ko**, **Lolei** and the pyramidal **Bakong**. But don't let their age fool you. These temples show an already highly refined level of art.

Bakong, the first Khmer pyramidal temple ›

Neak Pean

A satellite temple of Preah Khan, Neak Pean functioned as a 'healing temple' in Jayavarman VII's Angkor. It consists of a single *prasat* surrounded by a series of ponds, whose waters were believed to have curative properties. Don't miss the horse sculpture in the central pond, which was even mentioned by Zhou Daguan (p202). Neak Pean sits in the middle of the Jayataka Baray, beyond a long pathway.

You can visit Neak Pean together with the 'triad temples,' plus nearby Krol Ko & Ta Som

Around Angkor Thom

We've already covered the ancient walled city's main temples. But there's plenty more to explore, like the **Royal Terraces** and lesser-visited temples like **Preah Palilay** and the **Preah Pitus**. Also, be sure to stop and take a look at the 54 *deva* and *asura* statues in front of the **South Gate**, a depiction of the 'Churning of the Ocean of Milk' legend from Hindu lore (see p160).

‹ *The 'Leper King' statue*

Ta Keo

An impressive early prototype for Angkor Wat, this late 10th-century temple was ultimately left unfinished. It remains uncarved, revealing the stages in which Khmer temples were built. For similar 'temple-mountains,' check out **East Mebon** and **Pre Rup**.

Phnom Bakheng

Built around 907, Phnom Bakheng is a pyramidal temple built on top of a small mountain. The temple originally featured a multitude of *prasats* which added up to 108, a highly symbolic number in Hinduism. Today, Bakheng, located just south of Angkor Thom, is a popular gathering spot for sunsets.

The 108 prasats of Phnom Bakheng

Banteay Srei

One of the most eloquent temples in all of Angkor, Banteay Srei was built in 967 and its name means 'Citadel of Women.' This is a rare major temple to have been commissioned by a pair of Brahmin priests instead of a king. Made of high-grade sandstone of a pinkish hue, Banteay Srei has arguably the most beautiful and intricate carvings in all of Angkor.

The scenes largely focus on the Ramayana and Mahabharata epics. The central part of the temple, which contains statues of guardians and monkeys, is off-limits and can only be viewed from the periphery.

Indra riding the three-headed Airavata

Krishna and Arjuna try to burn down the Khandava forest as Indra makes it rain

The Mahabharata

The Mahabharata is the other of the two great Indian epics aside from the Ramayana (*see p153*). The main conflict of the story is between the five Pandava brothers and their cousins, the Kauravas, sons of the blind king Dhritarashtra.

The final conflict between the two sides, known as the Kurukshetra War, is foreshadowed from the very beginning. But there are plenty of subplots and unexpected twists along the way. In fact, the Mahabharata is the longest epic poem ever written!

Vishnu's avatar Krishna plays a major role in many of the epic's most important scenes. The Bhagavad Gita, the influential religious text, first appeared in the Mahabharata and is just one small part of it (length-wise, that is).

Scenes from the epic can be seen all over Angkor, some of the most beautiful being at Banteay Srei. And as mentioned, one entire section of the Angkor Wat bas-reliefs depicts the war (*see p209*).

Nowadays, the Mahabharata is not as popular as the Ramayana in countries like Cambodia, Thailand or Laos. But it's still worth reading to deepen your appreciation of Angkorian art.

The Fly and the Flood

The Khmer Empire reached its height of power while in possession of the Emerald Buddha, and the image was cherished by all. But everything would change once a king named Senaraja took the throne at Angkor.

Senaraja's son kept a fly as a pet, which he cherished and kept in a golden box. And the prince's best friend, the son of the king's head priest and advisor, kept a pet spider. But one day, when the children were playing with their creatures, the spider ate the fly. The loss of his little friend sent the prince into tears, which greatly alarmed the king.

'What happened?' the king asked his son. When the boy explained the incident, the king went into such a rage that he ordered to have his son's friend drowned in Tonle Sap lake. Saddened and disgusted by the king's behavior, Senaraja's head priest fled Angkor with his wife and other relatives.

And a king of the nagas who inhabited the lake was also incredibly upset. The serpent king caused a great storm to flood the city, killing all those who could not escape on boats, including Senaraja himself. As the heavy rains inundated Angkor, a venerable priest placed the Emerald Buddha on a junk, sailing to the North. Eventually, they arrived at an outpost village, and the statue remained there for a long time under the careful watch of local residents.

Eventually, however, the sovereign of the Kingdom of Ayutthaya began invading the Khmer Empire's frontier districts. And upon discovering the Emerald Buddha, the Siamese soldiers brought the statue back to Ayutthaya together with a great number of the village's inhabitants. Upon the image's arrival in the capital, the citizens of Ayutthaya were overjoyed, and people gathered from all over to make offerings.

Murals of the flood at Wat Phra Kaew, Chiang Rai

The Emerald Buddha Leaves Angkor

The incident involving the children, the fly and the spider is one of the most peculiar parts of the entire Chronicle. First of all, why would these children be keeping insects as pets? Surely, the son of the king could've had any exotic animal he wanted. Not only did he keep a fly as his pet, but he'd grown so attached to it that he was heartbroken at its loss.

Could the fly and the spider be a metaphor for something? Neither flies nor spiders seem to be especially significant in local Khmer folklore, nor in Hindu and Buddhist mythology. Interestingly, while most versions of the Chronicle mention insects, one version says that the pets were birds.

Naga serpents, on the other hand, have long played major roles in a wide variety of myths and legends. The Khmer people's own origin story, in fact, states that they're descendants of a princess who married a *naga*.

Floods were most definitely a common catastrophe in tropical Angkor. And taking local beliefs and superstitions into account, citizens would've likely seen such disasters as omens from the gods in response to the king's behavior. As mentioned on p206, the Khmer king even had to make love with a *naga* serpent on top of Phimeanakas every night, or else disaster was bound to strike the kingdom. Could this legend somehow be related to the story in the Chronicle?

But the story could also be an allegory for the Hindu iconoclastic period which followed Jayavarman VII's reign *(see p215)*.

And the fly devouring the spider might be a metaphor for Buddhism overtaking Hinduism and weakening the priesthood. Perhaps Senaraja's angry reaction represents the desecration of Buddhist art throughout Angkor. (No such king named Senaraja, by the way, exists in Khmer records.)

In the Chronicle, monks take the Emerald Buddha to safety after a major flood. But we also know that Buddha images all over Angkor were in danger at one point. Flood or no flood, the Emerald Buddha would've had to be taken into hiding during the destructive iconoclasm.

Experts generally agree that this destruction, while widespread, took place over a pretty brief period of time. The vandals, for example, missed plenty of Buddha carvings that were just slightly obscured by shadow, suggesting a rushed effort. Might they have been interrupted by heavy rains?

Whatever really happened, the Emerald Buddha was whisked away somewhere 'to the North,' according to the Chronicle. And it stayed at this undisclosed location for quite awhile.

Eventually, though, it was captured by the emerging Ayutthaya Kingdom, which did not even officially form until 1351.

While we don't know for sure when the iconoclasm took place, Jayavarman VII died in 1218. The Emerald Buddha, then, may have resided outside of Angkor, but within Khmer territory, for up to 130 years. But where? We'll go over some potential candidates from pp220-27.

BANTEAY CHHMAR • បន្ទាយឆ្មារ

Banteay Chhmar, some 170 km northwest of Angkor, was built by Jayavarman VII sometime in the late 12th century. It likely functioned as the Khmer Empire's 'second city' during his reign. While mostly in ruin today, the massive complex is about the same size as Angkor Wat, at least in area.

📍 65 km N of Sisophon
$ 5

Unlike at Angkor, the Buddhist imagery here was never damaged by vandals. Banteay Chhmar, then, was clearly a safe haven for Buddhism during the iconoclastic chaos. Could it have also hosted the Emerald Buddha at some point?

TRANSPORT: To get here from Siem Reap, take a bus or minivan to Sisophon, then a shared taxi to Banteay Chhmar ($5). Contact visitbanteaychhmar.org to arrange a homestay in town.

EXPLORING THE TEMPLE

Entering from the east, you'll encounter *deva* and *asura* sculptures like those outside of Angkor Thom. The temple's outer walls are adorned with bas-reliefs, with the eastern wall featuring battle scenes like those of the Bayon *(see p211)*. The western wall, meanwhile, is decorated with unique carvings of a multi-armed Avalokiteshvara (pictured below).

Exploring the disarrayed interior requires walking on top of massive piles of sandstone blocks, so proceed with caution. Banteay Chhmar, like many of Jayavarman VII's temples, utilized a complex and cluttered design. There were once over 40 face towers here, but only a few remain. Interestingly, the three *prasats* in the center reintroduced the *trimurti* layout *(see p203)* that was popular in the 9th and 10th centuries.

During your time in the area, also be sure to visit the impressive satellite temples of **Ta Prohm**, **Banteay Torp** and **Ta Nem**.

Preah Ko Preah Keo

According to the Chronicle, the Khmers possessed the Emerald Buddha for hundreds of years. But without any concrete evidence, some scholars suggest that it was all made up in order to boost the image's prestige. Be that as it may, a large number of Cambodians today are adamant that the Emerald Buddha resided in their country before being 'stolen' by the Siamese.

This brings us to a popular folktale called 'Preah Ko Preah Keo.' Passed down orally for generations, its true origins are unknown. Regardless, it's one of Cambodia's most beloved stories and has even been adapted to film.

The story begins when a village woman, pregnant with twins, is warned by an astrologer to avoid eating mangos. Unable to resist the temptation, she falls from a mango tree and dies. And out of her body emerge not just a regular baby, but also a calf. And not just any calf, but one with magical abilities. The calf, named Preah Ko, can manifest anything it desires from its belly. Later, after the passing of their father, the boys survive in the wild thanks to Preah Ko's abilities.

Eventually, Preah Keo (the boy) falls in love with the king's daughter. The king, upon finding out, has her beheaded for her actions, but she later gets revived by Indra. The princess, Neang Pov, then catches up with the brothers again and Preah Ko manifests an opulent palace for them to live in.

Meanwhile, the king of Siam, unbeaten in cockfighting, challenges the king of Cambodia to a battle. The Siamese king wins but agrees to a rematch. As the Cambodian king's minister searches for a new cock for the fight, he encounters Neang Pov, who offers assistance. Preah Ko then transforms himself into a cock and wins the fight.

A similar scenario repeats itself with elephants. Distraught by his defeat, the king of Siam consults with an astrologer who tells him of Preah Ko and his true nature. He also tells the king how to beat the magical bull: by building a mechanical bull of his own.

When the king of Siam goes and requests a bullfight, Preah Ko knows that it's all over. He fights anyway but escapes death at the last minute. Preah Ko, Preah Keo and Neang Pov run through the forest, but the princess loses her grip on the bull's tail and dies.

The brothers then hide in a bamboo forest outside of Lovek. The area is impoverished, and the king of Siam shoots silver coins into the region, knowing that the villagers will cut down the bamboo to find the coins. The brothers then get captured and brought to Siam. Locked inside of a palace, they long to return to Cambodia to this day.

But what does it all mean? The story is probably meant to help Cambodians cope with the downfall of their empire, as well as the looting of precious relics by the Siamese over several centuries. Preah Ko likely symbolizes Nandin the bull, and in a broader sense, the knowledge, texts and religious teachings of the Khmer Empire at the height of its prosperity.

And Preah Keo? Some scholars think that he's meant to symbolize a historical prince who was captured by Siam. But others, such as Kimly Ngoun, who wrote a thesis on the topic, suggest that this character represents a precious image or gemstone. In particular, the Emerald Buddha itself!

Nandin, the animal mount of Shiva

The Emerald Buddha In Isaan?

As mentioned on p219, the Emerald Buddha was taken out of Angkor at some point, though it remained elsewhere within Khmer territory for a time.

But where? We already covered one possibility on p220: Banteay Chhmar, Cambodia. But the Khmer Empire's reach at the time extended far into what now makes up Thailand. Therefore, if the Emerald Buddha was not taken to Banteay Chhmar, it likely ended up in the Northeast Thailand region known as Isaan.

According to the Chronicle of the Emerald Buddha, the statue would eventually be captured by the Ayutthaya Kingdom in the 14th century. And had it already been in Isaan at the time of Ayutthaya's founding, the Siamese wouldn't have had to go very far to find it. We'll be covering this topic more in-depth in the following chapter.

While the Emerald Buddha could've ended up anywhere in Isaan, let's look at a few likely candidates: Sakon Nakhon and Phimai.

Touring Isaan

Economically speaking, Isaan is one of the least developed areas of Thailand. And it's also among the least visited by foreign tourists. But those who make the visit often consider it Thailand's best-kept secret.

You'll encounter friendly and hospitable locals, delicious food, amazing scenery and well-preserved historic sites.

Overall, the Isaan region is huge, consisting of 20 provinces. Fortunately, some cities have airports while multiple provinces are linked by rail. Furthermore, Isaan is well-connected to Bangkok by bus.

> *i*
>
> *We briefly covered northern Isaan on p121. Isaan is easily accessible from Vientiane but can also be reached from major Thai cities.*

The Emerald Buddha in Sakhon Nakhon?

The old stone Khmer prasat of Phra That Narai Cheng Weng

In his book The Emerald Buddha: Its Mysteries and Chronicles, *Corrie Lamprecht writes that the Emerald Buddha was taken to the area that's now Sakhon Nakhon Province in Thailand's Isaan region. He writes that there, 'a temple, Phra That Phu Pek, was built to house the Emerald Buddha.' As Sakon Nakhon is exactly north of Angkor, could this be the 'North' referred to in the Chronicle?*

Unfortunately, no sources or references are listed in Lamprecht's book, while Sakon Nakhon is only mentioned a single time. Interested in where he got the information, I looked up the author's contact info to ask him. Sadly, I learned that he had just passed away.

I continued searching tirelessly for a possible connection between Sakon Nakhon and the Emerald Buddha, but ultimately came up with nothing. But the more research I did on Sakon Nakhon, the more the place intrigued me. And so, I bought a plane ticket to see what, if anything, I could find.

Visiting Sakhon Nakhon

Sakon Nakhon is a fascinating mix of Khmer, Lao and Thai cultures. As with much of the Isaan region, the Khmers controlled the area for hundreds of years. They left behind a handful of stone temples and even a trademark Angkorian *baray*, around which you can now find a peaceful public park.

Following the birth of Lan Chang in 1349, King Fa Ngum conquered everything between Vientiane and Roi Et, and Sakon Nakhon was part of Laos for a few hundred years *(see p82)*. And then later, the Siamese took over. Interestingly, to this day, many locals still identify as 'Lao' despite being Thai citizens.

In the town center, Phra That Choeng Chum has a Lao-style chedi (or that, see p116) built over an ancient Khmer prasat ▶

Wat Tham Phae Dan's carvings ▶

Though few tourists have ever heard of it, Sakon Nakhon has lots to do. In addition to ancient temples, the city has clean, spacious parks, beautiful scenery, friendly people and delicious food. The region is also famous for its indigo products, which are available all over town.

Visitors should plan for at least two full days here. Hotels can be booked online, but be prepared to rely on translation apps once you're there.

TRANSPORT: There are direct flights between Sakon Nakhon and Bangkok. Or, fly to Udon Thani first and take a 2.5-hour bus ride.

For outlying temples, it's best to arrange private transport at your hotel.

PHRA THAT PHU PEK · พระธาตุภูเพ็ก

Phra That Phu Pek is a rather unique Khmer temple for a number of reasons. The Khmers only built a handful of mountaintop temples in their empire, and this would've been the northernmost of them. At around 520 m above sea level, the temple requires a trek up nearly 500 steps to reach. But the climb is worth it, as visitors are greeted with stunning views of the lush green countryside.

Made of sandstone, the temple appears to have been left unfinished. The original plan was likely a basic layout of a single *prasa*t with a *gopura* attached to the front, all atop a raised platform *(see p203)*. The *gopura*, however, is missing, and the *prasat* doesn't even have a roof. While there isn't much leftover rubble, the original temple having collapsed long ago is not out of the question.

Local experts believe that the temple functioned as an astronomical calendar, built in alignment with both the solstices and equinoxes.

Phra That Phu Pek is also at the heart of a local legend, which tells of a competition held by men and women to see who could build the better temple. The deadline was the appearance of Venus in the morning sky, but the women used a lantern in a tree to trick the men, who stopped building upon seeing it. Their temple was named Phra That Phu Pek ('Venus Mountain Temple'). The women's temple, meanwhile, is supposedly Phra That Narai Cheng Weng (*pictured opposite*). A nearly identical story appears numerous times throughout the region, however, and it shouldn't be taken too seriously.

Estimates of the temple's construction date range from the mid-11th to the late 12th centuries, leaving a potential connection with the Emerald Buddha's story in the realm of possibility.

But it's difficult to imagine the Emerald Buddha being housed in such a barebones temple. Unless, of course, it needed to be built in haste.

Emerald Buddha connection or not, Phra That Phu Pek makes for a fun and rewarding visit. In addition to the views, you'll get to share the mountaintop with a large community of peacocks. And through a trail in the forest, you can also find an ancient stone quarry.

The Emerald Buddha at Phimai?

Prasat Hin Phimai • ปราสาทหินพิมาย

As for temples where the Emerald Buddha may have been taken after Angkor, Phimai is another potential candidate. Also known as Prasat Hin Phimai, the temple is situated in Isaan's Nakhon Ratchasima Province.

During Jayavarman VII's reign, he built a long road connecting it directly with Angkor Thom. Clearly, Phimai was a highly significant temple around the 12th century. And it also would've been a safe refuge for endangered relics.

But the temple is actually much older. It's often attributed to Jayavarman VI (r.1080-1107), but it might've been established even earlier by Suryavarman I (r.1002-1050).

As we went over on p201, the Khmer Empire was largely Hindu up until Jayavarman VII took the throne in 1181. While tolerated, the few Buddhist temples that existed at Angkor were small and relatively insignificant. Phimai, on the other hand, was not only a large and elaborate Buddhist temple, but it even had a city surrounding it. The area had long been inhabited by ethnic Mons who practiced both the Vajrayana (Tantric) and Theravada forms of Buddhism. Phimai is also one of the few Khmer temples adorned with Tantric symbols.

While it's certainly possible that the Emerald Buddha was taken to Phimai during Angkor's iconoclastic period (see p215), could it have also stopped here before?

Phimai wasn't on the trade route through which goods typically traveled to Angkor from the Malay Peninsula (see p182). The statue, though, may have been transported here following its arrival in the Chao Phraya River valley. Phimai, was, after all, the empire's only major Buddhist temple in the 11th century.

What's more is that some scholars believe that Jayavarman VI ruled the Khmer Empire out of Phimai, possibly while an unknown (to us) rival was in power at Angkor. We don't know exactly when the Emerald Buddha would've made its journey from (presumably) Nakhon Si Thammarat.

Vajrasattva, a Tantric symbol

But if it happened in the 1080s, Phimai would've been the de facto Khmer capital.

If the Emerald Buddha did stay at Phimai from the 11th century, it may have even remained there for quite awhile - possibly until Jayavarman VII took the throne in 1181. After all, the Champa Kingdom invaded and sacked Angkor in 1177, but they never got the Emerald Buddha. Perhaps Jayavarman VII later brought the jade image to Angkor after completing a major temple, such as the Bayon or Banteay Kdei.

Interestingly, at Phimai, there's a lintel carving depicting the Buddha statue that sits there now. The scene shows the *naga prok* image being transported from Angkor during the reign of Jayavarman VII (who also redesigned and expanded the temple). But the temple had already been a major Buddhist center for nearly a century. Surely, the central *prasat* would not have been empty that entire time. So what image was sitting there before?

This is all unprovable speculation, of course. But one thing we know for sure is that Phimai was one of the most elaborate and impressive temples in the whole empire, and it remains remarkably well preserved today.

VISITING PHIMAI

If you're in Thailand but unable to visit Angkor, Phimai is well worth your while. And for those who've been to Angkor and are craving more, Phimai is just what you're after.

Approaching the main entrance, visitors encounter an elaborate elevated *naga* balustrade. Structurally, Phimai is centered around three *prasats* enclosed by a concentric gallery. For some reason, though, the temple faces south and not east or west.

There's a considerable distance between the inner and outer enclosures, with a number of structures situated in between them. Some of them are what experts call 'libraries,' a common building at most Khmer temples. But their true function remains a mystery.

The current image being transported from Angkor

Phimai comprises of an interesting blend of Khmer architectural styles. Its central *prasat*, in particular, very much resembles those of Angkor Wat. Artistically, the temple is adorned with both Buddhist and Hindu imagery. And just like at Banteay Chhmar (p220), the Buddhist art has survived intact.

Visitors to the area also shouldn't miss the **Phimai National Museum** (150 baht), which houses numerous sculptures and artifacts from around the region. Also nearby the temple is **Sai Ngam**, Thailand's largest banyan tree.

- 📍 Ananthachinda Rd. Amphoe Phimai
- 🕐 7:30 - 18:00
- 📅 Daily
- ฿ 100

> **TRANSPORT:** Phimai, located in the town of the same name, can be reached by bus in 60 min from Nakhon Ratchasima. The city, also known as Khorat, is well connected to the rest of Thailand by either bus, train or plane.
>
> The province is home to **Khao Yai National Park** and the stunning **Wat Ban Rai** 'Elephant Temple.' Further east, **Phnom Rung** is another major Khmer temple in Buriram.

Central Thailand

*I*n this chapter, which places a special emphasis on archaeological ruins, we'll explore the regions commonly referred to as the North and South Central Plains. Together, they make up the central portion of modern Thailand and the heartland of historical Siam.

Our journey will take us to the former capital of Ayutthaya, which once enjoyed immense wealth and prosperity for centuries. Lopburi, meanwhile, is one of Thailand's oldest and most important cities. Farther north, Kamphaeng Phet served as a major outpost for both the Sukhothai and Ayutthaya Kingdoms. And once there, Sukhothai's splendid ruins are just a short ride away.

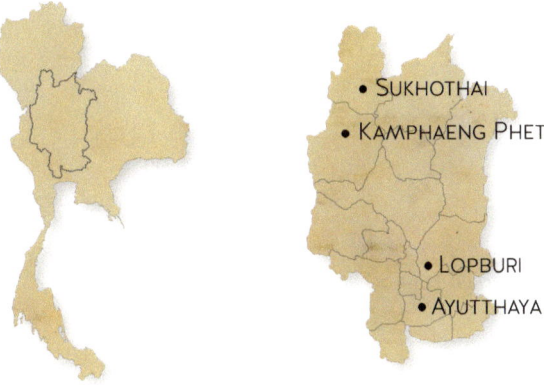

A Brief History of Siam	230
Ayutthaya	233
Lopburi	245
Kamphaeng Phet	255
Sukhothai	266

A Brief History of Siam

Over the next few sections, we'll be covering three city-states which were all once part of ancient Siam. The roots of Siam go back to the founding of Sukhothai in the 13th century. And it wasn't until 1939 that the country officially changed its name to Thailand.

Sukhothai: The Birthplace of Siam

The Sukhothai Kingdom first emerged in 1238. Before then, the area had been controlled by the Khmers. But with the death of Jayavarman VII and the gradual weakening of the Khmer Empire, the vassal state of Sukhothai seized the opportunity to rebel.

Sukhothai's first ruler was Si Inthrathit, who founded the Phra Ruang dynasty. He went on to transform Sukhothai from a city-state into an empire, conquering much of the territory throughout the upper Chao Phraya River valley. Meanwhile, he also began building his royal city centered around the temple of Wat Mahathat (see p266).

The Ram Khamhaeng Inscription

It would be Si Inthrathit's younger son, though, who would bring Sukhothai to its greatest height of power. King Ram Khamhaeng expanded the kingdom's territory as far east as Luang Prabang and as far south as Nakhon Si Thammarat. These territories were mentioned in the coveted 'Ram Khamhaeng Inscription' which is believed to be the first usage of the Thai script.

Sukhothai's annexation of Nakhon Si Thammarat, which maintained close relations with Sri Lanka, led to easier communication with the Theravada Buddhist stronghold. As Sukhothai was a Theravada kingdom, this was vital for its cultural development. But as a former Khmer territory, Brahmin priests still played a major role in civil and religious matters in accordance with ancient Khmer traditions.

The Sukhothai Kingdom established a number of nearby outpost towns like Kamphaeng Phet to the southwest and Si Satchanalai and Phitsanulok to the east. In addition to being militarily strategic, these towns built their own elaborate temples, turning into major cultural centers in their own right.

After King Ram Khamhaeng's death, Sukhothai lost much of its grip on its former territories. And over time, it reverted from a mighty empire to little more than a regional power. Eventually, in the mid-14th century, another Siamese kingdom would emerge to take its place.

The Rise of Ayutthaya

The city and kingdom of Ayutthaya were officially founded in 1351 by King U Thong (r.1351-1369), also known as Ramathibodi I. Surrounded by three different rivers on four sides, the island setting of Ayutthaya made it ideal for defense. And the Chao Phraya River also gave the kingdom access to the ocean and vital regional trading routes.

Nearby Lopburi, a longtime Khmer outpost, soon aligned itself with Siam. And U Thong quickly expanded his kingdom further east, likely capturing the Emerald Buddha in the process. We'll be covering his reign more in-depth from p234.

A Prosperous Ayutthaya

In 1431, the Ayutthaya Kingdom invaded and occupied Angkor. It also overtook Sukhothai in 1438, firmly establishing itself as the most powerful force in the region. And Ayutthaya would continue to remain dominant for hundreds of years.

The kingdom continued to expand, overtaking much of what makes up modern-day Thailand *(see map on pp24-25 for a look at the kingdom at its peak)*. And by the 17th century, the capital's population grew to over 1 million people, making it the most populous city in the world at the time.

In its heyday, Ayutthaya was also incredibly cosmopolitan. Portuguese, Dutch and Japanese settlements all formed around its outskirts. And visiting diplomats and merchants often boasted that it was among the world's most splendid and wealthy cities.

But that's not to say that Ayutthaya's time at the top was peaceful. Throughout much of the 15th and 16th centuries, the kingdom was embroiled in conflicts with Lanna to the north. The two sides regularly fought over Sukhothai's former territories. And the conflict grew so bad that the Siamese even shifted their capital up north to Phitsanulok for a couple of decades.

But no rival was as great as the Burmese. Throughout its history, Ayutthaya repelled over twenty Burmese invasions. And they were even occupied by Burma's Toungoo dynasty for a few decades in the 16th century. To this day, King Naresuan the Great is still honored for liberating Siam by defeating a Burmese prince in a legendary elephant battle. But eventually, after 417 years of prosperity, the Ayutthaya Kingdom would suffer a blow from which it could never recover.

A crown worn by Ayutthaya royalty

Ayutthaya's Fall

In 1767, the Burmese Konbaung dynasty, based out of their own island capital of Ava (or Inwa), breached Ayutthaya's defenses. They inflicted as much damage as they could, looting hundreds of temples and melting down the gold of the city's countless Buddha statues. Ayutthaya's last king, Ekkathat, even starved to death while in hiding.

After the siege of 1767, the city was considered damaged beyond repair. Instead of trying to restore what was lost, many of the remaining bricks were taken to subsequent capitals. The direct aftermath of Ayutthaya's destruction is described on p127.

From Siam to Thailand

King Taksin's Thonburi Kingdom succeeded Ayutthaya, but it only lasted for 14 years before the Rattanakosin Kingdom formed in 1782 *(see p143)*. Siam prospered throughout the 19th century. And unlike its neighbors, it managed to avoid being overtaken by European colonial powers.

In 1932, the 'Siamese Revolution' put an end to the absolute monarchy. For the first time in its history, the country became a constitutional monarchy led by a prime minister.

And it was Siam's third prime minister, Phibunsongkhram, an admirer of Mussolini, who changed the country's name to Thailand in 1939. His idea was to get the country's citizens, who belonged to various ethnic backgrounds, to start identifying themselves as a unified 'Thai' race.

Ever since, Thailand has gone back and forth between democratic and military governments near countless times. But the royal family of the Chakri dynasty, the founders of the Rattanakosin Kingdom, remains highly revered. And to this day, Thais generally regard Sukhothai and Ayutthaya as their first national capitals.

232 Central Thailand

Ayutthaya
1350s - 1380s

The Emerald Buddha In Ayutthaya

The Chronicle of the Emerald Buddha sums up the statue's arrival in Ayutthaya in just a couple of sentences. As we went over on pp218-19, the image was removed from Angkor after a great flood (or possibly during the iconoclasm that followed Jayavarman VII's death). The jade image then stayed in a Khmer outpost town for a period of time, until Ayutthaya captured it during a military campaign.

According to the story, Ayutthaya also abducted many of that town's inhabitants, which was actually quite common in those times. Rather than permanently occupy enemy lands, outside invaders typically preferred to bring back people to man the local rice fields. Furthermore, craftsmen and artisans were always in high demand. And as we'll go over shortly, the migration of people from the Khmer Empire to Ayutthaya would greatly shape Siamese architecture and culture.

One confusing part of the original Chronicle is the name given for the Ayutthaya king: Adicca. King Adicca happens to be a real historical king, but not of Ayutthaya. He was the ruler of Haripunchai during the 11th century and is credited with bringing a relic of the Buddha from the Himalayas to Lamphun *(see p61)*.

But as Haripunchai was part of Lanna by then, and the Chronicle clearly states that the king in the story ruled over Ayutthaya, we should dismiss this as an error. After all, this isn't the only time the Chronicle gets someone's name wrong!

But which king was it? Most likely, the Emerald Buddha was captured by U Thong, Ayutthaya's founder. Also known as King Ramathibodi I, U Thong's origins are mysterious. Some sources say he was a relative of the ruling family of Lopburi, while others even trace his family lineage back to King Mangrai of Lanna *(see p28)*. Meanwhile, other sources say he was the son of a Chinese merchant.

Whatever the case may be, Ramathibodi married a princess of the U Thong district in present-day Suphan Buri Province. A few years later, in 1347, he decided to move his capital roughly 80 km to the east due to a cholera epidemic (some say smallpox).

U Thong came across an 'island,' surrounded by rivers on all four sides, which he figured would be perfect for defensive purposes. He named his new city and kingdom Ayutthaya after Ayodhya, India, the hometown of Rama in the Ramayana epic *(see p153)*.

The Ayutthaya Kingdom was officially born in 1351, though U Thong had already been quite active before then. Around 1349, he even managed to get the king of Sukhothai to submit to him. Sukhothai would then long function as a vassal of Ayutthaya until 1438, when it was officially absorbed into the kingdom. Also around the time of the kingdom's founding, nearby Lopburi, a former Khmer frontier province, willingly aligned itself with Siam.

And after Ayutthaya replaced Sukhothai as the most dominant city-state in Siam, U Thong is believed to have gone after the Khmers.

Details of these early conquests,

A 14th-century image in the 'U Thong' art style

however, remain murky at best. The most widely documented of the early Siamese attacks took place in 1431, when Ayutthaya invaded and occupied Angkor. This is generally considered to mark the beginning of the end for the Khmer Empire, and its kings would start ruling out of Phnom Penh not long after.

But in regards to the Emerald Buddha story, the jade image would emerge in Chiang Rai in 1434, just a few years later *(see p33)*. Three years is not nearly enough time for it to travel up to Lanna, disappear and miraculously get discovered again. Therefore, Ayutthaya must've taken the image in an earlier attack.

As we went over in the previous sections, the statue was not in Angkor during U Thong's reign, but likely somewhere in Isaan (or possibly Banteay Chhmar). Many historians agree that U Thong led attacks on the western portion of the Khmer Empire from around 1352, just a year after the kingdom's official founding. And this date fits neatly within our timeline. While U Thong may not have gone as far as Angkor, he likely didn't need to travel a great distance to find the jade image.

The transfer of the Emerald Buddha from the Khmer Empire to Ayutthaya was likely a very real event. But it's also representative of a broader historical and cultural phenomenon: the emergence of Ayutthaya as the 'successor' to Angkor's legacy.

As seen in their culture, architecture, religion and system of government, Ayutthaya borrowed a lot from the Khmers. Furthermore, many of the early Ayutthaya nobles are believed to have been ethnic Khmers themselves. Therefore, the founding of Ayutthaya coincided with not just the migration of a relic from the Khmer Empire, but also that of people and ideas.

The Emerald Buddha, having spent time in both Sri Lanka and the Khmer Empire, was likely sought after by U Thong as a way to legitimize himself as ruler. Quite fittingly, Ayutthaya would go on to utilize not only elements of Khmer culture, but Sri Lankan culture as well.

Visiting the Ayutthaya ruins today, the influence of both countries remains clear. At many temples, Sri Lankan bell-shaped *chedis* stand alongside Khmer-influenced *prangs*. Like Sukhothai before it, Ayutthaya adopted the Theravada Buddhism of Sri Lanka while maintaining the *devaraja* (king as a god) cult of Angkor.

But while the Emerald Buddha would help legitimize the emergent Ayutthaya Kingdom, it wouldn't stay there for very long. It would end up traveling to two other Siamese city-states before its eventual emergence in Lanna.

Even if Ayutthaya's role in the Chronicle of the Emerald Buddha is rather brief, it's a must-visit destination for those with an interest in history and ancient ruins. And as mentioned earlier, the story of Ayutthaya's destruction in 1767 is directly tied to the founding of Bangkok.

As for which temple the jade image was likely kept at, Wat Phra Si Sanphet is the most probable choice. This was the royal temple of the Ayutthaya ruling elite, and it would even greatly influence the architecture of Bangkok's Wat Phra Kaew.

The architects of Ayutthaya took the Khmer prasat and made it taller and narrower ›

AYUTTHAYA TRAVEL TIPS

Ayutthaya was once among the world's most populated and cosmopolitan cities, with traders and diplomats from around Europe and Asia setting up base there. But that all came to an end in 1767 at the hands of the powerful Burmese Konbaung dynasty.

While the era of the Ayutthaya Kingdom may be long gone, the ruins of this once splendid city remain one of Thailand's most endearing travel destinations.

The highlights of the central 'island' can be seen in a single day, but at least two or three full days are recommended to discover all that Ayutthaya has to offer.

 ## GETTING THERE

Coming from Bangkok by **train** couldn't be easier. Simply head to Hua Lamphong Railway Station and buy a ticket for the next departing train. The ride lasts around 90 minutes and only costs around 15 baht! As the ride is so short, you'll be fine with the cheapest third-class ticket.

Ayutthaya's railway station is to the east of the island. Arriving at the station, you'll need to pay a small fee of five baht for a ferry to take you across the river. But if you have lots of luggage, tuk tuks can take you over the nearest bridge for around 60 baht.

Ayutthaya is also connected by **bus** with most major cities. If you happen to be staying near Mo Chit Bus Terminal in Bangkok, a bus will likely be an easier option than the train.

 ## WHERE TO STAY

Staying on the main island is ideal, as this would give you easy access to many of the town's most prominent ruins. As Ayutthaya is a popular tourist destination, you'll come across a wide range of hotels for all budgets. Staying by the train station would be another convenient option.

 ## GETTING AROUND

If you're centrally located enough, many of the main temples can be reached **on foot**. A **bicycle**, however, is probably the best option, as this would allow you to ride to some of the outlying temples as well. Bicycles can be rented for around 50 baht per day. Look out for rental shops around Naresuan Rd Soi 2.

Tuk tuks are another option, and you can generally hire one for around 200 baht per hour. Ayutthaya even has its own unique, futuristic style of tuk tuk!

The Rama Public Park area is great for cycling, but the main roads can be quite hectic

Crossing the river

THE COMBO TICKET

Most of the major temples cost 50 baht (for foreigners) to enter. Some minor temples are free, while other temples run by separate management have their own pricing systems.

Visitors have the option of buying a 220 baht combo ticket which includes the following six temples: Wat Mahathat, Wat Ratchaburana, Wat Phra Si Sanphet, Wat Chai Watthanaram and Wat Maheyong. But is it worth it?

The inclusion of Wat Maheyong is rather puzzling, as it's an obscure, hard-to-reach temple located a few kilometers east of the island. So while visiting all six temples would save you 80 baht, most people only make it to five, thus saving just 30 baht.

Whether you decide to buy the combo ticket or not, Ayutthaya's five main temples should definitely not be missed.

FOOD & MARKETS

Ayutthaya has a few local markets, such as the Chao Phrom Market near the intersection of Naresuan Rd and U Thong Rd. There's also a night market that appears outside of Wat Mahathat.

The Ayutthaya Floating Market is located to the east of the city, but many visitors feel that it's a tourist trap. With that in mind, you'd be better off visiting the floating markets of Thonburi *(see p138)*.

You can also find a plethora of restaurants along U Thong and Naresuan Rds. Wherever you go, you're bound to encounter a wide variety of traditional and delicious Thai dishes.

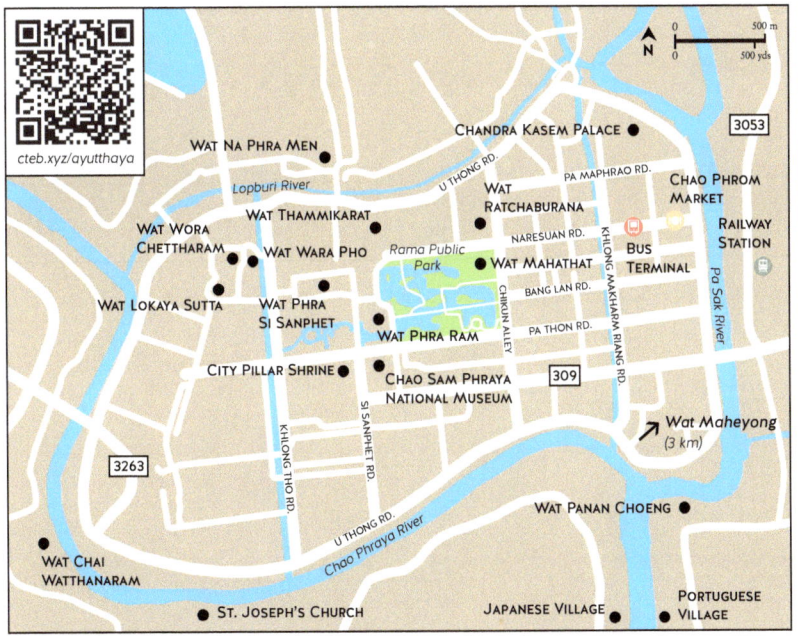

Wat Phra Si Sanphet • วัดพระศรีสรรเพชญ์

📍 Si Sanphet Rd.
🕐 8:30 - 17:00
📅 Daily
฿ 50

Wat Phra Si Sanphet functioned as the royal temple for the ruling class of Ayutthaya. Essentially, it was to the Ayutthaya Kingdom as Wat Phra Kaew is to Thailand today.

The temple dates back to the 15th century, but the site was once the location of Ayutthaya's royal palace. U Thong built his residence here, waiting until it was completed in 1351 to officially declare the establishment of the Ayutthaya Kingdom.

U Thong's royal palace featured three wooden structures. Would one of them have contained the Emerald Buddha? Notably, the Chronicle of the Phra Sihing states that the Sihing image was kept here *(see p191)* in the 14th century. And the two images would likely leave Ayutthaya together, a topic we'll cover more in-depth in a future section.

In 1448, King Borommatrailokanat constructed a new royal palace nearby. Then, on the site of the original palace, he built Wat Phra Si Sanphet. It remained the kingdom's most important temple until the Burmese sacking of 1767.

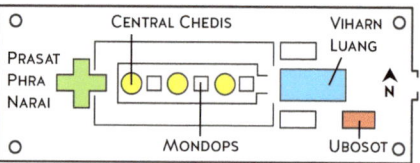

◀ A Buddha head found at the viharn

Viharn Luang

You can find the main *viharn* at the temple's eastern end. It once housed a massive golden Buddha statue called Phra Si Sanphet, after which the temple was named. But when the Burmese invaded in 1767, they looted all its gold.

While not much is left, you can still make out remnants of old columns and a Buddha image. The slit windows are also a trademark of this era. And nearby you can also find the ruins of the *ubosot*.

The Prasat Phra Narai

At the western end of the complex, on the other side of the three main *chedis*, stands the remnants of a cruciform-shaped structure. It was added in the 17th century by King Narai (after whom it was named). It likely would've looked similar to the Grand Palace's Dusit Throne Hall *(see p154)*.

The cruciform-shaped Dusit Throne Hall ▶

AYUTTHAYA

THE THREE CENTRAL CHEDIS

The highlight of Wat Phra Si Sanphet is the trio of bell-shaped *chedis* standing in the center of the complex. They originally would've been gilded with gold, just like Wat Phra Kaew's Phra Si Rattana Chedi *(see p150)*, which copies their design. The niches above each staircase would've contained standing Buddhas, while enshrined within the *chedis* were ashes of former kings.

The Phra Si Rattana Chedi of Wat Phra Kaew, Bangkok

MAKING MERIT

The Buddhist concept of merit is deeply related to the idea of *karma*. Performing certain actions to make merit can result in a better future incarnation, Buddhists believe.

The construction of *chedis* is considered an act of merit-making, which is one reason why Buddhist kings built so many of them.

But a person's actions can even help out their ancestors in the afterlife. By enshrining their predecessors' ashes in *chedis* like those at Wat Phra Si Sanphet, kings believed that their fathers would be reincarnated as one who's destined to become a future Buddha.

33 rings adorn the chedi's *spire, representing the 33 levels of heaven in Buddhist cosmology.*

At Wat Phra Si Sanphet, the colonnades around the square railing, or 'harmika,' is a first in Siamese architecture.

The entrance chambers of these particular chedis *were inspired by the gopuras that extended out of Khmer prasats (see p203).*

WAT MAHATHAT · วัดมหาธาตุ

📍 Chikun Rd.
🕐 8:30 - 17:00
📅 Daily
฿ 50

Originally established in 1374, Wat Mahathat was used for important royal ceremonies. It was also the seat of power for the Ayutthaya Kingdom's Supreme Patriarch of Buddhism.

According to ancient chronicles, numerous sacred images looted from Angkor were kept at this temple. Many of the images found in the crypt of the central *prang* are now on display at the **Chao Sam Phraya National Museum** (opposite Rajabhat University).

THE BUDDHA HEAD

Nowadays, Wat Mahathat is most known for the mysterious Buddha statue head that's permanently entangled in the roots of a tree. But how did it get there? Nobody knows for sure. But one popular theory is that thieves or looters hid it by the tree, intending to come back for it later. But they never did, and the head ultimately became one with nature.

THE PRANGS

Wat Mahathat was built in the quincunx layout of Angkor Wat *(see p203)*. The central *prang* collapsed in the 17th century and was rebuilt even larger. It managed to survive the Burmese invasion, only to collapse again in 1904. Today, nothing but the base remains. The smaller *prangs* around it, on the other hand, are still standing.

OUTER GALLERIES

The five *prangs* in the center of the temple were surrounded by outer galleries. While the roofs are no more, the galleries, including many of their original Buddha statues, can still be seen by visitors today. Many of the stone statues resemble the 12th-13th century Bayon art style of Angkor. But nobody's really sure of their true origin.

VIHARNS AND THE UBOSOT

The former *ubosot* stands to the west of the central *prangs*, while other areas of the temple feature numerous *viharns* added by various kings. Ancient Buddha images still sit in some of them - minus their gold coating, of course.

WAT RATCHABURANA • วัดราชบูรณะ ฿ 50

Wat Ratchaburana is just north of Wat Mahathat and is equally as impressive. Established in 1424, the temple was built as a memorial to the older brothers of King Borommarachathirat II.

According to legend, two princes fought with each other on elephants to determine the rightful heir to the throne. These kinds of skirmishes were fairly common, as the Ayutthaya Kingdom (along with many others in Indochina) had no clear-cut rules for succession. Tragically, both princes died in the battle, leaving their younger brother as the sole heir.

One of the most unique aspects of the temple is the central *prang's* crypt, which visitors can enter.

The frescoes inside are some of the oldest in all of Thailand, and many valuable gemstones and Buddha images were found here as well.

Reemerging from the crypt, turn around for a great view of the large *viharn*. And looking at the *prang* from below, check out the carvings of *garudas* and other guardian beings.

WAT THAMMIKARAT • วัดธรรมิกราช

📍 U Thong Rd.
฿ 20

Wat Thammikarat is not frequented by many foreign tourists, but it's one of Ayutthaya's most interesting temples, not to mention its oldest. It even predates the city's foundation, dating back to the region's time as a Khmer outpost. The lion statues around the base of the *chedi*, for example, may have been built by the Khmer Empire.

Much later, the temple is believed to have been the site of a cockfight between the roosters of a Burmese and Ayutthayan prince. The Siamese prince was victorious, and locals still bring rooster statues as offerings.

Wat Thammikarat remains a living temple, featuring a wooden *viharn* with a massive reclining Buddha image. Outside, you'll also find a bronze replica of a gigantic Buddha head that dates back to the U Thong period. The original can be seen in the local National Museum.

Exploring Further

There's still a lot more to do and see in Ayutthaya. In addition to the temples below, the city is home to the Chao Sam Phraya National Museum (150 baht) and the Chandra Kasem Palace Museum (100 baht). You can also visit the Japanese Village, the Portuguese Settlement ruins, and St. Joseph's Church.

Wat Na Phra Men
📍 *Opp. Royal Palace* ฿ *Free*

Wat Na Phra Men, located just north of the island, dates back to the early 16th century. Amazingly, it's one of the few structures in all of Ayutthaya to have survived the Burmese invasion of 1767.

As it was situated across from the royal palace, it made for a convenient base from which Burmese troops could fire their cannons. And he primary golden Buddha in the *ubosot* happens to be one of the only Ayutthaya Buddha images that wasn't looted by the Burmese.

The smaller *viharn* was added by King Rama III in the 1800s. The bronze image inside is actually around 1,500 years old, and was created by the Mon Dvaravati civilization (*see p253*). The small *viharn* is also adorned with beautiful murals of the Jataka Tales, or past lives of the Buddha.

A rare Dvaravati statue depicting the Buddha seated in a chair ▶

Northwestern Cluster
฿ *Free*

In the northwestern part of the island is a large grassy space with some interesting ruins. Entering the area, you'll first come across **Wat Wora Pho**, a small temple containing a white Buddha statue. Heading south, you'll encounter

Wat Wora Chetaram. Built in the late 1500s, you'll recognize it by its large bell-shaped *chedi*.

Next, you'll find **Wat Lokaya Suttha**, known for its giant reclining Buddha. We don't know for sure when it was built, but it likely dates back to the early Ayutthaya period. The temple was clearly once quite large, but it's been almost entirely destroyed. Remnants of the large Buddha did survive, but what we see today was mostly reconstructed in the year 1954. Nevertheless, it's sheer size is pretty awe-inspiring.

Wat Wora Chetaram

A 42 m-long reclining Buddha!

WAT PHRA RAM

📍 Si Sanphet Rd. ฿ 50

Located near Wat Phra Si Sanphet, Wat Phra Ram is recognizable from afar by its tall lone *prang*. While the *prang* was likely built in the 15th century, estimates of the temple's original construction date range from 1369-1434. According to one legend, the temple was originally built on the cremation site of Ayutthaya's founder, U Thong. The temple's name, meanwhile, was inspired by Rama, the hero of the Ramayana *(see p153)*.

WAT CHAI WATTHANARAM

📍 SW of island
🕐 8:30 - 18:00
📅 Daily
฿ 50

Built in the 1630s, this is one of Ayutthaya's most popular sunset viewing spots, though it officially closes shortly after 18:00.

The temple utilizes the popular quincunx layout of Angkor Wat *(see p203)*. But it was built on flat ground and not atop a tiered pyramid. Its style would greatly influence Thonburi's Wat Arun *(p131)*.

In the center stands the main *prang*. And the four shorter *prangs* around it symbolize the peaks of Mt. Meru, the abode of the gods.

The temple complex appears relatively well-preserved thanks to recent restoration efforts.

Located on the west bank of the Chao Phraya, it's accessible by tuk tuk or bicycle.

Lopburi
1380s

The Red Flower

After a number of years in Ayutthaya, the king of the city of Kamphaeng Phet, having heard about the miraculous Jewel Image, came to pay it homage. He begged the Ayutthaya king to let him have it, and he was permitted to take the Emerald Buddha back to his city. The inhabitants of Kamphaeng Phet, who were all of great faith, received it with much celebration.

The king of Kamphaeng Phet then had a son who was appointed governor of Lopburi. This prince could not stop thinking about the Emerald Buddha day and night. During his next visit to Kamphaeng Phet, he implored his mother to pass on his request to his father: 'Please, mother, ask my father to let me take it back,' he asked her again and again.

The prince's mother finally agreed. 'Oh, Your Majesty, your son can't take the Emerald Buddha off his mind. Can you please let him have it for just a little while?' she asked him. Eager to satisfy his first and favorite wife, he told her, 'If our son truly desires the Emerald Buddha, then I shall lend it to him. But does he even know what it looks like? Or does he only know of it through legend?'

'In the hall where the Jewel Image resides,' the king continued, 'are many other Buddha images together with it. If our son can properly identify the statue, then it's his.' The queen then went back to her son and told him to fetch the doorkeeper. 'Oh doorkeeper,' she said, 'my husband has given my son permission to take the Emerald Buddha. Regrettably, neither of us can identify it. Can you please help us?'

And the doorkeeper replied, 'Do not worry. I'll place a red flower in the hand of the Emerald Buddha, and when it comes time for your son to identify it, he'll know which one to choose.' Satisfied and relieved, the queen and her son gave the doorkeeper a great amount of gold to show their gratitude.

They later headed together to the hall where the Emerald Buddha was kept. Noticing the red flower, the prince of Lopburi was able to properly identify the statue, and he instructed his servants to carry it back home. The Emerald Buddha then stayed in Lopburi for one year and nine months before the prince returned it to his father in Kamphaeng Phet.

Previous p218

Next p268

The Emerald Buddha in Lopburi

For having spent such a short amount of time in Lopburi, the story of how the Emerald Buddha got there is certainly elaborate. It's even more detailed than what's written about the statue's entire time in Ayutthaya! According to Camille Notton, the Lopburi episode comes from the Siamese version of the manuscript, but is absent from others.

Notably, the scene bears a striking resemblance to one detailed in the Chronicle of the Phra Sihing. As described on p192, that event involves a queen (or maybe concubine) who gets asked by her son to send him the Sihing Buddha. She then bribes the doorkeeper to help her identify it.

And yet another version of this scenario occurs in the Chronicle of the Emerald Buddha itself. During the 16th-century scene where Setthathirath decides to take the statue from Chiang Mai to Luang Prabang (p87), one version of the story mentions that he needed help identifying it. But considering how it would've been in the niche of Wat Chedi Luang (p69), visible to all, it's highly unlikely that he'd need any assistance.

It's possible that these scenes in the Chronicle of the Emerald Buddha were influenced by the Chronicle of the Phra Sihing, which had been transcribed earlier. Be that as it may, the Chronicle of the Emerald Buddha is very specific about the length of time the statue spent in Lopburi: 1 year and 9 months. Therefore, while the circumstances remain mysterious, the statue could very well have been taken to the ancient city for that amount of time.

In the 14th century, both Kamphaeng Phet (the focus of our next section) and Lopburi were Siamese city-states. The transfer of the relic from one municipality to the other, then, likely occurred without any violence.

While its role in our story may be minor, Lopburi's overall historical significance is anything but. According to legend, the city, then called Lavo, was founded in the 7th century by a king from Gandhara (see p169). Mostly inhabited by ethnic Mons, Lopburi remained one of the most prominent cities of the Chao Phraya River valley for several centuries. The Haripunchai Kingdom's founder, Queen Chamathewi (see p61), also lived in Lopburi before migrating up north.

For many years, Lopburi and Haripunchai acted as the two prominent kingdoms of what we now call the Mon Dvaravati civilization. They thrived culturally and economically, spreading their art and language throughout most of present-day Thailand. The Dvaravati were largely Theravada Buddhists, though some regions also practiced Hinduism, as well as Mahayana and Vajrayana Buddhism (see p226).

Lopburi was later taken by the Khmer Empire in the 11th century. But following the death of Suryavarman II a century later, it regained independence for a time. Eventually, though, it was retaken by Jayavarman VII (see p210), who even placed his own son as governor. During their multiple occupations, the Khmers built numerous temples on top of prior Dvaravati foundations.

And a number of more recent structures were added in the Ayutthaya period. Most were built by King Narai (r.1656-1688) who preferred to spend most of the year there. Lopburi, a short train ride from Ayutthaya, remains a must-visit destination for lovers of history, temples and even monkeys!

LOPBURI TRAVEL TIPS

Lopburi is one of Thailand's oldest cities. And within the Old Town district, you'll find ruins from the Dvaravati, Khmer and Ayutthaya eras - sometimes all at a single site! Conveniently, most major landmarks can be visited in a single day on foot.

GETTING THERE

Lopburi is a three-hour **train** ride from Bangkok and just over an hour from Ayutthaya. It'd be wise to plan a stop here in between Ayutthaya and your travels further up north.

WHERE TO STAY

As mentioned, Lopburi's main attractions can be visited in a single day. But if you choose to spend the night in the city, the Old Town has several mid-range hotels to choose from, while the New Town area features a few higher-end options.

GETTING AROUND

All of the locations featured in the following section are located in Lopburi's Old Town and are easily accessible **on foot** from the railway station.

THE COMBO TICKET

Lopburi has a combo ticket for 150 baht. It includes three of the main Old Town landmarks (Wat Phra Si Rattana Mahathat, Prang Sam Yod and the Ban Wichayen House) in addition to the **Kraison Siharat Palace**, located 3.5 km out of town. Therefore, the ticket isn't of much use for those skipping the palace.

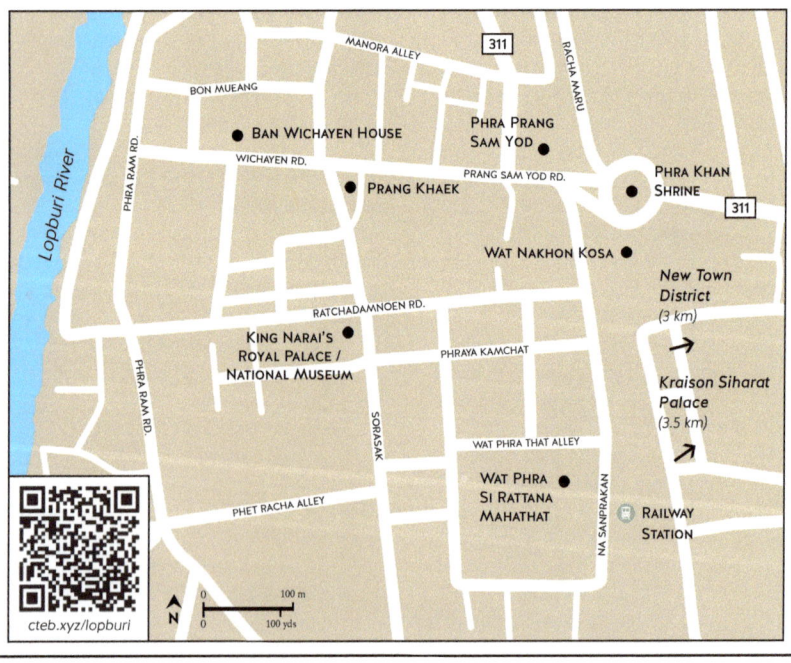

Wat Phra Si Rattana Mahathat • วัดพระศรีรัตนมหาธาตุ

Located just outside the train station, this impressive temple dates back to Lopburi's time as a Khmer outpost. It was likely built in the 12th century during the reign of the great 'builder king,' Jayavarman VII.

📍 Opp. train sta.
🕐 7:00 - 17:00
📅 Daily
฿ 50

Later, after the decline of Angkor and Lopburi's absorption into the Ayutthaya Kingdom, the temple was converted to a Theravada Buddhist *wat*. And new *viharns* were added in front. The temple was also a favorite of Narai, the 17th-century king of Ayutthaya who preferred to rule out of Lopburi. In fact, he even built his royal palace nearby *(see p253)*.

Though just speculation, this likely would've been the home of the Emerald Buddha during its brief stint in town.

The Central Prasat

The main sanctuary in the center more closely resembles a Khmer *prasat (see p203)* than an Ayutthauya-style *prang (see p20)*. Therefore, it likely dates back to the temple's founding. The *prasat* features Buddhist imagery but also a *linga* inside, mirroring the syncretic nature of Angkorian religion at the time.

The Viharn Luang

The Theravada Buddhist *viharn* was added sometime after Lopburi's absorption into the Ayutthaya Kingdom. It may have been built as late as King Narai's reign in the 1600s, or possibly shortly after the fall of Angkor. In any case, Narai is at least credited with restoring it. The structure is massive and its walls remain standing, revealing what an impressive temple this would've been in its day.

Phra Prang Sam Yod • พระปรางค์สามยอด

The 'Monkey Temple,' or Phra Prang Sam Yod, is arguably Lopburi's most popular landmark. The hordes of monkeys climbing all over the temple walls and main Buddha statue make this one of the most photogenic spots in all of Central Thailand.

As always with macaques, you'll need to keep your guard up. If given the opportunity, the monkeys will try to grab small objects and especially food. Fortunately, the monkeys are fed by the town at regular intervals, so they don't get too aggressive with tourists.

The architectural style of the Monkey Temple is clearly Khmer in origin. It implements the *trimurti* style of temple architecture, in which three *prasat*

- Wichayen Rd.
- 8:00 - 17:00
- Daily
- ฿ 50

sanctuaries stand next to one another in a row (see p203).

The layout was especially popular in 10th-century Angkor. But interestingly, Jayavarman VII brought it back into style hundreds of years later. This temple was likely built while Jayavarman's son governed Lopburi in the late 12th century.

Phra Khan Shrine • ศาลพระกาฬ

Located in the center of a roundabout, Phra Khan Shrine was built in 1951. However, it sits atop ruins which likely date back to the Dvaravati period, before the arrival of the Khmers.

Stepping inside, the central image is not a typical Buddha, but a golden Vishnu statue. Supposedly, the head was missing upon its discovery, so a Buddha head was added as a replacement. It turned out to be a pretty good fit!

It's also possible that the statue wasn't Vishnu, but none other than king Jayavarman VII, who sent numerous statues of himself as a multi-armed being to his empire's many outposts. Regardless, locals still highly revere the shrine and its statue.

Surrounding the shrine are benches, street vendors, and a community of playful monkeys.

- Opp. Prang Sam Yod
- 7:00 - 18:00
- Daily
- Free

Wat Nakhon Kosa • วัดนครโกษา

Just south of the shrine is another interesting temple called Wat Nakhon Kosa. It was first built by the Dvaravati and later added to by the Khmers. And then it was expanded yet again during the Ayutthaya Period.

The temple, in fact, is named after Kosathibodi, one of King Narai's officials who's credited with carrying out the restoration.

Today, the temple is not in the best of shape, but you can still get a good idea of its size and layout. Don't miss the standing Buddha carving that can still be clearly seen on the side of the *prang*.

Prang Khaek • ปรางค์แขก

- Wichayen Rd.
- Free
- *Right in the middle of a roundabout!* ⌄

Prang Khaek is widely regarded as one of the oldest Khmer structures in Lopburi. It's estimated to have been built in the 10th century, and just like Phra Prang Sam Yod, it features three *prangs*. In this case, they likely represent the Hindu trinity of Shiva, Vishnu and Brahma. And this would've been one of the very first instances of Khmer *prasats* in Thailand. As with many other Lopburi temples, some additional parts were later added by King Narai.

Ban Wichayen House • บ้านวิชาเยนทร์

Also known as the 'Wichayen Ambassador's House,' this large, well-preserved structure dates back to the 17th century during the reign of King Narai (1656-1688).

During Narai's rule, the Ayutthaya Kingdom had very close relationships with several foreign powers, namely the French and Persians. As mentioned earlier, Narai was the king of Ayutthaya but preferred to spend most of his time in Lopburi. Therefore, he had a large Ambassador's

House built in the center of town to house foreign envoys visiting Siam. Fittingly, the Ban Wichayen House appears more European than Thai in style.

One of the king's closest advisors, a Greek man named Constantine Phaulkon, became a permanent resident of the house. As such, it's also sometimes referred to as the 'Phaulkon Residence.'

A former merchant, Phaulkon was fluent in many languages and first became acquainted with Narai after serving as his translator. Eventually, he started working in the treasury and became so close with the king that

A young Phaulkon as depicted in William Dalton's 1862 biography, 'Phaulkon the Adventurer'

he was promoted to the position of prime counselor. Though of Greek origin, Phaulkon worked closely with the French and forged closer relations between France and Siam. But perhaps a bit *too* close, as France soon started demanding a number of concessions, such as French garrisons throughout the country.

- Wichayen Rd.
- 8:00 - 17:00
- Daily
- ฿ 50

Further controversy arose when other members of the king's cabinet suspected that Phaulkon, with the aid of French troops, was plotting to usurp the throne of Siam for himself.

Whether this was actually true, or merely jealousy (and to some degree xenophobia) on the part of the king's cabinet members remains up for debate. In any case, during a period when King Narai was sick and frail, his cousin Phetracha staged a coup to capture and execute Constantine Phaulkon. The king's appointed heir, Phra Pui, was also a victim, as it was feared that he might rule as a puppet with Phaulkon pulling the strings.

Upon Narai's death, Phetracha would be crowned as the Ayutthaya Kingdom's new ruler. He aggressively purged foreigners from the kingdom, and Ayutthaya remained relatively isolated from the West until its eventual demise in 1767.

King Narai's Royal Palace • พระนารายณ์ราชนิเวศน์

Throughout his reign, King Narai spent about 8 months of the year in Lopburi and the rest in Ayutthaya. That meant that he needed an additional royal palace.

Like his Ambassador's House, Narai's palace fused French and Thai architecture. It was finally completed in 1677 after a dozen years of construction. But as subsequent rulers shifted the seat of power back to Ayutthaya, the palace was left abandoned and unused after Narai's death.

It wasn't until the 1800s, during the reign of King Mongkut (Rama IV), that serious reconstruction efforts were carried out. Rama IV even built brand new lodgings for himself to stay in during official visits.

In addition to the palace ruins, the complex is now home to the **Somdej Phra Narai National Museum**. Inside, you can learn more about the building itself, while the museum houses various artifacts from the Dvaravati, Khmer and Ayutthaya periods. It even contains some European sculptures that once stood outside the Chapel of the Emerald Buddha.

- 📍 Ratchadamnoen Rd.
- 🕗 8:30 - 16:30
- 📅 Museum closed Mon., Tues.
- ฿ 150 (for museum)

Dvaravati Art

The term 'Dvaravati' refers to the culture prominent throughout most of Thailand before the arrival of the Khmers. Some of the major Dvaravati centers included Nakhon Pathom, Ratchaburi, Lopburi and Lamphun. While the major city-states of Lopburi and Lamphun (Haripunchai) were in contact with one another, scholars still aren't sure whether Dvaravati functioned as a unified empire or as separate but culturally similar city-states.

Most Dvaravati cities were Buddhist, and many of their early images were clearly inspired by Indian Gupta art, an influential empire that lasted from the 3rd - 6th centuries AD (see p169).

Throughout the Khmer occupation of the 11th-13th centuries, Dvaravati art styles merged with Khmer art. The term 'Lopburi style' often refers to this fusion.

Confusingly, however, many museums use the term 'Lopburi style' to refer to *any* sort of Khmer art found in Thailand - even if the piece was produced in Cambodia!

An 8th-century stele

◁ Found at Wat Phra Si Rattana Mahathat, this 13th-century image is a mix of Dvaravati and Khmer styles

See more examples of Dvaravati art on p156 and p242.

Kamphaeng Phet

1380s

The Emerald Buddha In Kamphaeng Phet

As mentioned on p246, the Emerald Buddha traveled from Ayutthaya to Kamphaeng Phet and then to Lopburi. And after less than two years there, it returned to Kamphaeng Phet yet again. According to the Chronicle, the king of Kamphaeng Phet merely asked Ayutthaya for the statue. This likely would've happened sometime in the 1380s.

An alternative telling of the story in the Chiang Mai version of the manuscript, however, says that the king of Kamphaeng Phet went with his army and took it by force.

But a third version of events can be found in the Chronicle of the Phra Sihing. That manuscript was written down while the Emerald Buddha was missing, and it doesn't mention the jade image directly. However, both the Phra Sihing and Emerald Buddha were in Ayutthaya at the same time, and both would end up in Kamphaeng Phet not long after.

As described on p192, the scene in which the Phra Sihing travels from Ayutthaya to Kamphaeng Phet is the one where King Nanatissa's mother bribes the pavilion doorkeeper. Could she have sent him *both* the Phra Sihing and Emerald Buddha? The truth probably lies somewhere in between the three variations.

Kamphaeng Phet was originally established by the Sukhothai Kingdom (*see p230*) and would eventually be controlled by Ayutthaya. But in the 1380s, Sukhothai's power was waning while the Ayutthaya Kingdom was still on the rise. Kamphaeng Phet, then, may have been semi-independent around this time, with both the Ayutthaya and Lanna kingdoms vying for control.

In its heyday, Kamphaeng Phet acted as a vital defensive outpost for both Sukhothai and Ayutthaya. The city's name translates to 'Diamond Wall' after the large walls built to defend it from Burma to the west. But as Kamphaeng Phet grew, it also gradually blossomed into an important cultural center.

Once Ayutthaya solidified control over the region, they expanded the city walls and continued building more and more grand temples. A large community of forest-dwelling monks prospered in the area, which explains why most of Kamphaeng Phet's temple ruins are situated outside the town center.

Kamphaeng Phet's most prominent royal temple, though, was located right in the heart of the city. And today, it's one of several temples throughout Indochina to be called Wat Phra Kaew, or Temple of the Emerald Buddha.

But what would eventually become of this once prosperous city? In the 1500s, the Burmese Toungoo dynasty finally broke through its 'diamond' defenses. Though Ayutthaya would later kick the Burmese out, Kamphaeng Phet was mostly left abandoned from the 16th century, with excavations not taking place until the 1800s.

And today, the town and its ruins have largely been left deserted by tourists as well. Despite its close proximity to Sukhothai and its designation as a UNESCO World Heritage Site in 1991, you'll likely find yourself roaming the archaeological park alone. But for many, the chance to enjoy these excellent ruins in relative isolation is all the more reason to visit. And among those who do make the trip, many consider Kamphaeng Phet to be one of Thailand's most underrated destinations.

KAMPHAENG PHET TRAVEL TIPS

The UNESCO World Heritage Site of Kamphaeng Phet features a plethora of well-preserved ruins amidst a picturesque setting. Dubbed the 'Diamond Wall,' Kamphaeng Phet is easily one of Thailand's most overlooked destinations.

If you're in a rush, all the main temples can be seen within a single day. But together with a visit to the National Museum and Shiva Shrine, taking things slowly over the course of two days is recommended.

While in the region, also be sure to visit the ancient Siamese capital of Sukhothai, which is just an hour's ride away *(learn more on pp266-67)*.

GETTING THERE

Located along Thailand Route 1, a major highway which connects Bangkok and Chiang Mai, Kamphaeng Phet is accessible from either city by **bus**. It takes about six hours from either place and bus tickets cost around 500 baht.

Before departure, be sure to tell the bus driver where you're headed, as relatively few people alight at Kamphaeng Phet on these cross-country journeys.

Alternatively, many people head over to Kamphaeng Phet after visiting Sukhothai, which is just about an hour away. There are regular buses in addition to blue **songthaews** which depart every hour, with tickets costing around 70 baht. Many also visit Kamphaeng Phet from Sukhothai as part of a group day tour.

The nearest **train** station to Kamphaeng Phet is Phitsanulok, which is situated along the national railway's Northern Line *(see p279)*. Buses from Phitsanulok to Kamphaeng Phet depart every couple of hours and the ride lasts around two hours.

From the Kamphaeng Phet Bus Terminal, a **motorbike taxi** can take you to your hotel for around 50 baht.

WHERE TO STAY

Kamphaeng Phet is nowhere near as visited as neighboring Sukhothai and tourism infrastructure is relatively limited. Fortunately, however, there are a few hotels catered toward foreign tourists, the most popular among them being Three J Guesthouse.

At a few hundred baht per night, the rooms are fairly standard, but they open up to a spacious courtyard with tables and benches for relaxing. You can order a Western-style breakfast before going out exploring, while a Thai restaurant with an English menu is located right across the street.

Three J Guesthouse house is located just a few kilometers southeast of the Central Zone ruins, and they offer bicycle rentals for around 50 baht per day.

If you're looking for something a little more upscale, you may want to try searching online. Just make sure that you'll be within a reasonable distance of the ruins.

Sunset over the Ping River

Kamphaeng Phet

 ## TICKETING SYSTEM

The temple ruins are all situated within the Kamphaeng Phet Historical Zone, which itself is divided into two zones. The **Central Zone** ruins are right in the middle of the city, while the **Forest Zone** ruins (also called Ariyabot) lie about 1 km north of the center.

You can buy a combined entry ticket to visit both zones for 150 baht. Unfortunately, this ticket is only valid for the day of purchase. Therefore, if you want to visit each zone on separate days, you'll need to purchase two individual tickets for 100 baht.

 ## GETTING AROUND

Getting around Kamphaeng Phet is best done by **bicycle**, which can be rented from your hotel (recommended) or at the Central Zone ticket gate.

The Central Zone ruins are walkable from most places in town. Some people also walk to and around the Forest Zone, though cycling is ideal. When exploring the area, be on the lookout for territorial dogs who inhabit the forest.

Those traveling independently to Kamphaeng Phet as a day trip can hire a taxi to the Central Zone and then rent a bike from there. Note that you may be asked to hand over your passport. Alternatively, you could also try hiring a private driver for the day.

Pp260-61 cover the Central Zone ruins, while pp262-63 cover temples of the Forest Zone

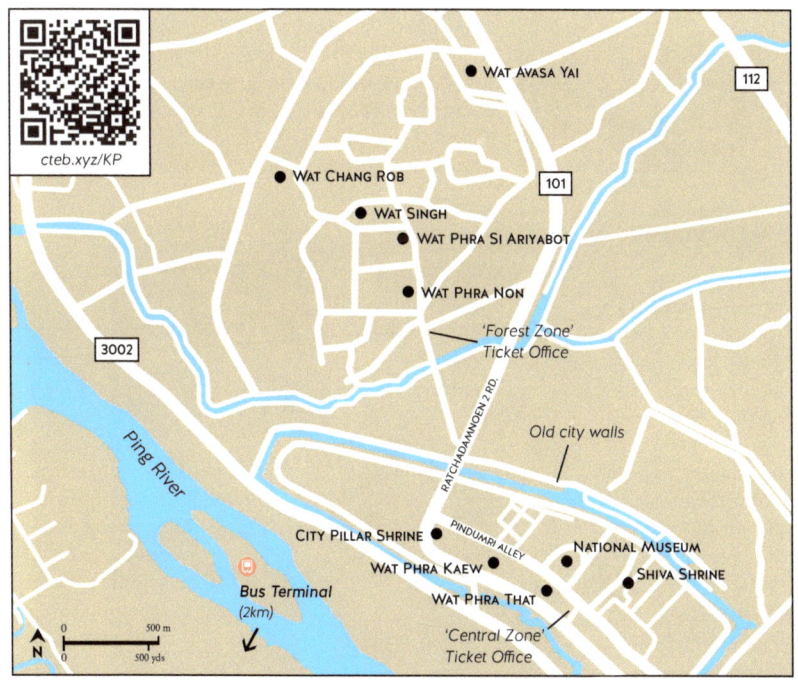

Wat Phra Kaew · วัดพระแก้ว

> The Emerald Buddha was here

While Wat Phra Kaew was undoubtedly the most prominent temple of ancient Kamphaeng Phet, its exact construction date remains a mystery. Located in the very center of town, access to Wat Phra Kaew would've been restricted to local royalty, much like Ayutthaya's Wat Phra Si Sanphet *(see p238)*.

The *wat's* current name translates to Temple of the Emerald Buddha, but it was given retroactively by Prince Mongkut (future King Rama IV) in the 1800s. While traveling the country as a monk, he came across Kamphaeng Phet, still unexcavated at the time. After discovering the central temple, he decided that it must be the same one referred to in the Chronicle, and thus gave it its current name.

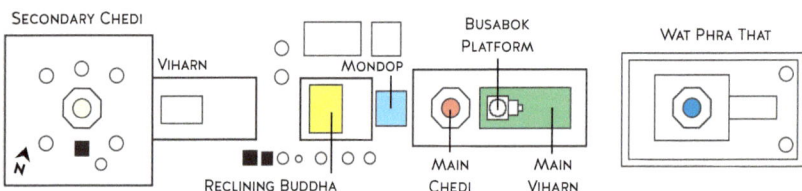

Wat Phra That

Entering the compound from the east, you'll first pass by Wat Phra That, known for its massive Sri Lankan-style *chedi*. While little else remains intact today, the temple originally had a long rectangular *viharn* in addition to two smaller *chedis* at its eastern end. And all that was surrounded by a gallery housing Buddha statues and other artwork.

The Main Viharn

Wat Phra Kaew's main *viharn* was situated at its eastern end, just west of Wat Phra That. Though the wooden structure is long gone, the raised brick platform on which it stood is still clearly visible. In its center is a seated Buddha image made of laterite. It remains surprisingly well-preserved, though it's clearly seen better days.

At the western end of the platform is a jagged-edged structure with a small staircase leading to 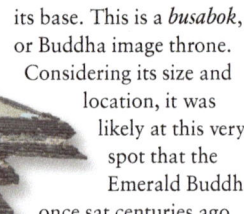 its base. This is a *busabok*, or Buddha image throne. Considering its size and location, it was likely at this very spot that the Emerald Buddha once sat centuries ago.

The Main Chedi

Just west of the *viharn* is the temple's bell-shaped main *chedi*. Built in the Sri Lankan style, it remains in good shape today. Look out for the small Buddha images remaining in some of its 16 niches. The base originally featured 32 lion and elephant sculptures, though many are now missing.

Reclining Buddha

Past the *chedi*, you'll find the base of a small *mondop* containing another weathered statue. And beyond that is a massive reclining Buddha in front of two large seated ones. These huge Buddhas were constructed with brick and then covered in stucco.

Looking closely, you can even see remnants of gold leaf on the reclining Buddha's face. Regarding the statues' style, there's still debate over whether they're representative of Sukhothai or Ayutthaya-style sculpture. But they may be a mix of both.

Subsidiary Chedis

Further west, you'll find the base of another large *chedi*, now collapsed. Many of the elephant sculptures surrounding it, however, remain in good condition. You'll also see many more laterite Buddhas at the bases of other smaller *chedis*. And there were likely a number of smaller wooden *viharns* and *mondops* in this western portion as well.

Elephant motifs were common at both Sukhothai and Kamphaeng Phet temples ›

Wat Phra Non • วัดพระนอน

Located near the Forest Zone entrance, this 15th-century temple once contained a huge reclining Buddha image. While it hasn't survived, we can imagine something similar to the one in Wat Phra Kaew. The *viharn's* twelve gigantic laterite pillars, on the other hand, are still standing tall. Each one is estimated to weigh as much as 30 tons!

Walking past the *viharn*, you'll come across a large *chedi* and the remnants of a brick seated Buddha image, along with the bases of other former structures. Clearly, Wat Phra Non was quite an elaborate temple back in its day.

Wat Singh • วัดสิงห์

Visitors to Wat Singh will first encounter the elevated laterite base of what was once its *viharn*. Supposedly, it used to be surrounded by lion statues, but none are evident today. And at one point, the *viharn* structure was converted into an *ubosot*, or ordination hall for monks.

The highlight of this temple as we see it today is its large seated Buddha image. It's mostly survived intact except for one broken arm.

Further along, you can also find another seated Buddha statue inside of the temple's main *chedi*.

Wat Phra Si Ariyabot • วัดพระสีอิริยาบถ

The head of a Buddha image found at the temple

Wat Phra Si Ariyabot is famous for its well-preserved 9 meter-high standing Buddha statue, originally contained within a huge *mondop*. Walking around the platform, you'll see outlines of other Buddha poses, such as sitting, reclining and walking. The name of this temple, in fact, translates to the 'Four Postures of the Buddha.'

WAT AVASA YAI • วัดอาวาสใหญ่

Located at the far northern end of the Forest Zone is the expansive Wat Avasa Yai temple complex. The temple was centered around a large *viharn*, with two L-shaped platforms situated in front and around its sides. Behind the *viharn* was a large *chedi*, the base of which can still be seen. A series of smaller *chedis*, meanwhile, once adorned the top of the platforms.

Wat Avasa Yai is one of the more exciting temples to explore in the area, as the platforms and numerous other structures are climbable. The temple even once contained a large pond, which has clearly been empty for some time.

WAT CHANG ROB • วัดช้างรอบ

Wat Chang Rob is arguably the Forest Zone's top highlight. This 15th-century temple was named after the dozens of elephants surrounding its massive *chedi* in a style that was influenced by Sri Lanka. The base spans 31 by 31 meters. And while its top no longer exists, the huge platform is sturdy enough to be climbed.

Though influenced by Sri Lanka, elephant-encircled *chedis* were also very popular in neighboring Sukhothai. But visiting Sukhothai today *(see p266)*, you'll find that most of its elephant motifs have been recently refurbished and don't quite fit in with their surroundings. Temples like Wat Chang Rob, on the other hand, allow visitors to see the animals how they were first discovered by archaeologists.

‹ *Singha lions, like this one on display at the National Museum, were found here as well*

Around Town

There's still more to see in central Kamphaeng Phet. Aside from the National Museum, all the locations mentioned below are free. Kamphaeng Phet Province is also home to the Khlong Wang Chao and Khlong Lan national parks, both known for their waterfalls.

Shiva Shrine (San Phra Isuan) ▶

Southeast of the National Museum, on a small street off of Pindumri Alley, is a tall bronze statue of Shiva. Interestingly, it was installed in 1510, when Kamphaeng Phet was a vassal of Ayutthaya. This was in spite of Theravada Buddhism being the dominant religion. And even now, the small shrine remains ever-popular with locals.

An old inscription reads that it was built to protect all two-legged and four-legged creatures in town. Therefore, many come to pray for the health of their furry friends.

In the 1800s, the head and arms of the statue were stolen by a German visitor but were eventually found and reattached.

The statue at the shrine today is actually a more recent replica, while the original can be found inside the National Museum.

Kamphaeng Phet National Museum

Located just next to Wat Phra Kaew, this museum contains ancient artifacts discovered all over the city. There are also informative English exhibits on the cultural influence left by both the Dvaravati and the Khmer Empire. Entry costs **100 baht**. And just next door is the **Thai House Museum**, which requires a separate entry fee.

The City Pillar Shrine

To the west of Wat Phra Kaew is the local city pillar shrine. In fact, there are two of them – the new one, installed in 2007, and the original, which dates back 700 years to the Sukhothai era. In Thailand and neighboring countries, city pillars are venerated as protectors of a municipality and its inhabitants *(see p17)*.

The Old City Walls & Moat

While cycling around Kamphaeng Phet, you'll encounter numerous sections of the city's original walls. As mentioned earlier, Kamphaeng Phet was built as a defensive outpost, with its name even translating to 'Diamond Wall.' Eventually, though, the walls could not withstand repeated Burmese attacks.

Exploring Sukhothai

Located just an hour from Kamphaeng Phet, Sukhothai is one of Thailand's most historically significant cities. The first kingdom of Siam, Sukhothai was founded in 1238 after gaining independence from the Khmer Empire.

But it was eventually overtaken by the Ayutthaya Kingdom. As such, the city contains a plethora of 13th-century ruins in addition to later Ayutthaya-style temples.

The Sukhothai ruins are divided into five different zones. The **Central Zone**, comprised of the original Royal City, and the **North Zone** are the most essential. The two can be explored in the same day by bicycle. Officially, each zone costs 100 baht to enter, though the lesser-visited zones are sometimes unstaffed. There are also many interesting free temples in between the zones as well.

Wat Mahathat

Situated in the heart of the walled Royal City, Wat Mahathat was the Sukhothai Kingdom's most important temple.

The central *chedi* was built in a traditional Sukhothai lotus-bud shape by the kingdom's very first ruler, Si Inthrathit. Successive kings continued to contribute to the temple, bringing the total number of *chedis* to around 200 by the time of Sukhothai's abandonment! The temple complex is so large that it feels like its own city within a city.

The temple also features other structures inspired by Haripunchai, Khmer and Lanna architecture.

It's here that King Mongkut discovered the Ram Khamhaeng inscription *(see p230)*. And this also likely would've been home to the Phra Sihing after King Ram Khamhaeng had it delivered from Nakhon Si Thammarat *(see p190)*.

Sukhothai Art & Architecture

Sukhothai artists developed the walking Buddha image, which is meant to symbolize the Buddha walking among his people. And the Buddha's raised hand represents the *abhaya mudra* posture, or dispelling of fear *(see p19)*.

Meanwhile, the lotus-bud shaped *chedi* was an integral part of Sukhothai architecture. Known for their tall and narrow shape with a spire at the top, these *chedis* did not remain popular for long. But some can also be seen in the neighboring ruins of Si Satchanalai, a former Sukhothai Kingdom outpost.

Wat Sa Si

Located on a small island within an artificial lake, Wat Sa Si is one of the Central Zone's most picturesque temples. You'll find the ruins of a *viharn* in front of a large Sinhalese-style *chedi*, originally built to enshrine the ashes of a former king.

Wat Si Sawai

Before Sukhothai became an independent kingdom, this temple was built by the Khmer Empire, likely in the late 12th century. The central *prasat* (see p203) is dedicated to Shiva, the temple's main deity. And the other two represent the other gods of the Hindu trinity, Brahma and Vishnu (see p16).

Wat Phra Pai Luang

Located on an island in the North Zone, Wat Phra Pai Luang was built by the Khmers as a Vishnu temple but was later converted to a Theravada Buddhist one.

Of the three original *prasats*, only one remains. Behind it is the large base of the former *viharn*, also mostly in ruin. But despite its dilapidated state, this still remains one of Sukhothai's most impressive temples.

Wat Si Chum

Inside this North Zone temple's *mondop* is a gigantic 15 m-high Buddha image known as Phra Si Achana. In the late 16th century, when Sukhothai was the site of fighting between Burma and Ayutthaya, King Naresuan once ordered a soldier to give a speech from atop the image. The acoustics of the *mondop* (which then had a roof) were so good that many of the soldiers were convinced the statue itself was speaking!

The massive brick and stucco image was restored in the 1950s

The Emerald Buddha Vanishes

Over in the Lanna Kingdom, the prince of Chiang Rai, Maha Proma, heard of the wondrous nature of the Emerald Buddha and the Phra Sihing images. Both were being kept in Kamphaeng Phet, and the prince greatly desired to take them back to his city.

Maha Proma was the younger brother of the Lanna sovereign, King Kue Na. With his brother's blessing, he marched down to Kamphaeng Phet with a huge army of 80,000 men. He seized both statues and brought them back to Chiang Rai. These events transpired just as described in the Chronicle of the Phra Sihing.

Later, after his older brother's death, Maha Proma was unsuccessful at taking the Lanna throne from his young nephew, Saen Muang Ma. He was forced to retreat, and following the altercation, King Saen Muang Ma went on to invade Chiang Rai in a counterattack.

The young king seized the Phra Sihing image, bringing it back to the capital and installing it at Wat Phra Singh. But he did not return with the Emerald Buddha.

Why not? Because during the fighting, the Jewel Image had been disguised by the local people. They smeared the Emerald Buddha with lime plaster, concealing its identity. And it was kept among many other relics at the temple known as Wat Pa Yeah.

For a long time, there was no way of knowing that such a unique and beautiful image was hidden beneath the stucco. However, strange dangers came to those who tried to touch it, and nobody could say why.

Eventually, the image was secretly enshrined within the temple's chedi where it would stay for over fifty years. And over the next several decades, the Emerald Buddha's whereabouts would remain a complete mystery, even to the local monks.

That is until a chance event occurred that would change the fate of the region forever.

Previous
p246

Next
p32

From Kamphaeng Phet to Chiang Rai

As we know, the Emerald Buddha was discovered in the *chedi* of Wat Pa Yeah, Chiang Rai in 1434 *(see p32)*. But how did it get there?

The Jinakalamali version of the Chronicle says that the statue traveled from Kamphaeng Phet to Chiang Rai together with the Phra Sihing. The text even tells readers to check the Chronicle of the Phra Sihing for the full version of the story! If you missed it, be sure to read the summary on pp190-93.

The two statues were likely brought to Chiang Rai sometime in the 1380s after Prince Maha Proma marched to Kamphaeng Phet with 80,000 men.

Later, after the death of his older brother, King Kue Na, Maha Proma would attempt to usurp the Lanna throne from his young nephew, Saen Muang Ma. He failed, however, and in a counterattack, Saen Muang Ma captured the Phra Sihing and brought it to the Lanna capital. But not the Emerald Buddha.

At some point, either local residents or Maha Proma himself covered the image in stucco and placed it inside the *chedi*, keeping it safe amidst the chaos. And it wouldn't be discovered again until a chance lightning strike destroyed the *chedi* around five decades later.

Curiously, the Chronicle of the Emerald Buddha references the Phra Sihing, yet the Chronicle of the Phra Sihing never mentions the Emerald Buddha. This is likely because that manuscript was transcribed in 1417, when the Emerald Buddha had already been missing for around thirty years.

Yet, as we'll go over from pp170-3, some believe that the Emerald Buddha never even existed at all prior to the 15th century, and that the first half of the Chronicle is pure fiction. In fact, the veracity of the Chronicle and the true history of the Emerald Buddha remain controversial and hotly contested topics to this day.

A mural at Chiang Rai's Wat Phra Singh shows Maha Proma taking the Phra Sihing image from Kamphaeng Phet to Chiang Rai.

According to the Chronicle of the Emerald Buddha, the prince returned with the 'Jewel Image' as well. ▸

Other Possible Locations

Throughout this book, we've covered over a dozen locations that the Emerald Buddha has traveled to. But was that everything? Not quite.

Taxila, Pakistan

As mentioned on p170, the Chiang Mai version of the manuscript says that from Pataliputra, India, the statue first traveled to Taxila, Gandhara (now Pakistan). And from there it was taken to Sri Lanka. It then went back again to Pataliputra and back to Sri Lanka for a second time.

Tak Province, Thailand

According to the Chronicle of the Phra Sihing, Nanatissa of Kamphaeng Phet arranged for the handoff of that image to be carried out in Tak (see p192). If the Emerald Buddha was handed over together with the Phra Sihing, then, of course, it would've traveled there as well.

Pang, Mae Hong Son Province

The Emerald Buddha story also appears in an ancient manuscript called the 'Chronicle of Phra Dhatu Chomtong.' According to that text, after a great war (not flood) ensued at Angkor, a lone priest took the image to safety. He first traveled to Ayutthaya and then to Pang in Mae Hong Son Province.

Later, when Maha Proma brought the Phra Sihing to Chiang Rai, the same priest also discreetly brought the Emerald Buddha there without telling anyone. This priest covered the image in stucco and even constructed a new monastery to hide it in.

Phayao Province

Continuing the same 'Phra Dhatu Chomtong' version of events, the Emerald Buddha was brought to Phayao upon its discovery in Chiang Rai. And from there it was later brought to Lampang and then Chiang Mai.

Phetchabun Province

After the Emerald Buddha's installment at Wat Phra Kaew in Bangkok, did it ever leave at any point? According to one theory, it may have. During World War II, Thailand was ruled by Prime Minister Phibunsongkhram, better known as Phibun. And in those uncertain times, Phibun concocted an elaborate plan to move the Thai capital out of Bangkok. As Bangkok was being bombed by Allied forces, he hoped to build a brand new city in the jungles of Phetchabun Province in the country's center.

The plan, of course, would never come to fruition. According to an article in the *Borneo Post*, however, the government went ahead with moving valuables and riches to hide in Phetchabun's caves. The article even mentions that around 1943, the Emerald Buddha was taken to Phetchabun as well, before being returned to Bangkok after the war's end. No other sources seem to back up this particular claim, however.

In addition to moving the capital to Phetchabun, Phibun also hoped to create a new 'Buddhist capital' in his hometown of Saraburi.

Saraburi Province

Speaking of Saraburi, the Emerald Buddha stayed there for a brief period of time in 1779. Following the Thonburi Kingdom's siege of Vientiane, the exhausted soldiers, who were in possession of the Emerald Buddha, rested for awhile in Saraburi Province upon their return. King Taksin then sent his son on a royal barge to retrieve the image and bring it to Wat Arun. Written records of the command survive to this day.

Where Does the Emerald Buddha Really Come From?

While nobody questions the importance of the Emerald Buddha to Thailand today, many aspects of its history remain hotly disputed. Could the statue possibly be 2,000 years old? How accurate is the Chronicle? And where does the Emerald Buddha really come from? While we may never know the answers to any of these questions for sure, let's examine some popular theories.

A 'Chiang Saen' Image?

Visitors to Bangkok's Wat Phra Kaew receive a free brochure upon entry to the temple. In addition to information on the *wat's* various structures, the pamphlet also gives a brief summary of the Emerald Buddha's backstory. It reads: 'Judging from the image's style, the Emerald Buddha is of the northern Thai workmanship and was probably made in the 15th century.' Wait, what?

Yes, that's right. According to this official source, the image was carved in Lanna. If so, that would make everything the Chronicle describes, from the statue's creation in India, up until the image's arrival in Kamphaeng Phet, complete fantasy. We already went over, of course, how the Chronicle's story isn't corroborated by other documents until the 15th century. But does that really mean that the Emerald Buddha was nothing more than a crude block of stone before that point? Quite a few scholars seem to think so.

Most fine arts experts who believe the Emerald Buddha to be a Lanna creation attribute it to the 'Chiang Saen' school of Buddhist sculpture. Chiang Saen is now a small town in Chiang Rai Province. But several hundred years ago, it was a major cultural and political center, and the city developed a unique style of Buddhist sculpture and architecture *(see p40)*.

Among those in favor of the Chiang Saen theory was French scholar R. Lingat. He also believed that the material used to make the image was not jade, but a type of green quartz found in Nan Province. Reginald Le May, author of *A Concise History of Buddhist Art in Siam*, agrees. He also claims to have seen similar green Buddha images in the markets of Nan himself. It's worth pointing out, however, that he doesn't provide any photos of these green images, nor do similar ones seem to be on display at Nan's prominent temples.

Carol Stratton, author of *Buddhist Sculpture of Northern Thailand*, is yet another proponent of the theory. She writes:

> 'In defense of the North as the homeland of the Emerald Buddha, we marshal the following facts: quality jadeite comes from Shan States or Nan; [...] Northern facial features can be noticed in the salient ears, thick nose, and the handling of the area above the upper lip with its wide indentation...'

When looking at the Emerald Buddha side-by-side with northern Thai images from the 15th century, there are certainly some similarities. In addition to the lips, the Emerald Buddha also has a chin and arched eyebrows like those of typical Chiang Saen images.

But while the Emerald Buddha and Chiang Saen sculptures do share a lot in common, there are some notable differences as well.

First is the posture. The Emerald Buddha is carved in the *dhyana mudra*, or seated meditation posture, which is actually quite rare for Lanna images. A large majority were carved in the *bhumisparsa*, or 'Calling the Earth to Witness' pose *(see p19)*. *Bhumisparsa* isn't just the most common posture in Lanna, but in all of Indochina.

In another pamphlet that's available for sale at Wat Phra Kaew, Professor M.C. Subhadradis Diskul acknowledges that the statue's posture is more similar to those of India and Sri Lanka than the typical Thai image.

Furthermore, in the middle of the Emerald Buddha's forehead is an *urna*, marking the Buddha's 'third eye.' This is also rare in Thai Buddha images, and is much more commonly found in South Asian or even Northeast Asian ones. While today, the Emerald Buddha's *urna* is a diamond that was placed there by King Rama IV, a photo of the statue completely without costume reveals that an indentation was indeed carved at the spot.

That's not to say that there have been absolutely no Buddha images with *urnas* and in the seated meditation posture carved in Thailand. But they're definitely in the minority.

Next, let's consider the statue's material. Whether it was made of jadeite, nephrite, jasper or quartz *(see p39)*, how many other similar green Buddha images have been found in Thailand? The number seems close to zero.

Indeed, there are some recent jade images, such as the replicas now on display at Wat Phra Kaew in Chiang Rai, that were carved as a tribute to the Emerald Buddha. And the 'Watermelon Emerald Buddha' of Lampang *(see p55)* was likely carved well after the Emerald Buddha's discovery.

But if jade or any other type of green stone from the Shan States or Nan Province was so widely available, why have no similar images from the 14th or 15th centuries ever surfaced? Unless, of course, there are more out there hidden within *chedis* or under layers of stucco!

It's also worth noting that the Chiang Saen style cannot be proven to predate the Emerald Buddha's arrival in Lanna. As far as we know, the earliest Lanna images created with similar facial features to those of the Emerald Buddha date from around the time of the green image's emergence in Chiang Rai. Therefore, it's possible that the Emerald Buddha influenced the style of Chiang Seen images and not the other way around.

The fact of the matter is, we'll likely never be able to prove the Emerald Buddha's true age or place of origin. Nobody but the Thai royal family is allowed to touch it, while jade is a very difficult mineral to age test anyway. So unless a very similar green image appears somewhere in the future, our understanding will remain limited. And that brings us to the Chronicle.

How Accurate is the Chronicle?

As mentioned, no other historical sources prior to the 15th century name the Emerald Buddha, unless we count Faxian's 5th-century travel diary *(see p171)*. When it comes to studying the statue's early history, the various versions of the Chronicle are all we have to go by. And even they can't agree with one another on numerous details! So just how reliable are they?

The Chronicle of the Emerald Buddha is, without a doubt, rife with errors. In some cases, events described in the story are off by several years. But at other times it may be centuries! And at some points, it's difficult to distinguish history from mythology, as guardian *yaksha* giants, a flying horse and an angry *naga* serpent all make appearances.

The number of inaccuracies, combined with the mythological and fantastical elements, have prompted some academics to disregard the Chronicle entirely. But that may be going too far.

The Chronicle of the Emerald Buddha is by no means unique among Asian chronicles in terms of its historical errors and grandiose embellishments. Take the Mahavamsa, for example. The Pali epic poem chronicles the history of Sri Lanka up until the 4th century. But it's full of historical inaccuracies and fantastical elaborations. And as a result, some scholars completely dismissed it at first. That is until archaeological findings in both Sri Lanka and India proved many of the stories to be true. Nowadays, scholars recognize that while the Mahavamsa contains many errors, it also holds lots of truth.

Likewise, the Chronicle of the Emerald Buddha contains many mistakes. But it also provides surprisingly accurate accounts of various events from South and Southeast Asian history. And as paradoxical as it may sound, the Chronicle's errors suggest that the story may be rooted in a much older tale - one that long predates the 15th century.

The scenes involving King Anawrahta of Pagan, for example, are mentioned as having taken place 1,000 years after the Buddha's passing, or around 457 AD. That's 500 years off!

But if the authors had absolutely no idea of what time period Anawrahta ruled Burma, how could they have known the intricacies of his dealings with Sri Lanka *(see p173)*? Or that the Khmer Empire was the other dominant power at the time?

One possibility is that the story was passed down orally from generation to generation, and also from one geographical location to the next. And while details like names and dates got mixed up along the way, the overall gist of the story was mostly preserved up until its initial transcription in the 15th century.

THE EMERALD BUDDHA & MODERN POLITICS

As mentioned on p221, many Cambodians still feel that the Emerald Buddha was stolen from their country. Resentment over Cambodian relics ending up in Thailand even prompted the creation of the legend Preah Ko Preah Keo. Furthermore, a number of Lao citizens still decry the Emerald Buddha's capture from Vientiane in the 18th century. To this day, the topic remains a sensitive subject between the two neighbors.

With that in mind, we can't overlook the convenience of the Chiang Saen theory in regards to current-day diplomatic relations. Lanna is now part of Thailand. And if the statue was created there, then no 'theft' could've taken place, as it was Thai all along!

But if the image really is from India, as the Chronicle describes, then numerous countries have valid claims.

Of course, as mentioned earlier, there's certainly merit to the Chiang Saen theory from a fine arts perspective. And it would be unfair to presume that proponents of the idea are politically motivated in any way. But it's also not hard to see why the theory has become so mainstream in Thailand nowadays.

But amidst all the confusion, one thing's for sure: the Chronicle of the Emerald Buddha is a fascinating story that blends history, geography, mythology and adventure. It's about much more than just the travels of a single relic, but the historical and cultural evolution of an entire region. And regardless of what percentage of the story is truth or fiction, it can still serve as the blueprint for an unforgettable journey.

The Emerald Buddha's Complete Journeys

1 c. 150 BC
In Pataliputra, India, Nagasena calls for the creation of the Emerald Buddha to keep Buddhism alive.

2 c. 300s
Due to internal strife, the king sends the statue to Anuradhapura, Sri Lanka for safekeeping.

3 993
The Chola Empire invades Anuradhapura. The Sri Lankan elite retreat to Ruhuna, likely taking the Emerald Buddha and tooth relic.

4 1060s
Vijayabahu I of Sri Lanka gives King Anawrahta of Pagan the Tripitaka scriptures and the Emerald Buddha. But the boat with the statue gets blown off course, likely ending up on the Malay Peninsula. Anawrahta goes to retrieve them but only ends up with the scriptures. Eventually, the statue arrives in Angkor, but probably with some stops along the way.

5 1200s
A devastating flood (or religious iconoclasm) puts the Emerald Buddha in danger. Monks take it to a northern outpost town for safety. Possibilities include, Banteay Chhmar, Phimai or Sakon Nakhon.

6 c. 1352
Upon founding the Ayutthaya Kingdom, King Ramathibodi I (U Thong) invades the western Khmer Empire and takes the Emerald Buddha.

7 Early 1380s
During the reign of King Borommaracha I, the king of Kamphaeng Phet requests to take the Emerald Buddha (and probably the Phra Sihing).

8 1380s
The king of Kamphaeng Phet's son, the governor of Lopburi, is allowed to have the statue for 1 year and 9 months before returning it.

9 1380s
Prince Maha Proma obtains the Emerald Buddha and Phra Sihing from the king of Kamphaeng Phet and takes them to Chiang Rai. The image is then covered in stucco during a later civil war.

10 1434
Lighting strikes Wat Pa Yeah's *chedi*, revealing a Buddha statue inside. Its stucco covering then comes off, exposing the Emerald Buddha beneath.

PATALIPUTRA

ANURADHAPURA

RUHUNA

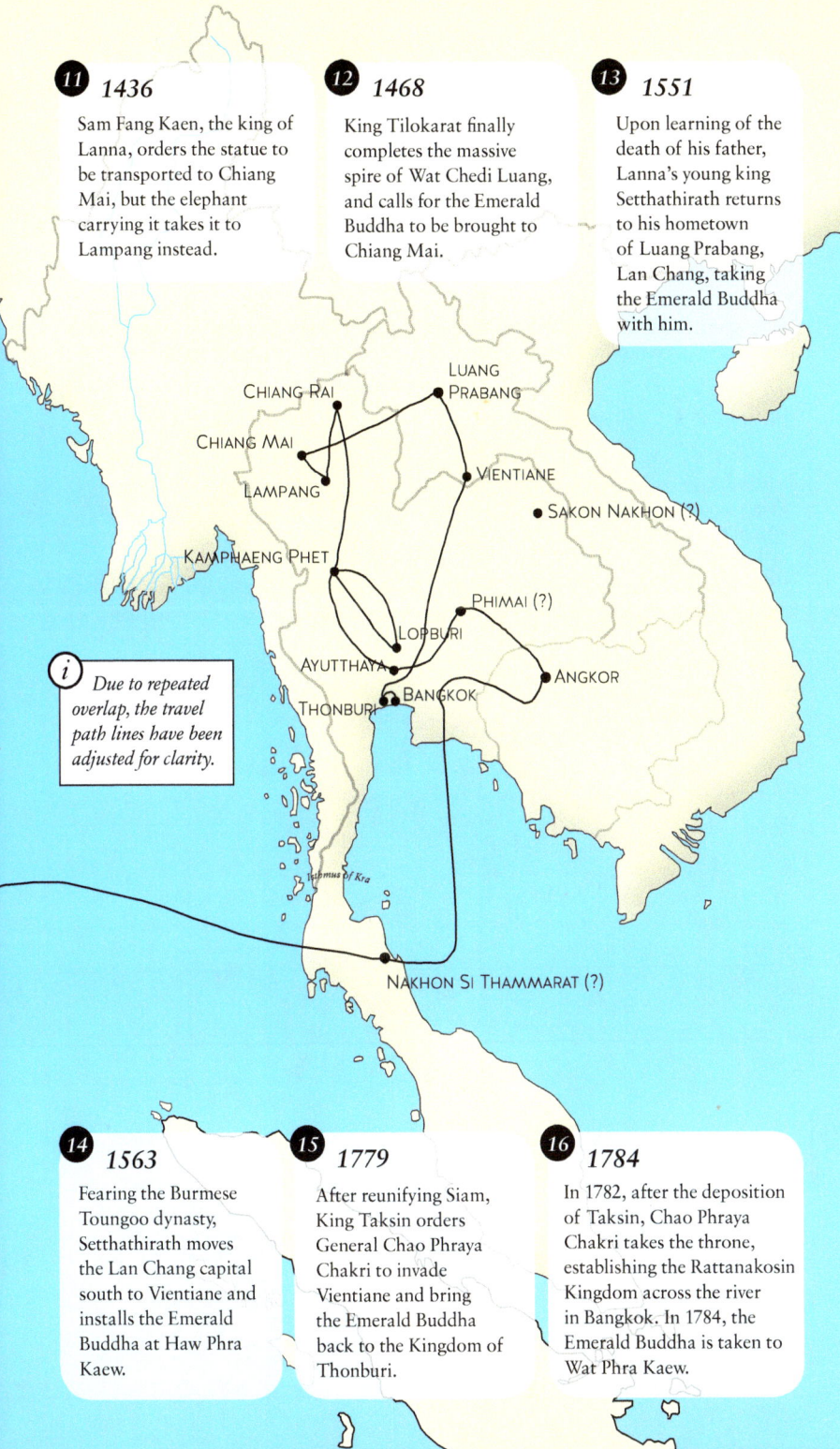

ITINERARY IDEAS

Visiting the locations in the order they appear in the story isn't necessary, nor even recommended. You should plan your trip according to whatever works best for you, price-wise and logistically. Most travelers won't end up making it to every single place, while no two itineraries are going to look exactly the same. But with that said, below are some ideas, tips and general information to help you plan your journey. You can also learn more about long-distance transport on p279.

Bangkok & Central Thailand

Many travelers will start and end their trip in Bangkok, as it's one of Southeast Asia's main transport hubs. It's up to you whether you want to visit Wat Phra Kaew to see the Emerald Buddha in person before carrying on with the rest of your journey. You may prefer to save it for the very end of your trip. If you don't mind paying double the entrance fee, you could even visit twice!

You'll need at least 2-3 days in Bangkok to see the sights around the Rattanakosin and Thonburi areas. And throw in a couple more if you want to tour downtown and visit some outlying sites like the Erawan Museum *(p158)*. Note that the traffic, heat and chaotic atmosphere of Bangkok can wear on people after a few days. Two shorter stays might be better than one long one.

Moving on from Bangkok, you can take a Northern Line train from Hua Lamphong Station to Ayutthaya (2 hrs). Spend two nights or more there, as you'll want at least one full day to explore the ruins. Depending on your level of interest, you could easily fill up three days.

From Ayutthaya, take the train to Lopburi (about 1 hr). There's no need to spend the night there, as the main locations can be seen within a day. Later in the evening, hop on the train again and head north, but be sure to book your sleeper berth in advance *(see p279)*.

From Lopburi you have two options: ride to Lampang and proceed to make your way around the Lanna region. Or, get off at Phitsanulok. From Phitsanulok, take a bus (1 hr) to Sukhothai, explore the ruins there for 1-2 full days, and then make the short journey to Kamphaeng Phet. After a couple of days there, you can then take a bus to Chiang Mai (6-7 hrs).

Note: From Ayutthaya, it's also possible to take a Northeastern Line train to Nakhon Ratchasima (near Phimai). This line also goes on to Udon Thani (from where you can take a bus to Sakon Nakhon) and Nong Khai (from where you can travel overland to Vientiane).

Thailand's Lanna Region

If you're entering the Lanna region by train, you'll probably start in Lampang. Spend one or two days exploring the sites there. On your last day, hire a taxi to take you to Wat Phra That Lampang Luang and then onto the bus or train station. If you wish, spend a day exploring Lamphun on your way to Chiang Mai.

Chiang Mai deserves at least 2-3 days, but those who stay for longer won't run out of things to discover. From Chiang Mai, you can head to the Arcade Bus Station to reach the other major towns of Lanna. Chiang Rai is a little over three hours away, and many people also spend a few days in Pai.

In Chiang Rai, at least 2 full days is ideal. The city has an airport (but no train) and you may want to fly to your next destination. For those wishing to explore the South, there are direct flights from Chiang Rai to Krabi. And from Krabi, you can head over to Nakhon Si Thammarat by bus (more below).

You could also fly to Bangkok, from where you can start your Central Thailand journey or embark on bus or train travel to the Isaan region (and from there, possibly head overland to either Vientiane or Siem Reap, Cambodia).

Many head directly from Chiang Rai to Luang Prabang, Laos by taking a popular riverboat cruise along the Mekong *(read more on p88)*.

Laos

For those starting in Luang Prabang (via flight or river cruise), you can see the sights within town in just a couple of days. However, staying awhile is ideal, as the town's slow pace of life is one of its main appeals. Heading onward to Vientiane, you can travel by bus, though a stopover in Vang Vieng is recommended. You can also fly directly to Vientiane.

In Vientiane, 1-2 days is ideal, though you might want to reserve a whole extra day just for the Buddha Park *(p119)*.

You could also start your Laos journey in Vientiane, either by direct flight or via an easy bus ride from Nong Khai in Thailand's Isaan region *(see p121)*. Or, end your Laos trip in Vientiane and enter Thailand via Nong Khai.

For those doing more extensive travels around Laos and Cambodia, you could potentially travel overland by bus from Pakse (southern Laos) into Cambodia.

Cambodia

For most people, the easiest way to get to Siem Reap is via direct flight from Bangkok. You can also take a bus, shared minivan or train to the border, but watch out for scams.

Spending at least three days exploring the Angkor Archaeological Park is ideal, though up to five days is recommended if you love ruins and have the time.

Banteay Chhmar is an easy trip from Siem Reap *(see p220)* and the nearest city, Sisophon, is close to the Thai border. To see other outlying ruins like Koh Ker and Preah Vihear, consider hiring a private driver (around $100 a day) to take you around. You can see most of the major sites in three days *(learn more on p205)*.

While not covered in this guidebook, many travelers also visit Phnom Penh, an easy bus ride from Siem Reap. From either Siem Reap or Phnom Penh, you can head onto your next destination by bus or plane. Many travelers also visit the southern beaches of Sihanoukville.

South Thailand

You can fly to Krabi directly from Chiang Rai, Chiang Mai, Bangkok or other cities. You can also start or end your South Thailand excursion in Nakhon Si Thammarat via flight from Bangkok. Alternatively, you could fly to Surat Thani first and head westward from there. For those doing even more extensive travels around the region, there are even direct flights from Krabi to Kuala Lumpur. Learn more about what to see in South Thailand and getting around on pp196-97.

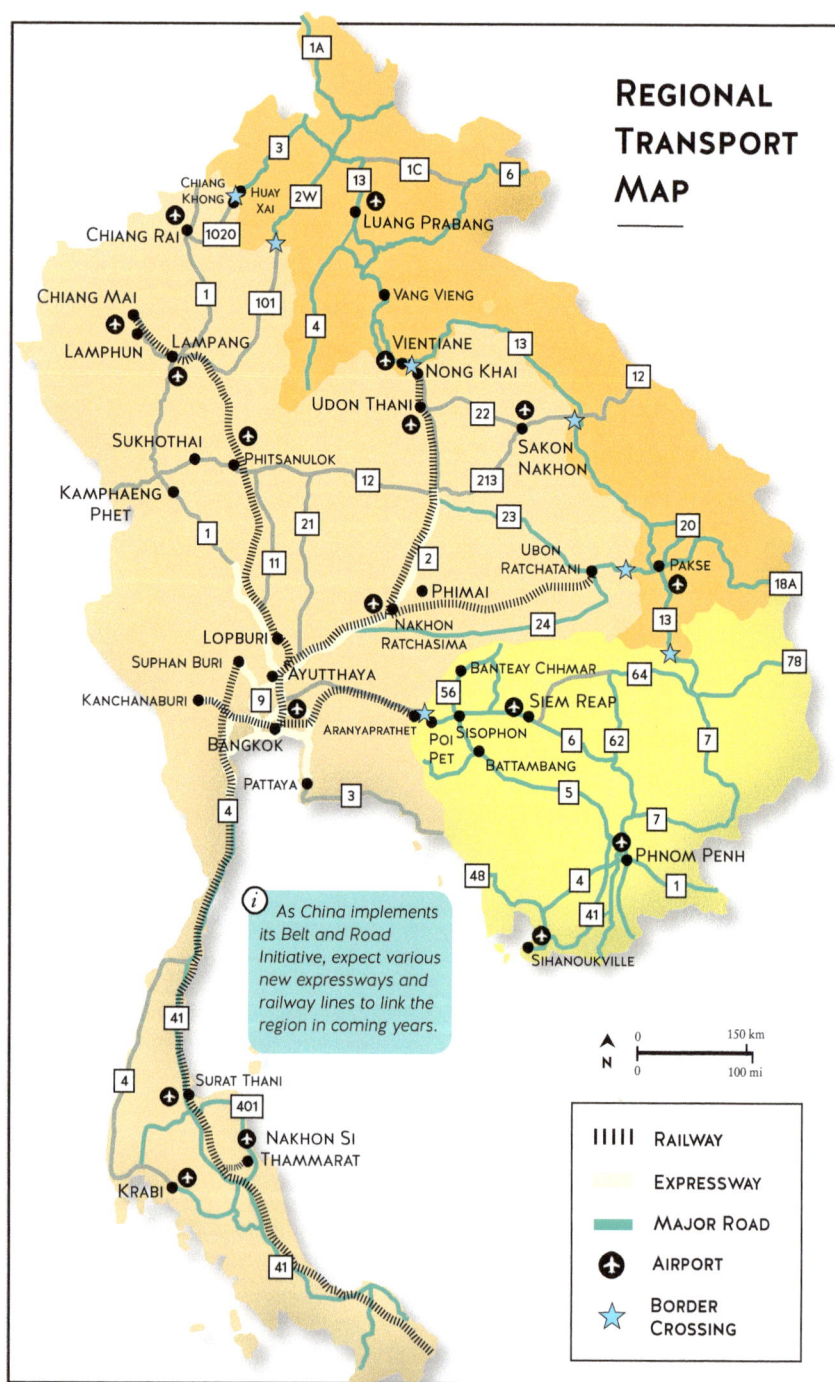

TRANSPORTATION TIPS

Thailand

Flights: Thailand is an excellent country for cheap and reliable air travel. Budget airlines such as Nok Air, AirAsia, Thai Lion Air and others are great ways to get around the country for not much more than a train ticket!

You can travel between Bangkok and Chiang Mai, for example, for just around 1,000 baht (roughly $30 USD) one-way, provided you book in advance.

The budget airlines, though, are strict with luggage restrictions. In addition to charging extra for checked luggage, the carry-on limit is usually around 7 kg. In practice, they often won't bother to weigh your bags, but sometimes they might. And if your bag is over the limit, you could potentially be faced with a hefty fine.

If you anticipate doing a lot of plane travel around the country (or the region in general), pack accordingly and save your souvenir shopping until the very end.

Trains: Trains can be a fun and convenient way to travel long distances in Thailand. Many of the locations in this guide book are accessible by train. But if you're traveling long-distance, it's vital that you get a ticket in advance, as many trains sell out.

Seats on the trains are divided into three classes. Third class seats don't have air conditioning, and the seats are benches which are first come, first serve. These are fine for traveling relatively shorter distances, such as from Bangkok to Ayutthaya. They're also a good way to meet locals.

Second class seats are a mix of seated and sleeper berths. Generally, everyone will be seated in the daytime, and then fold out their beds after dark. First class seats, meanwhile, are private cabins and can be as expensive as flights.

During long journeys, train staff will come around with a menu and ask if you'd like to order a meal. Someone will then come by to collect your dishes. Newer trains may also have dining areas that you can visit when hungry. And vendors frequently enter the train selling food, snacks and drinks.

Bookings can be made up to 60 days in advance of your departure date at either a train station or through a travel agent (for an added fee). You can also book online at **railway.co.th**.

While not an absolute rule, trains and buses generally leave close to their scheduled departure time. But they may also be late, so keep that in mind if you have a transfer somewhere.

There are four main train lines: **Northern**, **Northeastern**, **Eastern** and **Southern**. All four are linked at Bangkok's Hua Lamphong Station. The Northern Line should be of particular interest to most, as Bangkok, Ayutthaya, Lopburi, Phitsanulok (near Sukhothai), Lampang and Chiang Mai are all stops on it.

Bus: Bus travel is one of the easiest and cheapest ways to get around. The country has many competing companies and with so many direct routes, you can get to most places without needing to transfer. There are few towns that don't have direct routes to Bangkok, while many mid-sized cities also have direct routes to one another.

While you can buy tickets in advance, it's often fine to just show up at the bus station on the day of your departure. Even if you're traveling long-distance (such as Chiang Mai to Bangkok), you shouldn't normally have to wait around for more than an hour until the next bus leaves.

Of course, for peace of mind, you may still wish to purchase advance tickets. The easiest way to do so is at the station itself. But if your accommodation is too far away, services like **ThaiTicketMajor** or **12GoAsia** allow you to book online.

Songthaews and Minivans: When traveling to a city an hour or two away, another option is to take a songthaew (converted pickup truck) or a shared minivan. It's generally hard to find timetables for these online, so your best bet is to show up at the station and ask.

Tip: Buses or minivans will rarely deny an extra passenger if there's room. And even 'full' vehicles will always have room for one more! If you find yourself needing to get to the next town over but are far from the nearest station, try standing by the main road and flagging down the next songthaew, minivan or bus you see. If they're going in that direction, they'll gladly let you on and collect your money.

Boats: When traveling around the southern islands, you have the option of ferries, speedboats or wooden longboats. After deciding where you want to go, be sure to research the best way to get to that particular place, as transport options may vary from island to island.

LAOS

Flights: The main airports in Laos are Vientiane, Luang Prabang and Pakse, and there also some additional smaller airports. The main cities all have frequent flights to and from Bangkok.

Domestic flights, meanwhile, are served by either Lao Airlines or Lao Skyway, and are considerably more expensive than the domestic flights in Thailand. But given Laos's size and state of its roads, flying is often the easier and safer option.

Bus: Depending on where you're going, you'll likely have the option between a VIP bus for tourists (often a sleeper bus) or a standard local bus. VIP buses can usually be booked through your hotel or at a travel agent. But at the time of writing, not online.

Laos also has a minivan system similar to that of Thailand (see above). Just show up at the local bus station and find out when the next one departs.

CAMBODIA

Flights: The main airports in Cambodia are Siem Reap, Phnom Penh and Sihanoukville. There are daily flights between them and prices are reasonable. And the major cities are also fairly well connected internationally *(see p204)*.

Bus: There are numerous long-distance bus routes throughout the country of varying comfort levels. Asking at your hotel is often the easiest way to book.

Train: After many years, Cambodia's railway network is once again in use. At the time of writing, however, the only regular route is between Phnom Penh and Sihanoukville. A route between Poi Pet and Phnom Penh has also just reopened, but services are very limited.

Private Driver: There are many fantastic ruins outside of Angkor, but no public transport to get there. And due to the state of the roads, a 4x4 might be required. Expect to pay around $100 a day for a private driver.

VISAS

Before your trip, it's imperative that you take the time to research each country's visa system and how it pertains to your nationality. Also be sure that your passport is valid for at least six months from the time of your trip.

And before crossing any borders, be mindful of scams by either tour operators or taxi drivers who insist on 'helping' you process your visa. While there are some honest agents out there, exercise due diligence.

Thailand Visas

Many visitors to Thailand have the option of entering the country for up to 30 days with a visa exemption. Be sure to check whether this applies to you.

When planning out your itinerary (see p276), you may find that it's most convenient to enter Thailand more than once. While it's not against the rules to enter the country multiple times using the 30-day visa exemption, the immigration officers always have the final say. And some repeat visitors complain of having been denied entry for no apparent reason.

Generally speaking, the authorities want to make sure that you're not working in the country illegally. To avoid suspicion, it's best not to stay for the full limit before coming right back again. Also bear in mind that even if you have no issues with re-entry, you can only stay a total of 90 days within a six month period.

If you want to stay in Thailand longer than 30 days on a single entry, you have a couple of options. You can extend your 30-day visa exemption stamp at an immigration center for a fee of 1,900 baht.

Depending on your nationality, you can also apply for a 60-day tourist visa. This can only be done at a Thai consulate or embassy outside of Thailand. These visas can also be extended for an additional 30 days using the same process mentioned above. Be sure to check with the embassy or consulate for what documents you need.

Thailand also offers a 6-month multiple entry tourist visa. The average person won't be eligible, though, as you must show proof of current employment while also promising not to work. Furthermore, you can only apply in your home country or country of residence.

At the time of writing, an eVisa system has recently been launched, but only for select nationalities. As visa rules and regulations are always changing, be sure to check online or with your local embassy before your trip. The web site **thaivisa.com** also provides regular updates.

Laos Visas

Most nationalities require a tourist visa to enter Laos. As of 2019, Laos has an eVisa system which you can apply for at **laoevisa.gov.la**. But be sure to check whether your desired entry port accepts it.

Otherwise, visas can easily be obtained at the border. You'll need to bring a separate passport photo (or in some cases two). However, some airports let you pay an extra dollar for them to simply copy your passport. Be sure to research if this is a possibility at whatever port of entry you'll be coming through.

At the time of writing, 30-day visas for Laos can range from $30-45 depending on your nationality. These visas can be extended up to two times at an immigration office, with the cost being around 20,000 kip per day.

If you'll be entering Laos multiple times, you'll need to pay the fee for a new visa each time. But citizens of numerous Asian countries can enter Laos visa-free.

You can also apply for a visa in advance at a Laos consulate or embassy for a slightly cheaper fee.

Cambodia Visas

Cambodia has a visa on arrival system like that of Laos. Most people can purchase a 30-day visa for $30 USD at airports and land crossings. You're supposed to have a passport photo with you but can usually avoid this by paying a few extra dollars.

eVisas can be applied for online, though the extra processing fee (around $6) makes it more expensive. And eVisas are not accepted at all ports of entry, though they are at most.

For those wishing to stay even longer, a tourist visa can be extended for an additional month through an agent.

CURRENCY

As this guide covers three countries, you'll have to deal with three different currencies throughout your journey. Nowadays, many travelers simply withdraw money from the local ATM upon arrival at the airport. This will, of course, incur fees from your bank, and you'll also have to pay a fee for each withdrawal. You may want to look into setting up an account with a bank that reimburses ATM fees.

As far as exchanging cash, you can do it at all airports. And in Thailand in particular, there are currency exchange counters all throughout big cities.

Regarding Lao kip, you will not be able to exchange them after leaving the country. Therefore, be sure to exchange all your kip to baht or dollars before leaving Laos.

Cambodia, meanwhile, uses American dollars (but also Cambodian riel for smaller exchanges). Before entering Laos or Cambodia, it would be wise to have some $USD on you to pay the visa fee.

SIM CARDS & WIFI

Obtaining a SIM card in each country you visit is highly recommended. This will allow you to access maps and travel info or make calls in case of an emergency. Fortunately, SIM cards in Southeast Asia are very cheap and there's no long-term commitment.

At all of the major airports of Thailand, Laos and Cambodia, you can simply sign up for a prepaid SIM card that lasts up to a month. While it varies slightly depending on company and location, you can often get several gigabytes of data for somewhere between $5 and $15. The option to make calls may cost extra.

Many people throughout Southeast Asia use a chat app called LINE, which may come in handy for communicating with staff at your accommodation. WhatsApp is also fairly popular.

WiFi is now a standard amenity at nearly all accommodations throughout the region, and it's also very common at cafes. Coworking spaces are also quite popular.

HEALTH, SAFETY & SECURITY

Safety & Scams

Generally speaking, Thailand, Laos and Cambodia are all safe countries. You rarely need to worry about random acts of violence or muggings. Pickpockets or occasional bag-snatchers are not unheard of, however. Be sure to bring a small lock for your luggage for long journeys.

Taxi drivers throughout the region are infamous for rigged meters or taking extra long routes. And if a driver tells you that the destination you're going to is closed due to a holiday, it's probably not true.

And if anyone recommends you buy an item (like a gem) to sell back home for a profit, it's a scam. In Cambodia, you'll likely be approached by strangers asking for donations for a local orphanage. Sadly, these are often scams as well.

Staying Healthy

In Indochina nowadays, there's not too much to worry about in terms of illnesses or infectious diseases. Malaria is uncommon in most regions, though there may still be a risk in rural areas that are far off the beaten path. And speaking of isolated jungle areas, some parts of Laos and Cambodia still contain unexploded ordinances. Be sure to thoroughly research each isolated region you plan to visit.

You shouldn't drink from the tap anywhere in the region. Thankfully, bottled water is readily available. But some people have no issues brushing their teeth with tap water.

Food poisoning is not unheard of in Indochina, though food safety standards are gradually improving. Spicy food may also cause stomach upset for new visitors.

Also be on the lookout for street dogs. Whether they're stray or just unleashed, dogs can sometimes be very territorial and aggressive, especially when gathered in packs. Rabies is a serious concern, and if you do end up getting bit, you're likely going to be the one paying the hospital bills. While this isn't an issue everywhere, it can be a problem in Ayutthaya, the forest ruins of Kamphaeng Phet and certain alleyways of Bangkok.

Road Safety

If you plan on riding a motorbike or scooter, note that Thailand is now ranked second in the world for road traffic deaths. While the rate may be lower in Laos and Cambodia, traffic is just as chaotic.

Many motorbike rental shops will rent you a bike even if you don't meet all the legal requirements. But if you end up getting in an accident, your travel insurance probably won't cover you. Only experienced and licensed riders should consider getting around this way.

Emergency Numbers	Thailand	Cambodia	Laos
Police	191	117	1191
Ambulance & Rescue	1554	119	1195
Fire Emergency	199	118	1190

SELECTED BIBLIOGRAPHY

- Coedès, George, *The Indianized States of Southeast Asia*, trans. by Susan Brown Cowing, Australian National University Press, 1975
- Daguan, Zhou, *A Record of Cambodia: The Land and Its People*, trans. by Peter Harris, Silkworm Books, 2007
- Diskul, M.C. Subhadradis, *History of the Temple of the Emerald Buddha*, Bureau of the Royal Household, 1980
- Fa-Hien (Faxian), *Record of Buddhist Kingdoms*, trans. by James Legge, Buddha Dharma Education Association Inc., 1886
- Garnier, Francis, *Voyage d'exploration en Indo-Chine*, Hachette, 1873
- [Brochure] *Guide to the Grand Palace*
- Hall, Kenneth R., *A History of Early Southeast Asia*, Rowman & Littlefield Publishers, 2011
- Hargreave, Oliver, *Exploring Chiang Mai: City, Valley & Mountains*, Within Books, 5th Ed., 2017
- Lamprecht, Corrie, *The Emerald Buddha: Its Mysteries and Chronicles*, Corrie Books, 2016
- Le May, Reginald, *A Concise History of Buddhist Art in Siam*, Tuttle, 1962
- Lingat, R., *Le Culte du Bouddha d'Emerude*, The Journal of the Siam Society, Vol. XXVII, 1934
- Narula, Karen Schur, *Voyage of the Emerald Buddha*, Oxford University Press, 1994
- Ngoun, Kimly, *The Legend of Preah Ko Preah Keo and its Influence on the Cambodian People's Perception of the Thais*, Chulalongkorn University, 2006
- Notton, Camille, *The Chronicle of the Emerald Buddha* (translation of original Pali manuscript, author unknown), Bangkok Time Press, 1933
- Notton, Camille, *P'Ra Buddha Sihinga* (translation of original Pali manuscript, author unknown), Bangkok Time Press, 1933
- Petrotchenko, Michel, *Focusing on the Angkor Temples: The Guidebook*, Amarin Printing & Publishing, 2017
- Roeder, Eric, *The Origin and Significance of the Emerald Buddha*, University of Hawaii, 1999
- Stratton, Carol, *Buddhist Sculpture of Northern Thailand*, Silkworm Books, 2004
- Thera, Ratanapañña, *Jinakalamalipakaranam (The Sheaf of Garlands of the Epochs of the Conqueror)*, trans. by N.A. Jayawickrama, Pali Text Society, 1968
- Vickery, Michael, *Cambodia and Its Neighbors in the 15th Century*, Asia Research Institute Working Paper Series No. 27, 2004
- Viravong, Maha Sila, *History of Laos*, Paragon Book Reprint Corp., 1964
- Woodward, Hiram W., *The Sacred Sculpture of Thailand*, River Books, 1997

INDEX

This index begins with full chronological lists of rulers of the major kingdoms featured in this book. The individual kings mentioned are highlighted in bold. From the category titled 'Other Monarchs & Government Officials' onward, however, entries are ordered alphabetically.

KHMER EMPIRE

Jayavarman II *(802-835)* 200
Jayavarman III *(835-877)*
Indravarman I *(877-889)*
Yashovarman I *(889-910)* 200
Harshavarman I *(910-923)*
Ishanavarman II *(923-928)*
Jayavarman IV *(928-941)*
Harshavarman II *(941-944)*
Rajendravarman II *(944-968)* 201
Jayavarman V *(968-1001)*
Jayaviravarman *(1001-1002)* 182
Suryavarman I *(1002-1050)* 182-3, 200-2, 206-7, 226
Udayadityavarman II *(1050-1066)* 202, 207
Harshavarman III *(1066-1080)* 202
Jayavarman VI *(1080-1107)* 226
Dharanindravarman I *(1107-1113)*
Suryavarman II *(1113-1150)* 200, 208-9, 247
Dharanindravarman II *(1150-1160)*
Yashovarman II *(1160-1167)*
Tribhuvanadityavarman *(1167-1177)*
(Champa occupation - 1177-1181)
Jayavarman VII *(1181-1218)* 116, 200-2, 210-16, 219-20, 226-7, 247, 250-1
Indravarman II *(1218-1243)*
Jayavarman VIII *(1243-1295)*
Indravarman III *(1295-1308)*
(*little is known of 14th and 15th-century Khmer rulers)

LANNA KINGDOM

Mangrai *(1292–1311)* 28-29, 70, 73. 77
Chaiyasongkhram *(1311-1325)*
Saenphu *(1325-1334)*
Kham Fu *(1334-1336)* 75
Phayu *(1336-1355)*
Kue Na *(1355-1385)* 64-65, 68, 76, 192, 268
Saen Muang Ma *(1385-1401)* 68, 72-4, 192-3, 268-9
Sam Fang Kaen *(1402-1441)* 33, 48-49, 68
Tilokarat *(1441-1487)* 29, 64-65. 68
Yotchiangrai *(1487-1495)*
Mueang Kaeo *(1495-1525)*
Ketklao *(1525-1538 - 1st reign)*
Saikham *(1538-1543)* 87

Ketklao *(1543-1545 - 2nd reign)* 86-7
Chiraprabha *(1545-1546 - queen's reign)* 87, 109
Setthathirath *(1546-1547 - also king of Lan Chang)* see Setthathirath (Lan Chang)
(interregnum - 1547–1551)
Mekuti *(1551–1558)* 108-9, 193

LAN CHANG KINGDOM

Fa Ngum *(1353-1373)* 82-83, 98, 224
Samsenethai *(1372-1417)*
Lan Kham Deng *(1417-1428)*
Phommathat *(1428-1429)*
Yukhon *(1429-1430)*
Khon Kham *(1430-1432)*
Kham Tam Sa *(1432)*
Lusai *(1432-1433)*
Khai Bua Ban *(1433-1436)*
Kham Keut *(1436-1438)*
Nang Keo Phimpha *(1438)*
(interregnum - 1438-1441)
Chaiyachakkapat *(1441-1479)* 24, 83, 98
Souvanna Banlang *(1479-1486)*
La Sen Thai *(1486-1496)*
Somphou *(1496-1500)*
Visoun *(1500-1520)* 83, 86-7, 90-2, 98
Photisarath *(1520-1528)* 83, 86-7, 90, 93
Setthathirath *(1548-1571 - also Lanna king)* 86-7, 94, 103, 108-9, 112-18, 193, 247
Sen Soulintha *(1571-1575)*
Voravongsa *(1575-1579)*
Sen Soulintha *(1570-1582)*
Nakhon Noi *(1582-1583)*
(interregnum - 1583-1591)
No Muong *(1591-1598)* 83
Voravongsa II *(1598-1622)*
Oupagnouvarath *(1622-1623)*
Photisarath II *(1623-1627)*
Mon Keo *(1627)*
Tone Kham *(1627-1633)*
Vichai *(1633-1637)*
Suriya Vongsa *(1637-1695)* 83, 127
Tian Thala *(1695)*
Ong Lo *(1694-1698)*
Nan Thara *(1698-1699)*
Setthathirath II *(1699-1707)*

Kingdom of Vientiane

Setthathirath II *(1707-1735)*
Ong Long *(1735-1760)*
Ong Boun *(1760-1778)*
(Siamese takeover - 1778-1780)
Ong Boun *(1780-1781)* 99
Nanthasen *(1781-1794)* 99
Intharavong *(1795-1805)*
Anouvong *(1805-1828)* 112-15, 120

Ayutthaya Kingdom

U Thong (Ramathibodi I) *(1350-1369)* 191, 230, 234-5, 238, 243
Ramesuan *(1369-1370 - 1st reign)*
Borommaracha I *(1370-1388)* 191
Thonglan *(1388)*
Ramesuan *(1388-1395 - 2nd reign)*
Ramracha *(1395-1409)*
Intharacha *(1409-1424)*
Borommaracha II *(1424-1448)* 241
Borommatrailokanat *(1448-1488)* 238
Borommaracha III *(1488-1491)*
Ramathibodi II *(1491-1529)*
Borommaracha IV *(1529-1533)*
Ratchadathiratkuman *(1533-1534)*
Chairacha *(1534-1546)*
Kaeofa *(1546-1548)*
Mahachakkaphat *(1548-1568)*
Mahinthrathirat *(1568-1569)*
Mahathammaracha *(1569-1590)*
Naresuan the Great *(1590-1605)* 231, 267
Ekathotsarot *(1605-1610)*
Sisaowaphak *(1610-1611)*
Songtham *(1611-1628)*
Chetthathirat *(1628-1629)*
Athittayawong *(1629)*
Prasatthong *(1629-1656)*
Chaofa Chai *(1656)*
Sisuthammaracha *(1656)*
Narai the Great *(1656-1688)* 83, 238, 247-53
Phetracha *(1688-1703)* 252
Sanphet VIII *(1703-1708)*
Phumintharacha *(1708-1732)*
Borommakot *(1732-1758)*
Uthumphon *(1758)*
Ekkathat *(1758-1767)* 126-7, 231

Thonburi Kingdom

Taksin the Great *(1767-1782)* 69, 126-7, 130-7, 142-3, 189, 270

Rattanakosin Kingdom (Chakri Dynasty)

Rama I (Phra Phutthayotfa Chulalok f.k.a. Chao Phraya Chakri) *(1782-1809)* 126-7, 142-3, 146-57, 193
Rama II (Phra Phutthaloetla Naphalai) *(1809-1824)* 133, 149
Rama III (Nangklao) *(1824-1851)* 114, 136, 149, 151, 155, 242
Rama IV (Mongkut) *(1851-1868)* 39, 49, 149-52, 253, 260
Rama V (Chulalongkorn) *(1868 - 1910)* 133, 151, 154, 194
Rama VI (Vajiravudh) *(1910 - 1925)* 143, 150, 156
Rama VII (Prajadhipok) *(1925 - 1935)*
Rama VIII (Ananda Mahidol) *(1935 - 1946)*
Rama IX (Bhumibol Adulyadej) *(1946 - 2016)* 77
Rama X (Vajiralongkorn) *(2016 - Present)*

Other Monarchs & Government Officials *(alphabetical)*

Adicca (Haripunchai) 234
Alexander the Great 166
Anawrahta (Pagan) 172-5, 180-3
Ashoka (Maurya Empire) 14, 116, 164-7, 170
Bayinnaung (Toungoo dynasty) 109
Queen Chamathewi (Haripunchai) 52, 61, 73, 247
Chao Kawila (Lanna) 29, 70-1
Guhasiva (Kalinga) 170-1
Kanishka the Great (Kushan Empire) 168
Kitti Sri Meghavanna (Anuradhapura) 170
Lithai (Sukhothai Kingdom) 191
Maha Proma (Prince of Chiang Rai) 41, 74, 192-3, 268-9
Menander I (Indo-Greek) 163, 166-7
Nanatissa (Kamphaeng Phet) 192
Phaulkon, Constantine (Narai's advisor) 252
Phaya Ngam Mueang (Phayao) 28
Phi Fa (Pha Ngum's father) 82
Phibun (Thai Prime Minister) 231, 270
Princess Hemmali & Prince Danta 170-1, 188
Ram Khamhaeng (Sukhothai Kingdom) 28, 156, 190-1, 230, 266
Si Inthrathit (Sukhothai Kingdom) 230, 266
Sisavang Vong (Kingdom of Luang Prabang) 95
Souvanna Phouma (Prime Minister of Laos) 112
Vijayabahu I (Sri Lanka) 172-4
Zakarine (Kingdom of Luang Prabang) 91

Other Notable Figures

artists and architects
   Chinitz, John 154
   Delaporte, Louis 91, 114, 116
   Duchanee, Thawan 34, 41-2
   Kavindrarimathana 201
   Khrua In Khong 149
   Kositpipat, Chalermchai 34, 43
   Sayasthsena, Tham 115

Sulilat, Bunleau **119**, 121
Tornarelli, Alfonso 156
Cheewok Komaraphat 152
Daguan, Zhou **202**, 206-7, 216
Jayawickrama, N.A. **7** *see also* Jinakalamali
Mae Suchada 54-5
see also 'Watermelon Emerald Buddha'
monks and religious figures
    Acharn Mun Bhuridatto 72
    Dhammarakkhita 164, 168
    Faxian 171
    Maha Pasaman 82, 98
    Nagasena **163-8**
    Ratanapañña **6** *see also* Jinakalamali
    Siwichai, Khruba 73, 75
    Shin Arahan 172-3 *see also* Anawrahta
Notton, Camille **7**, 190 *see also* Chronicle of the Emerald Buddha, Chronicle of the Phra Sihing
Thompson, Jim 158
Viriyaphant, Lek 158

Historical Kingdoms & Ethnic Groups

Anuradhapura Kingdom
    see Anuradhapura (Sri Lanka)
Ayutthaya Kingdom 127, 191-2, 230-31, 233-43, 252 *see also* Ayutthaya (Thailand)
Black Flag (Haw Chinese marauders) 90-1, 94
Champa Kingdom 200, 210-11, 227
Kingdom of Champasak 83, 127
Chola Empire **174**, 176, 181-3, 195
French colonial empire 83, 91, 95, 112-15, 252
Greco-Bactria Kingdom 166-7
Gupta Empire 169, 253
Han dynasty 39, 168
Haripunchai 28, 53, 61, 73, 176, 247
    see also Lamphun (Thailand), Queen Chamathewi, Mon Dvaravati
hilltribes **45**, 104
    Akha 44-45
    Hmong 45, 77
    Karen 45, 77
    Khmu 104
Indo-Greek *see* Menander I
Kalinga 170
Konbaung dynasty 127, 175, 231
Kushan Empire 168-9
    see also Kanishka the Great
Lan Chang Kingdom **82-3**, 87, 109, 127
Lanna Kingdom 24, **28-9**, 65, 87, 109
Lawa people 73
Ligor / Tambralinga **181-3**
Kingdom of Luang Prabang 83, 94-7, 127
Maurya Empire 166-8

    see also Ashoka, Pataliputra
Mon Dvaravati 16, 226, 247, 251, 253
    see also Haripunchai, Dvaravati art
Mon people 28, 173, 247
    see also Mon Dvaravati, Thaton (Myanmar)
Kingdom of Pagan *see* Anawrahta
Persian Empire 166, 168, 252
Portuguese Empire 137, 231, 242
Rattanakosin Kingdom **142-3**, 146-57, 231
Sailendra dynasty 181
Shunga dynasty 166-7
    see also Nagasena, Pataliputra
Srivijaya Empire 181-3, 187, 195
Tai people 28
Teochew Chinese 132
Thonburi Kingdom **126-7**, 130-7, 142-3, 231
    see also Taksin (Thonburi)
Toungoo dynasty 29, 83, 109, 175, 231, 256
Kingdom of Vientiane 83, 98, 114-15, 126-7
    see also Anouvong (Vientiane)
Yuan dynasty 28, 202

General Travel Info

cuisine
    Isaan 11
    Lanna 35
    Lao 89, 101, 104, 110
    southern Thai 185
festivals *see* holidays and festivals
health and safety **283**
internet 282
modern art 42-3, 78, 138, 159
money 282
Muay Thai 78, 159
nightlife 51, 78, 89, 158-9, 197, 205
outdoors
    beaches 184, **196-7**, 205
    caves 77, 103, 196
    diving 197
    hiking 60, 76-7, 100, 102, 120-1, 194, 197, 225
    rafting 77
    waterfalls 76-7, 102, 194, 264
    wildlife 77, 102, 197, 250
photography 148
scams 88, 144, 197, 283
shopping
    general 51, 78, 159, 185,
    markets 59, 78, 104, 120, 138, 157, 237
temple etiquette 23
tipping 11
transport 278-80
trip planning **10-11**, 276-83
weather 10, 196
visas 121, 281

Thailand

Ayutthaya 126-7, 153-4, 191-3, 218, **230-43**, 252
Bangkok 99, 114, **123-59**, 168, 193, 231
   Rattanakosin 134, **141-59**, 231
   Thonburi 98, **125-39**, 142-3, 189, 231, 270
Chiang Mai 6-7, 28-9, **63-79**, 86, 108-9, 192-3
   Wiang Kum Kam 28, 77, 193
Chiang Rai 28, **31-45**, 88, 192-3, 268-9
   Chiang Saen 38, 40, 108-9, 271-3
Kamphaeng Phet 192, 230, 246-7, **255-69**
Kra Isthmus 177, 181-2
Krabi Province **196-7**
Lampang 29, **47-61**, 64-5, 193, 272
Lamphun 28, **61**, 73 *see also* Haripunchai
Lopburi 73, 182, 230, **245-53**
Mae Hong Son
   Pai 77
   Pang 270
Nakhon Ratchasima 114, 226-7
   see also Phimai
Nakhon Si Thammarat 126-7, **179-97**, 230
Nan Province 65, 271-2
Nong Khai 49, 110, 121, 223
Phayao 28, 270
Phetchabun 270
Phimai 126-7, 182, 223, **226-7**
Phitsanulok 18, 126-7, 191, 230-1, 258, 276
Phuket 196-7
Sakon Nakhon 17, 72, 223, **224-5**
Samut Prakan 158
Saraburi Province 151, 270
Sukhothai 28-9, 190-2, 230-1, 261, **266-67**
   Si Satchanalai 230, 266
Surat Thani Province 184, **197**
Tak Province 192, 270 [birthplace of Taksin]
Takua Pa 181-3
Udon Thani 121, 223

Laos

Champasak *see* Kingdom of Champasak
Luang Prabang 82-3, **85-105**, 108-10, 126-7, 193
Vang Vieng 88, 110
Vientiane 82-3, 98-9, **107-21**, 126-7, 224

Cambodia

Angkor 82, 98, 152, 181-3, **199-221**, 226-7, 234-5, 247-51
   Harihalaya 200, 216
   Mt. Kulen 200
Banteay Chhmar 220
Battambang 182, 205
Koh Ker 200, 205
Lovek 221
Phnom Penh 204-5, 235

Siem Reap 204-5 *see also* Angkor
Sihanoukville 205
Sisophon 182, 220

India

Ayodhya 153, 234
Bihar Province 73
   Bodh Gaya 65, 170
   Mt. Vipula *see* Rajagriha
   Pataliputra (Patna) 161-70
   Rajagriha (Rajgir) 162-4
Dantapura 169, 171, 188
Kashmir 166, 168
Tamil Nadu 174
Telangana 39

Sri Lanka

Anuradhapura 165, 169-71, 174, 190
   Abhayagiri 171
   Jetavana Monastery 190
   Meghagiri 165, 170-1
Kandy 170, 188
Polonnaruwa 176-7
Ruhuna 174

Myanmar

Ava (Inwa) 127, 231
Mergui 181-2,
Pagan (Bagan) 172-5, 180-2, 273
Pegu (Bago) 109
Shan 6, 65, 87
Thaton 173-4, 181-2

Other Locations

China 39, 65, 127, 132, 168, 171, 202
   Guangdong Province 132
Gandhara (Pakistan & Afghanistan) 150, 166, 168-70, 247
Indonesia 153, 181, 200
Vietnam 83, 90, 200, 210 *see also* Champa

Religion, Culture & Architecture

amulets 61, 157
apsaras (celestial nymphs) 209, 213
architecture
   Ayutthaya architecture 235, 239
   Burmese architecture 53-4, 58, 61, 173-5
   Chinese architecture 38, 40
   colonial architecture 44, 132, 137
   dok so faa 114
   Haripunchai architecture 61
   Khmer temple architecture 203, 211, 250-1
   Lanna-style houses 59
   Lanna temple architecture 40, 56-7, 72

Index

Lao *that* 116-7, 224
modern-style temples 42-4, 78, 158
Siamese houses *see* Thompson, Jim
Sinhalese (Sri Lankan) style 69, 92, 170, 263
Srivijaya architecture 181, 191
Sukhothai architecture 261, 266
Theravada Buddhist temples 20-2
arhat (enlightened being) 14, 163, 167
Aruna 130
Avalokiteshvara 14, 201-2, 214-5, 220
Bhumi (Earth goddess) 19, 187
bodhisattva 14 *see also* Avalokiteshvara
Brahma (creator god) 16
Brahman (ultimate reality) 15-16
Brahmin (priests) 15, 157, 171, 200-2, 215, 230
Buddhist sculpture
    'Bayon Buddha' 212
    Chiang Saen style 40, 271-3
    'Crystal Buddha' 73
    Dvaravati art 156, 242, **253**
    Emerald Buddha **5**, 157-9 *see also* Chronicle of the Emerald Buddha
    Emerald Buddha replicas 38-40, 55-7, 69, 96-7, 114, 132, 205
    Gandhara images 150, 168 *see also* Gandhara
    'Golden Buddha' 33, 159
    jade 39, 168, 271-3
    Lao style 92, 113
    Lopburi style 253
    Luang Phor Phra Sai 49, 121
    meaning and significance 18
    Phra Bang **98-9**, 126, 159
    Phra Fon Saen Ha 71
    Phra Si Achana 267
    Phra Sihing 41, 74-5, 156, 189, **190-3**, 268-9
    Phra Sila 73
    postures 19
    'Reclining Buddha' (Wat Pho) 155
    Sukhothai style 261, **266**
    U Thong style 212, 234, 241
    'Watermelon Emerald Buddha' 55, 57, 272
chinthe (guardian lions) 22, 186
chronicles
    Chronicle of the Emerald Buddha **6-7** *see* contents page
    Chronicle of the Phra Sihing *see* Phra Sihing
    Glass Palace Chronicle 174
    Jinakalamali 6-7, 49, 269
    Mahavamsa 27
    Yonok Chronicle 33
'Churning of the Ocean of Milk' 209, 216
city pillar 17, 70-1, 118, 157, 264
dharma 13, 164
dharmaraja (righteous king) 14, 18
Eightfold Path 12-13
Erawan (Airavata) 113, 131, 217, 158
Four Noble Truths 12
Ganesha 15-16
Garuda / *garudas* 22, 143, 148, 186
Guan Yin 14, 44-5 *see also* Avalokiteshvara
holidays and festivals
    Boun That Luang Festival 117
    Inthakin Festival 71
    Loi Krathong / Yi Peng **79**
    Songkran 10, 74, **79**, 93, 99, 103, 193
    Vassa (Buddhist lent) 121
Indra 15, 36, 70-3, 113, 142, 163-5, 217
karma 12-14, 239
kinnara / kinnari 131, 152
Krishna 16, 217 *see also* Rama, Vishnu
kumbhanda (genie) 162, 164 *see also yaksha*
linga 15, 195, 203-7, 211 *see also* Shiva
Mae Suchada 54-5
Mara 19
moksha 15
Nandin (Shiva's bull mount) 221 *see also* Shiva
naga (serpent) 19, 22, 69, 120, 190, 206, 218-19
nirvana (enlightenment) 12-15, 165
Pali 6-7
phi (spirits or ghosts) 17, 48-9, 86-7, **93**, 103
pradakshina 117, 180
Prajnaparamita 213-14 *see also bodhisattva*
Preah Ko Preah Keo **221**, 273
Prince Vessantara 13 *see also* Jataka Tales
Rama 14, 16, 104, 153, 234 *see also* Ramayana
religions
    animism 17, 18, 45, 49, 71 *see also phi*
    Hinduism **15-16**, 195, 200-3, 215-17, 264
    Mahayana Buddhism **14**, 163, 202, 210, 214
    Tantra / Vajrayana 226-7, 247
    Theravada Buddhism **14**, 20-1, 65, 173, 215
religious texts
    Bhagavad Gita 217 *see also* Mahabharata
    Jataka Tales **13**, 74, 133, 149, 242
    Mahabharata 15, 153, 168, 209, **217**
    Ramakien / Phra Lak Phra Ram *see* Ramayana
    Ramayana 14-16, 104, 138, **152-3**, 209, 234
    Tripitaka **13**, 14, 113, 172-4
    Vedas 15
sangha (monkhood) 13-14, 108, 142-3, 164, 172
Sanskrit 15, 200
Shiva 15-16, 157, 195, 200-1, 264-5
Siddhartha Gautama (Buddha) 12-14, 19
tooth relic 169-71, 174, 183, 188
trimurti (Hindu trinity) 16, 203, 220, 250
Vayu (wind god) 131
Vishnu 16, 22, 148, 156, 181, 208, 251
    see also Krishna, Rama, Ramayana
Vishwakarman (divine architect) 142, 163-5, 168
yaksha (guardian giant) 22, 131, 134, 146, 162-5

ABOUT THE AUTHOR

Ken Lawrence is a writer, photographer and designer with a passion for world cultures, art and literature. He's lived in several different countries spread across four continents and has explored dozens more.

He is also the author of the Japan-based travel guide '**The Murakami Pilgrimage: A Guide to the Real-Life Places of Haruki Murakami's Fiction**,' available in both paperback and digital formats. You can learn more at **murakamipilgrimage.com**.

Furthermore, he's also written numerous guides and articles for **sailingstonetravel.com** about fascinating destinations throughout the world.

The original concept for this book, in fact, began as a three-part series of online articles. Eventually, though, the author realized that only a full-length book could do the Emerald Buddha's backstory justice!

You can find the author's city, culture and art guides for the various locations featured in this guide book by scanning the QR code found above each area map.

www.ingramcontent.com/pod-product-compliance
Lightning Source LLC
Chambersburg PA
CBHW041503010526
44118CB00001B/1